3 1994 01115 4587

SANTA ANA PUBLIC LIBRARY

D0116358

Treasures in Your Attic

For B. F. and R. C.
Thanks for your love and support.

Contents

Foreword

My father was an antiques dealer. He owned a firm in New York City called Arthur S. Vernay, Incorporated. The firm dealt in seventeenth- and eighteenth-century English furniture, porcelains, pottery, glass, silver, and paintings; it also provided and installed architectural interiors and paneled rooms for many an American tycoon during the first half of the twentieth century. (One of Dad's great loves was the restoration and preservation of many historic buildings and sites. He devoted hours to helping his friends in the museum world with their various "projects," as he called them. And he always donated his time and expenses. He worked on some amazing projects: The White House; Blair House, the president's guest house; Gracie Mansion, the mayor's residence in New York City; Colonial Williamsburg; Ainsley Hall, the Robert Mills house in Columbia, South Carolina; and Tryon Palace in North Carolina, among others.)

Although I sort of grew up in the business, it was rather mysterious in some ways. Like many children, I really didn't know—and certainly never understood until much, much later—what it was my father did for a living. All I knew for several years was that Dad "went to New York."

I have a fond memory of going to New York City for the very first time—to the "office" (it was never a shop). I was five years old. The business was a grand antiques emporium housed in a grand wide town house on a tree-lined side street in the mid-50s just off Park Avenue. It had four floors filled with truly splendid things: what I remembered most was walking into the shop with my mom at noontime. Dad was passionate about old English clocks, and there were a lot of them. They were all running, of course. They all struck the noon hour at once—a cacophony indeed! It was wonderful. And my father *never* called them grandfather clocks! (More about this later.)

Like my eight brothers and sisters, I never had any intention of going into the antiques business, Dad's business, and the family business—never had any interest in it at all. Just like my brothers and sisters, I thought it was bor . . . ing. *But,* a little more than fifteen years after that first visit—and I had not made very many visits there at all in the intervening years—I went to work in the shop "to help Dad out." (How smug and self-assured we all are at twenty-two.) My intention was to stay for a few months at the most. I had moved back home to lick my wounds after a failed romance, and it had been my intention to go on to law school the following autumn. But after a few weeks, time began to stretch a bit, and it was two months after going to help out that I went to Dad and said, "Gee, I really like this; I think I'd like to stay." He was thrilled, of course, and my so-called temporary job lasted a very long time—more than twenty years—and became my career. In short, the antiques bug bit me! There is no known cure, you know.

Now remember how I talked about the long case clocks in Dad's shop. Well, when I read the remark in this manuscript that Joe made about their being properly called long case clocks, I knew it was a good book! And yes, just in case you are wondering, there are "litmus tests" we antiques folks conduct on each other—it's a ritual (which is one of the few things not mentioned in the book!).

If the antiques bug has bitten you, then this is the book for you. It is the book that gives you the real skinny, from Important Criteria to Consider to the Crux of the Matter—Condition. This book ought to be a bible for every beginning collector. It takes you on a marvelous journey through all the main categories of items you are likely to see on any beginner's journey in collecting: that is, from Belleek to Belter, from Hummel to Hepplewhite, from terra-cotta to Tiffany and tabletop, from scrimshaw to smalls. It teaches you the beginner's basics. It teaches you how to become knowledgeable about all sorts of different antiques. The Treasure Hunt provides an invaluable guide to what to look for as you walk through your house, what you are likely to find in various areas, and what *not* to overlook. It teaches you that frequently there are treasures everywhere in the house.

I enjoyed reading this. I learned some things—I learned a lot, actually. And that's really what's great, and fun, about collecting antiques. You *never* stop learning. It goes on forever. There is always that treasure around the corner, that Treasure in the Attic. I won't say don't leave home without it—just don't leave home without reading it first.

Happy reading, happy learning, and happy hunting.

—Chris Jussell

Sotheby's.com, former host of *Antiques Roadshow*

Introduction

We have a friend—a smart, savvy lady—whose mother died, leaving a big house full of furniture and bric-a-brac that needed to be cleaned out, with the contents to be divided between two siblings. The things her brother wanted went into one pile, the things she wanted went into another pile, and then the things that neither of them wanted went into either a Goodwill box or what she called a "Joe and Helaine box."

The idea was that we could sell these items on her behalf. One day, while going through a bathroom closet, she came across an old hooked rug that had been used as a bathmat for years. It was small and rather ugly, and showed a dogsled mushing across snowdrifts. In short, it had no apparent appeal. She dithered about which pile it belonged in. Was it a Goodwill item, or did it belong in the "Joe and Helaine box"?

Fortunately, she finally tossed it into "our" box, and it was picked up and sent to auction, where the so-called bathmat was immediately recognized as a very collectible item made by the highly regarded Canadian Grenfell Company. When sale day came, the small hooked rug sold for $1,000, and both brother and sister were flabbergasted that such an "insignificant" item could sell for so much money.

This sort of thing is all in a day's work for us because we are professional appraisers who routinely advise clients (in person, on national television, and in newspapers and magazines) about the value of what they own, when to insure an item, and how to sell what they no longer want. We have found that many average American homes are treasure troves of items that are easily overlooked and undervalued, and so in this book we present you with information that will help you separate your treasures from your trash.

In the process of appraising house contents, it is not unusual for us to arrive at the front door while the owner is going out the back door to the garbage can with some wonderfully valuable, but unrecognized and unappreciated, possession. We have literally picked diamond rings, Fiesta ware, eighteenth-century documents, and much, much more out of the rubbish because people just did not understand what they had.

If you think this does not happen and we are exaggerating to make a point, consider the case of two brothers whose mother had just died. They decided that they had to clean out the family home as quickly as possible, so they hired a dump truck and began pitching. Out went the extensive baseball card collection, out went the toys and children's books, out went the Victorian Christmas decorations, out went everything but the furniture, and, for some reason, the dolls.

Somehow, local antiques dealers got wind of this carnage and began hiding in the bushes and following the truck to the dump in order to "rescue" these valuable discards. How could this happen?

Many, many people believe that their most valuable possessions are the big things, such as furniture; the things of obvious intrinsic value, such as the sterling silver flatware; or the things that cost a lot of money to begin with, such as fine china. In some cases, this may be true, but all too often these items represent only about one-half (or perhaps a bit less) of the cumulative worth of their household goods.

In fact, in many instances it is the vintage fountain pens hiding in a desk drawer; the old letters, documents, postcards, and photographs tucked away in a trunk upstairs; the out-of-date radios with colorful plastic cases in the garage; the war souvenirs thrown in the back of a closet; the corkscrews, bottle openers, and toasters tucked away in the back of a kitchen cabinet; and the sewing items gathering dust in Grandma's old mending basket that are actually worth more money than many other household items that are perceived to be the most valuable.

It is amazing how valuable some little things can be, and how eagerly sought after they are by collectors. While fine antique furniture is always both in demand and hard to find, the usual furnishings found in most homes turn up in quantity every day. Because of this, collectors and antiques dealers are always looking to find high-quality "smalls" (trade talk for accessories and easily portable items), and these are the very items that often go underappreciated, undervalued, and undersold by their owners.

In *Treasures in Your Attic,* we go exploring for the valuable objects that can be found in many ordinary American homes. We focus on the things that many people actually own, not on the rarefied items that only turn up once in a blue moon—although some of these will be covered as well.

Treasures in Your Attic is divided into three parts. In the first part we address the basics of the antiques trade, which many collectors and noncollectors alike find mystifying and daunting. We take an insider's look at how the antiques market really works, how value is determined, and the role that such things as age, condition, and fashion play.

It is hard to understand antiques and collectibles unless you speak the language, so in this first part we define 175 of the most important words every collector should know. Being able to "talk the talk" like a connoisseur is vital when you are researching a cherished possession or listening to an auctioneer describe an item being offered for sale.

Part two, the largest section of the book, is a room-by-room exploration of an ordinary American home. As we take you through the house we are looking for items of value that you might find in your own home. We talk prices, prices, and more prices as we examine the no-longer-played-with toys in the children's room, the costume jewelry in the master bedroom, the furniture in the living room, the old gadgets and appliances in the kitchen, and even the concrete garden ornaments in the backyard.

The last part of *Treasures in Your Attic* focuses on buying and selling antiques and collectibles at auction and on the Internet. We also discuss when you should hire a professional antiques appraiser and how to find a competent one whom you can trust.

Our goal for *Treasures in Your Attic* is to provide an entertaining and insightful, "everything you always wanted to know" guidebook to antiques and collectibles. In the process, we hope that you really will find some treasures in your attic—or perhaps in your kitchen, living room, bathroom, or backyard.

Part One: The Basics

CHAPTER ONE

Collecting 101

The American public is fascinated with antiques and collectibles. Turn on the television, open a magazine, scrutinize a newspaper, or switch on a computer, and you are sure to find an array of "experts" who will tell you about the objects in your home and how much they are worth.

In many cases, we are bombarded with information that is very hard to understand, evaluate, and associate correctly with the items that we actually own. All too often viewers and readers sitting at home are shown an object that vaguely resembles something in their possession, which falsely kindles a hope that riches—or an unexpected windfall at least—are just around the corner.

Not long ago, Joe was evaluating at an appraisal clinic and a couple came to his table with a Civil War sword that had belonged to the gentleman's great-great-great grandfather. The couple had traveled to the appraisal event because they had seen a television show that valued a sword similar to theirs at $50,000, and they were certain that they had a treasure.

Unfortunately, theirs was a fairly common Union cavalryman's sword worth about $850 at retail. The couple's disappointment was palpable, and they seemed unsure of what to believe. Joe dealt with their reservations by encouraging them to get a second opinion (and telling them where and how to get it), and by explaining exactly why their particular sword was in fact a family heirloom to be treasured, not a monetary treasure in itself.

The difference between a $50,000 sword and an $850 sword is a matter of details. To the untrained eye, one sword looks pretty much like another, but individual traits such as who made the piece, whether it is Confederate or Union, the engraving on the blade, the overall condition, and whether or not it has its original scabbard, not to mention what type of sword it happens to be, are of paramount importance.

As the saying goes, "Close only counts in horseshoes and hand grenades." "Close" certainly does not count in antiques. In determining the value of any given antique or collectible, the smallest circumstance can make the biggest difference. Color—or the lack thereof—counts, as does size. Sometimes bigger is better, but sometimes smaller is more valuable. The content of the decoration is also very significant as is the skill of the person who did it.

Who the maker was can be of great importance, and anonymous pieces are seldom as valuable as those created by a known or famous craftsman. In addition, the history of a piece can be very meaningful. Knowing who owned a given piece over the years (this information is called "provenance") can add considerable interest and value.

Valuing an antique or collectible can be a very difficult and convoluted task that requires a lot of specific information about the object in question. But before we can accompany you on your treasure hunt and help you spot the valuable items among your possessions, you'll need to master a few basic concepts.

The "Old" Myth

Two of the most destructive ideas that television and the media have knowingly or unknowingly conveyed to the public are that everything over a week-and-a-half old is potentially valuable, and that everything around the house will be collectible sooner or later. Neither one of these concepts is true.

It needs to be pointed out vigorously that not everything found around the house is a potential treasure, nor is everything that is "old" valuable! Age is *not* the major criterion for determining whether or not an object has any significant monetary worth.

We receive thousands of letters every year from people asking how much their possessions are worth, and we talk to many thousands more who have the same burning question on their lips. All too often, people try to impress us by declaring in a grave tone of voice that they know for certain that their cherished heirloom has to be valuable because it is "over one hundred years old!"

This statement is usually followed by a pregnant pause while the inquirer waits for us to be impressed by this piece of chronological information. Although we usually smile and graciously acknowledge this assertion of age, most people would be surprised to learn that we are not nearly as impressed by this number as they think we ought to be.

In the fascinating real-life adventure game of collecting, the only part that age plays in the all-important equation of an object's desirability and monetary worth is that the item under consideration must be as old as it is supposed to be. For example, an American Chippendale chair needs to have been made between about 1750 and 1780 to be of real interest to serious collectors. Those made in the 1870s or 1920s are also "old," but they do not command the same interest or the prices of pieces from the original period.

Years can add value to wine, and years of experience can add value in the job market, but years do not necessarily add value to objects, and they are not the primary yardstick by which collectors judge or assess monetary worth. Do not confuse age with value, and remember not to equate the two in your mind. When a seller tells you that you should buy something ". . . because it's one hundred years old," do not be so impressed that you automatically reach for your checkbook.

Your reaction should instead be to focus on the real criteria that can make a given object valuable.

Important Criteria to Consider

Ask yourself:

Does this piece have artistic merit?
For example, the famous Rookwood Pottery of Cincinnati, Ohio, made some artistic wares that were designed and hand-executed by highly skilled artists. But Rookwood also made "production-line"

wares that were mass-produced with little or no handwork. The very best of the artist-designed pieces can bring tens, or, in very rare cases, hundreds of thousands of dollars each at auction, but some of the production-line pieces can be purchased for less than $200 at the retail level.

Was the piece made by the company whose name it bears?
Recently, Helaine was watching one of the numerous appraisal programs on television, and the appraiser was evaluating an American Belleek tankard mug made by the Ceramic Art Company, which was the predecessor of Lenox. After the mug was thoroughly discussed and evaluated, it was appraised at $300. This would have been correct except Helaine recognized that the appraiser had missed an important point: The mug had been painted outside the Ceramic Art Company factory, by an amateur china painter, and this made it worth about half the $300 quoted. In other words, the piece was only partly made by the company whose mark it carried. This situation applies to much of the Limoges china offered for sale in this country. It also applies to items made for Tiffany and Company to be sold in their retail outlets. Many of these items bear the Tiffany name but were actually made by another company.

Does the item carry the name of a designer?
Even in the nineteenth century, individuals such as the English designer Dr. Christopher Dresser had their names or initials affixed to their creations, and this can raise the interest of collectors and the value of items significantly. Most "designer labels" are twentieth century, however, and a few to look for are Charles and Ray Eames, Georges Briard, Sascha Brastoff, Marc Bellaire, Vera, Russel Wright, and Royal Hickman.

Does the piece speak of the time in which it was made?
Is it in a particular style, such as the Adam style of the 1790s, the Aesthetics style of the 1880s, or the Art Deco style of the 1920s? Also think of the Danish Modern furniture from the 1950s, psychedelic

items from the 1960s, platform shoes from the 1970s, and Memphis-style objects from the 1980s.

Is it in fashion? Do people want to buy it? Is it popular with today's collectors?

This is often one of the primary components of a valuation equation. It may seem like a no-brainer to some, but too many people do not realize that the antiques and collectibles market, like any other market in this society, is based on supply and demand. Fashion and fad are often the demand side of this relationship. If nobody wants a given object, its value will be relatively low.

Is this piece uncommon or hard to find?

This is the supply side of the valuation equation. But remember, collectors must really want to own the piece before a rare item can have significant value. The rarest item in the world is not worth a proverbial plugged nickel unless someone wants it and is willing to pay the price the owner wants for it. There are also times when an object is so rare that few people recognize its significance. When this happens, the collectors who appreciate this sort of object must be made aware of its existence—and that can be a difficult and frustrating task.

Does it have some historical significance?

A letter written by most of you or by either one of us has very little monetary value either now or in the future unless we happen to do something really significant in our lives. On the other hand, a simple handwritten letter signed by Orville Wright of airplane fame might bring close to $2,000—and if its content had historical import (i.e., a statement such as "I told Wilbur the dang thing wouldn't fly, but he insisted we go to Kitty Hawk anyway!"), the value of that letter could jump to as much as $15,000!

These are some of the major factors that need to be taken into consideration when the value of any collectible object is being assessed. Other things to think about are size and condition.

Size is very important, but just because object A is 6 inches tall and similar item B is 12 inches tall does not mean that item B is twice as valuable as A. Sometimes miniatures are rarer, more sought after, and more expensive than their full-size cousins. Also, objects such as 12-foot-tall beds that are too big to fit comfortably into modern environments are often valued less because of this circumstance.

The Crux of the Matter—Condition

Condition is one of the most critical considerations in the whole realm of collecting. Serious collectors insist on perfection, unless the article in question is exceedingly rare and cannot be found in pristine shape. In real estate, the primary rule is said to be location, location, location. In collecting, it is condition, condition, condition!

Too often we have clients show us some poor, bedraggled artifact that is chipped, cracked, discolored, threadbare, and/or missing a significant part. When they see our distress over the condition of their cherished heirloom, they say, "Oh, if you were that old, you would have things wrong with you, too!" While that may be true on the surface, it is not a good analogy in the world of antiques and collectibles.

The rule of thumb here is that if an object can be found in perfect condition, collectors will resist accepting a less than perfect example. But if the item in question is rare enough, and is usually found damaged in some specific way, collectors are more inclined to accept a degraded condition.

A good example of this is the delicate porcelain figure groups made in several European countries during the eighteenth century. These often had delicate little fingers, fragile ruffles and bows, and other precarious protrusions that were easily dislodged. Collectors expect there to be some damage on these pieces and, as long as the flaws are not unsightly or too extensive, they refer to these flaws as "minor losses."

These "minor losses" do reduce the value a bit, but not the whopping 50 to 90 percent that more serious damage would demand.

Some deterioration is also acceptable on period furniture (basically, pieces made before 1830), and in fact is generally expected on these truly old pieces.

Collectors of furniture tend to frown upon objects that have been refinished, objects that have been repainted, objects with replaced tops, objects that have been altered or converted from one use to another, and objects that have been extensively repaired or restored. Just remember, condition is vital on all types of antiques and collectibles, and when you are in the marketplace, do not let some sharp salesperson convince you that a little crack or a small chip is unimportant. Do not allow him or her to euphemize a serious flaw by calling a chip a "flea bite," or a crack a "hairline" or "age crack." This last term in particular implies that such things are a normal result of age, and while cracks (and chips) *are* common, they are not something that collectors normally excuse without very good reason. So, do not be deceived: A chip or a crack by any other name is still a chip or a crack.

Reality Check

We need to inject a moment of painful reality here and make it clear once again that the majority of things found in the average American home may never interest most collectors and may never have a significant value on the secondary market (at least not in our lifetimes).

These items are now and will forever remain too mundane—too lacking in style or "pizzazz free" if you will—to excite us now or in the foreseeable future. Given that most of the things in our homes are not going to excite future generations, how can you know what to keep an eye out for? Here is a quick overview of some of the types of household items that might spark interest in the near future and beyond.

We suggest you pay special attention to:

Objects that strike some kind of nostalgic chord

This very diverse category ranges from kitchen wares to items that showcase emblems of entertainment or popular culture, such as characters from *Star Trek* or *Star Wars,* or Marilyn Monroe, Elvis Presley, and the Beatles. These items usually captured the collector's attention when he or she was young, and in later years these lunchboxes and ticket stubs push real psychic "hot buttons."

Personality items

Three entertainment icons were mentioned above, but items related to other, less luminary public figures—be they from the stage, screen, television, music, sports, political, military, scientific, literary, or fictitious worlds—are also highly desirable.

Obsolete objects

Things such as shaving brushes, straight razors, record albums, slide rules, photographs on metal and glass, fountain pens, late-nineteenth- and early-twentieth-century typewriters, and pre-World War II television sets are all obsolete today (or virtually so), and are either already very collectible, or on their way to becoming collectible in the near future. In other words, obsolescence, like evolution, is an ongoing process.

Recent objects made by venerable companies with long-standing reputations for quality

Companies such as Steuben, Tiffany, Orrefors, Cartier, Gorham, Stickley, and Baker are prime examples of such makers. Good art and good craftsmanship today will be good art and good craftsmanship tomorrow.

Items that fall into established collecting categories

Examples of these might be sewing collectibles (such as thimbles and sewing birds), toys, jewelry (both fine and costume), advertising items, and art glass.

Sports and sporting-event memorabilia

The range here is enormous. It includes unused tickets, programs, golf balls, footballs, tennis rackets, uniforms, and almost anything else to which fond memories of hard-fought contests can be attached.

Objects from world's fairs, the theater, opera, important historical events, and the military

Yes, that old army uniform might actually be worth something, as well as any memorabilia closely associated with such diverse happenings as the launching of a space shuttle or the impeachment of a president.

Objects with great graphic quality

Think of Currier & Ives prints, and how these images represent the way we would like to remember the nineteenth century. These prints have great "graphic" quality and, similarly, a lot of items being produced today will, in years to come, have a "look" that will remind people of the last half of the twentieth century and the beginning of the twenty-first. This may include such seemingly odd things as cereal boxes with pictures of Michael Jordan or Yogi Bear on them, or postcards, or, yes, even your kid's music posters. Do not throw any of these things away; that would be the same as running $100 bills through the garbage disposal!

Any item that is hand-crafted, or made from a luxurious or exotic material

A general rule is that if an item is expensive today and is finely made from top-quality materials, although it may go out of style for a while, it will probably be valuable once again one day. Quality is always quality.

By now it should be fairly obvious that collecting can be rather complicated. To make matters more challenging, there are people out there trying to take advantage of you. There are, however, a few simple rules that will help you protect yourself.

First of all, *never discard or sell anything until you know exactly what you have*. Do not make assumptions about value until you have something concrete and factual upon which to base that assumption.

Second, *if someone comes into your home to appraise your goods and he or she gives even a hint about wanting to buy one of the objects, ask that person to leave*. It is absolutely unethical for appraisers to buy from clients. They are being paid to work for you, not for themselves. In addition, never enter into an arrangement in which you trade your possessions for an appraiser's services.

Third, *do not believe anything that anyone tells you without checking it out*. Do your homework—a little research is always in order, and reference librarians are usually eager to help. Remember, getting a second opinion is never inappropriate.

These are just the basics, but they will help you swim through a sea of sharks without getting big bite marks taken out of your derrière. (It sounds so much nicer when you say it in French!) There are, of course, many other rules that will help keep you out of trouble while playing the collectibles game, but the principles mentioned above are the ones that are most likely to be helpful to the homeowner who is trying to evaluate, understand, and value his or her possessions.

"Insurance Replacement" Versus "Fair Market" Value

Before we start talking dollars and cents, it should be explained that antiques and collectibles do not have just one price or just one value. There are, in fact, a number of widely varying pricing, or valuation, levels, but for our purposes, we are going to talk about just two: "fair market value" and "insurance replacement value."

In simplest terms, "insurance replacement value" refers to the amount of money it would take to replace a given item if it were lost, stolen, or extensively damaged in some sort of disaster. This is the amount of money it would cost for someone to go out, find a comparable replacement piece, and purchase it from a retail source in the most appropriate marketplace, within a limited amount of time.

"Fair market value," on the other hand, represents the amount a willing seller can expect to receive from a willing buyer, both having a reasonable knowledge of the relevant facts (e.g., what the piece is, its condition, and so forth). In short, it is the actual amount of money that an individual can realistically expect to obtain from the sale of a given item within a reasonable time frame.

Generally, fair market value for most objects is approximately 40 to 60 percent less than insurance replacement value. We hasten to remind you, though, that any antiques or collectibles appraisal is an *opinion* based on research, experience, and the vagaries of the current marketplace and, as such, is not chiseled in stone.

Contrary to popular belief, the values of antiques and collectibles go up and down all the time, due to the ebb and flow of fad, fashion, and other economic forces. Prices are also influenced by the region of the country in which you live, and something that is quite sought after in New York City, Los Angeles, or Chicago may go unrecognized and unappreciated elsewhere.

Also, and perhaps more important, what appeals to tastes in the western part of this country may not appeal to the tastes of midwesterners or northeasterners, and vice versa. This is referred to as "regionality," and it can significantly affect the fair market value of almost any given item.

In this book, we will be citing insurance replacement value unless otherwise noted, because that value tends to price objects on a "best market" or "most valuable" basis. It is important for readers to remember that these values do not normally represent the sum that an individual might actually receive for his or her possession.

The prices quoted throughout this book are values garnered primarily from our experience and research. They are true and correct to the best of our knowledge at the time this book was written. Prices can change very rapidly (both up and down), and the ones found in *Treasures in Your Attic* are intended to serve as a guide to how much certain objects *might* be worth. Under no circumstances should any price be construed as a hard and fast "appraisal" of a given object.

CHAPTER TWO

Some Words and Phrases You Need to Know

Antiques and collectibles have a language all their own. It is impossible to identify and understand old glass without knowing what a "pontil" is; old silver without being able to spot and interpret the "hallmarks"; or old furniture without knowing what a handmade "dovetail" looks like.

Knowledge is power in the world of collecting, and knowing what things are and what they are called can save you money—and it can make you money, too. Knowing what the "lingo" means gives collectors the tools not only to understand but also to evaluate what they see, and it allows enthusiasts to communicate with one another and share vital information.

Not long ago, Helaine received a telephone call from a very excited young woman who breathlessly wanted to know if what her sister had seen the previous evening on a television show was correct. It seems the sister had seen a blue vase that had been valued at $2,000, and she thought it was exactly like a piece owned by her family.

In search of the facts, Helaine asked, "What did they say the object was?" "I don't know," she replied. "Well," Helaine continued hopefully, "what is it made from: Is it glass, pottery, porcelain, or what?" "I don't know," came the reply, and at that point Helaine realized that she could not help this caller because her lack of knowledge of even the simplest terms made it impossible for

Helaine to know what she was talking about. Two thousand dollars was at stake, but because the caller could not convey enough information to be understood, she could not get the confirmation she so urgently wanted.

In this chapter we will introduce you to some of the words and phrases that you need to know to "talk the talk," as well as those words and phrases that will help you understand what you see on the Internet, what you are told in antiques malls, and what you hear at auctions and flea markets.

This chapter is divided into seven separate sections: pottery and porcelain, glass, silver and other metals, furniture, paper, textiles and needlework, and a general compilation we call "catchall." The terms and phrases we will discuss are those that will be the most helpful to novice collectors. We will not only explain *what* the words mean, but *why* they are important. The words are given in alphabetical order for easy reference.

Pottery and Porcelain

The term "pottery" applies to any product made of baked clay—i.e., earthenware, stoneware, and porcelain. More narrowly, and more reflective of common usage, "pottery" usually refers to any item made from baked clay that is not porcelain or stoneware. Specifically, the terms "porcelain" and "stoneware" are usually separated from "pottery" and are considered to be an entirely different category by many collectors.

Pottery, as opposed to porcelain or stoneware, is always porous, and a pottery vessel must have a glaze on it in order for it to hold liquids. Pottery is also opaque, and so soft that it can be scratched with a knife. Pottery is generally fired at relatively low temperatures and can even be hardened in the sun or an open fire.

True porcelain, on the other hand, is not porous even if it does not have a glaze on it, and the body cannot be scratched even with a steel knife. It can be—but is not always—translucent, and must be fired in a kiln at temperatures around 1,300 to 1,450 degrees centigrade. It is also the material we often call "china."

Porcelain is called "china" because it was invented in China more than one thousand years ago (no one is exactly sure when). This very special material is principally made from two essential ingredients that are correctly called "petuntse" and "kaolin," but the English simplified these two hard-to-remember terms and called them "china stone" and "china clay," respectively.

In the days of Rembrandt and the great Dutch painters of the seventeenth century, Europeans were so enamored of Chinese porcelain that they often commissioned portraits in which they were depicted with a single piece of china such as a small bowl or cup. The idea was to demonstrate to the world that they were sophisticated and wealthy enough to afford this very expensive commodity.

In the eighteenth century, Europeans tried desperately to copy this Asian material, but, not knowing the proper ingredients, they had to settle for making a substitute that collectors call "soft-paste" or "artificial" porcelain. In contrast, the Chinese-style product made with the proper ingredients is generally referred to as "hard-paste" porcelain.

Soft-paste porcelain was made in Italy first, then in France and England, and its production usually entailed mixing "frit," or ground glass, into clay to achieve a translucent finished product. A few manufacturers in England, such as the famous Worcester factory, used soapstone instead of glass, and others added bone ash to achieve the desired effect.

Soft-paste porcelain is indeed softer than hard paste and it can be scratched with a steel knife. It has a tendency to warp during the firing process, and, if you look at it in a bright incandescent light, it can appear to be greenish, grayish, or even a bit orangish. Often unmarked by the maker, soft-paste porcelain is eagerly collected, but it is seldom found in the average American home.

Europeans did not learn how to make true Chinese-style hard-paste porcelain until 1709, when alchemist Johann Böttger stumbled upon the secret of the two essential ingredients while being held a virtual prisoner by the Elector of Saxony, Augustus the Strong, near Dresden in what is today Germany. Shortly after the discovery, the new porcelain-making operation was moved a few miles down the road to Meissen, where it continues to this day.

This discovery was more valuable than any of the recipes for gold that Böttger had once tried to concoct. Slowly the secret recipe for china (called the "arcanum") spread across Europe, mainly through theft and betrayal of trust. By the late eighteenth century, most European potters knew how to make hard-paste porcelain, but it was not manufactured in the United States until the nineteenth century.

There is one last complication you need to be aware of. Collectors have traditionally called a kind of early-nineteenth-century English earthenware "soft paste." Usually, this term is used in conjunction with such categories as "spatterware" and "Gaudy Dutch," but we think it is something of a misnomer. It is not a designation used by scholars as far as we can see, but it is an expression occasionally heard in the trade.

Now let's move on to some other words and phrases connected to pottery and porcelain.

Art pottery Technically, any type of pottery that was made for decorative rather than utilitarian purposes is art pottery, but when collectors use the term "art pottery," they are generally referring to an artistic movement that started in the late nineteenth century. The roots for this movement in America can be traced to the Philadelphia Centennial Exposition of 1876, the first successful world's fair, when Americans saw the treasures of the world firsthand. In attendance were the Robertsons of Chelsea, Massachusetts, who were impressed by the Greek and Chinese pottery they saw; and Mary Louise McLaughlin of Cincinnati, Ohio, who was fascinated with the slip-decorated faience sent by the Haviland Company of France ("Faience" is a type of pottery, and "slip" is liquid clay that can be colored and applied to pottery the way oil paint is applied to canvas). Soon, the Robertsons were making art pottery in Massachusetts and McLaughlin was making art pottery in Ohio and from there art pottery spread rapidly to such companies as Grueby, Rookwood, Wheatley, Owens, Matt Morgan, Paul Revere Pottery, Newcomb College, and others. The American Art Pottery movement emphasized underglaze hand-painting, hand-sculpting and carving, and special glazes. Several companies that produced wares that are eagerly collected today started out making true art pottery, but as time went by, switched over to making molded wares that are sometimes called "art pottery" but are really more correctly referred to as "commercial art wares." The leading makers of these commercial art wares were Roseville, Weller, A. E. Hull, and McCoy.

> **TIP:** Some of these commercial art wares, which were produced into the 1950s, can be very expensive. An A. E. Hull 12-inch Bow knot basket can retail for $2,800, and a Roseville Futura vase ("Arches #411–14") brings about the same.

Belleek D. McBirney & Company, which was located in the town of Belleek in County Fermanagh, Ireland, started making this distinctive type of porcelain about 1863. The body of this creamy white porcelain was called "parian" because it is said to resemble Parian marble. Statuary was often crafted from parian porcelain, and while D. McBirney and Company did make some figures from this material, their more common practice was to form it into very thin vessels that they covered with an iridescent glaze. The pieces were often decorated with applied three-dimensional flowers or aquatic motifs such as seashells and coral branches. This ware became so popular that the company had trouble filling its orders, which prompted numerous companies in the United States to make wares that bore the Belleek name (some similar, most not) as part of their mark. Some of the more famous American companies making so-called Belleek wares are Ott & Brewer; Willets; American Art China Works; Columbian Art Pottery; Knowles, Taylor and

These are the marks found on Irish Belleek that are of most interest to collectors. All are printed in black—you could say this is one time when a "black mark" is a good thing.
A: First black mark in use, 1863–1890
B: Second black mark in use, 1918–1926
C: Third black mark in use, 1926–1946

Knowles; and Ceramic Art Company, which became Lenox. Lenox used the name Belleek on its china until 1926, when the Irish company sued to make them stop.

> **TIP:** Irish Belleek pieces with various marks in black (used from 1863 to 1946) are the most desired. Earlier pieces of Irish Belleek are usually unmarked. Among the American Belleeks, the ones by Ott & Brewer are generally the most desired.

Bennington Americans customarily call pottery with a mottled brown-and-yellow glaze "Bennington," but this is not correct. The correct terminology for this type of glaze is "Rockingham," after Earl Fitzwilliam, Marquis of Rockingham. Reportedly, it was on his property in Yorkshire, England, that these products were first made. Many companies in America made Rockingham-glazed wares. Some of the best were produced by several companies in Bennington, Vermont, and the name of this town came to be widely applied to these items. The Bennington companies that interest collectors the most today are the Norton Pottery and the Lyman Fenton Company, which later became the United States Pottery Company (look for their "USP" mark). Fenton came up with a variation of the Rockingham glaze that they called "Flint Enamel." These wares were harder than normal Rockingham pieces, and besides brown and yellow, their mottled glaze incorporated flecks of other colors such as blue, green, red, and black. Flint Enamel pieces are highly sought after by collectors.

> **TIP:** The rarest and most valuable Fenton Flint Enamel pieces are said to be the figure of a lion with one paw on a ball and his tail curved over his back, and the figure of a poodle with a basket in its mouth.

Bisque From the French word "biscuit," "bisque" refers to porcelain that is only fired once and has no glaze. After this first firing, the porcelain has a soft, grainy look that reminds some people of the texture of human skin. This has led to its extensive use in making dolls' heads and other doll parts as well as decorative figures of children and adults. Bisque is often painted or colored, but this is an applied decoration, not a glaze.

> **TIP:** Bisque dolls' heads to look for are the ones with closed mouths; these tend to be the most valuable.

Blanc-de-Chine Literally "Chinese white," this porcelain was first made during the Ming Dynasty. The color of the clay ranged from a creamy white to a bluish white. Variously styled figures of the goddess Guanyin (Kuan Yin) are the most commonly found objects, but other figures are also found, as well as vases, bowls, censers, and libation cups.

> **TIP:** The vast majority of all blanc-de-Chine found on today's market is twentieth century, and this ware is still being made.

Bone china This is a type of artificial porcelain made with bone ash, usually from the bones of cows. Bone ash was reportedly introduced to European manufacturers at either the Chelsea or Bow factory in England in the mid-eighteenth century, but bone china as we know it was developed at the Spode factory in the 1790s. It was made in an attempt to provide a substitute for Chinese hard-paste porcelain tea wares that were expensive and in short supply at the time. Bone china is famous for being very white, very thin, and very delicate.

> **TIP:** All pieces actually marked "Bone China" are twentieth century.

Chinese Export This rather broad term refers to wares made in China that were designed to be exported to various countries in the West. These items were never intended for use in China because they did not appeal to Chinese tastes—in fact, the people who made them thought they were tasteless and barbaric. Most Chinese Export porcelain found on the market today dates from the eighteenth, nineteenth, or twentieth centuries, but earlier examples do exist. Encompassed by the term Chinese Export are such wares as Rose Medallion, Rose Canton, Canton, Nanking, and Armorial (Armorial pieces have real or imagined family crests as part of their decoration). To understand Rose Medallion and Rose Canton, it is necessary to know that the Chinese did not have a pink enamel in their color palette until Europeans brought them the method for making it in the second half of the seventeenth century. This "foreign" color formed the basis for a new palette known to collectors as Famille Rose ("rose [or pink] family"), and both Rose Medallion and Rose Canton belong in this grouping. The porcelain bodies for these wares were often made at the great Chinese pottery center, Ching-te Chen, and sent undecorated to the city of Canton, where they were painted to fill the specific orders of European merchants. The designs on Rose Medallion and Rose Canton are quite similar. Both have panels—or medallions—with images arranged around a central reserve (blank area "reserved" for decoration) on plates and bowls. In Rose Medallion, panels with floral arrangements (often with birds and/or butterflies) alternate with scenes that contain people. Rose Canton is all floral. When collectors just say "Canton," they are referring to the blue-and-white china that was decorated with a landscape consisting of a teahouse, a bridge, trees, perhaps a boat or two, and

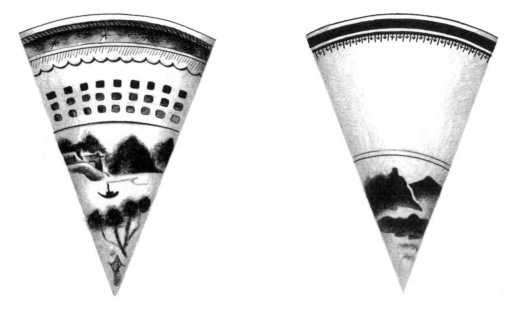

a cloud border around the rim. Nanking is much the same, only it has a different border, called "spear and post," around the edge.

> **TIP:** Rose Medallion and Rose Canton are still being produced, and collectors should be careful not to pay nineteenth-century prices for twentieth-century pieces. Examples of Rose Medallion marked "China" were made between 1891 and 1920, but pieces marked "Made in China" were made after 1920 and can be quite recent.

Creamware This is a relatively lightweight, whitish or cream-colored English earthenware that was introduced in the 1740s. It has a lead glaze, and was produced to compete with delft and salt-glazed wares. By the 1760s, it was the most produced English pottery. Its original name was "cream-colored," but in 1767, Josiah Wedgwood renamed it "Queen's Ware" in honor of Queen Charlotte, the wife of George III. Other than Wedgwood, the most famous maker of creamware was Leeds Pottery, located in Yorkshire.

left: A section of a Chinese Export Canton plate. Note the cloud border around the rim.
right: A section of a Chinese Export Nanking plate. Note the spear-and-post border that is somewhat exaggerated in this view for the sake of clarity.

TIP: It should be noted that Wedgwood's "Queen's Ware" was very popular in the early twentieth century, and the company is once again making tableware in that body. The newest wares (circa 2000) are made using eighteenth-century designs and are very beautiful. They are also very expensive.

Delft Unable to make Chinese-style porcelains, the Dutch created an alternative that involved covering an earthenware body with a thick lead glaze whitened with tin oxide. Much of this tin-glazed earthenware was manufactured in the Dutch town of Delft. Tin-glazed products made in Holland (and similar wares made in England) have been known by this town's name since the mid-sixteenth century. Dutch Delftware is properly spelled with a capital D, while the English product is spelled with a lowercase d. The very first European tin-glazed earthenwares were made in Spain and Italy in the fifteenth century, and these wares are called "Maiolica." Tin-glazed earthenwares made in continental European countries such as France and Germany are customarily called "faience."

TIP: Delft is so fragile that perfect pieces are very uncommon. Pre-1800 examples are almost always chipped or cracked, and specimens with rare decorations that have been broken in several pieces and repaired can still have a significant value. Even with major cracks, a circa 1700 English delft "blue dash" charger (a large plate with cobalt blue dashes or spots around the rim) that has a naive painting of Adam and Eve in the center is worth around $2,000.

Dresden Contrary to popular belief, porcelain was never manufactured in Dresden, the capital of the province of Saxony. So-called Dresden porcelain was only decorated there. Somehow, however, the name "Dresden" has been attached to the porcelain made fourteen miles down the road at Meissen.

TIP: Despite the fact that Dresden-decorated wares are generally less expensive than items made and decorated at Meissen, a circa 1900 pair

A sampling of marks used by Dresden decorators in the late nineteenth and twentieth centuries. The fish was used by A. Hamann, and the crown over the word "Dresden" by Donath and Company. Originally, the conjoined *A* and *R* was a rare, early Meissen mark; the initials stand for Augustus Rex, or Augustus the Strong, Elector of Saxony and King of Poland. Later, this particular mark was used by Helena Wolfsohn and fools many novice collectors, who think the item in question must therefore be an eighteenth-century piece. The "RPM" mark was used by H. Richter, and the lamb over the word "Dresden" was the play-on-words mark of A. Lamm.

of 25-inch-tall covered jars by Dresden artist Helena Wolfsohn with panels of courting scenes and flowers is still worth approximately $3,500 to $4,000.

Flow blue This type of dinnerware is characterized by a runny blue, transfer-printed decoration. To create flow blue, a chlorinated vapor was introduced into the kiln during firing. This made the blue "bleed," or run, and produced a sort of hazy, soft, and dreamy image that consumers found very attractive. This technique is said to have been perfected by Josiah Wedgwood II, and the first pieces reportedly appeared in the mid-1820s. Flow blue designs can be found on porcelain, semi-porcelain, and stoneware, and it enjoyed two great periods of popularity. The first, which ran from about 1825 until the 1860s, tended to feature Asian scenes rendered in a dark, almost inky blue. The second period started in the late nineteenth century and continued well into the twentieth century. Most of the patterns made during this time frame were floral and geometric. Flow blue was widely made in England, but American, French, German, and Dutch examples can also be found. It is estimated that there are approximately 1,500 flow blue patterns.

left: This is the central motif of the Gaudy Dutch pattern called "War Bonnet." It does indeed look something like a hat, but on closer inspection it is clear that it depicts a bowl of flowers and leaves.

right: The Gaudy Dutch pattern called "Oyster." This odd designation was derived from the amoeba shape found in the center of the design.

TIP: Flow blue is very popular with collectors and can be very expensive. As with most kinds of dinnerware, plates tend to be the least expensive items and serving pieces the most expensive. Plates generally run in the $65 to $100 range, but a Scinde pattern sauce tureen and underliner might fetch $1,200, and an Amoy teapot should be valued at about $1,400.

Gaudy Dutch Collectors call it "gaudy" because the patterns are bold and colorful, but why they call this English-made earthenware "Dutch" is a little more difficult to understand. The term "Gaudy Dutch" refers to a type of "soft-paste" earthenware decorated in the manner of Japanese and Chinese Imari. Imari was introduced to the European marketplace by the Dutch East India Company, and these wares became somewhat identified with the Dutch. Eventually, that nationality's name became attached to the English imitation. It is

also thought that when the English took these items to America, the only port at which they could find buyers was Philadelphia. There, the Pennsylvania Germans—called "Deutsch," or "Dutch"—liked the colorful dishes and bought them in some quantity. As a result, the dishes became known as "Gaudy Dutch," in reference to the bright colors and to the "Pennsylvania Dutch." Gaudy Dutch was in production from about 1810 (although some say it was made as early as 1790) to 1830, and most of it was made in the English Staffordshire district. It came in sixteen distinct patterns with names such as Butterfly, Carnation, War Bonnet, Oyster, Urn, Zinnia, and Dove. Decorations on Gaudy Dutch were usually painted in shades of cobalt blue, bright yellow, green, red, and pink.

TIP: Gaudy Dutch can be very expensive; and if you have a coffeepot in one of these patterns, the price could go well above the $5,000 mark. Even plates can be expensive, and a 9¾-inch-diameter example in Oyster should be valued in the $1,500 range, while a 10-inch diameter in the Butterfly pattern might bring as much as $2,000 if the butterfly motif is in the center with spread wings.

Gaudy Welsh and Gaudy Ironstone These wares are related to Gaudy Dutch, but they are later and less valuable. Gaudy Welsh was made at any number of potteries in England and Wales from about 1820 to 1860. This ware was also influenced by Japanese and Chinese Imari, but Gaudy Welsh is more Victorian-looking than Gaudy Dutch and the design is less spontaneous. In addition, Gaudy Welsh has a wider range of colors, and copper, pink, and gold luster were used in some of the more than three hundred patterns. Gaudy Ironstone is similar to Gaudy Welsh but is characterized by its heavy ironstone body. It was made between about 1850 and 1865.

A variant Gaudy Welsh pattern called "King's Rose Oyster."

TIP: A Gaudy Dutch plate in the Oyster pattern is worth about $1,500, but a Gaudy Welsh plate in Oyster is worth only about $150.

Historic Blue and White Staffordshire In the early nineteenth century, Americans began to want to serve their meals on something other than pewter or wooden plates. The new fashion was to use dishes made from pottery, but since there really were no companies on this side of the Atlantic that could make this dinnerware as well or as cheaply as the English potters in the Staffordshire district, those enterprising gentlemen sent us boatloads of dishes. Much of it in the 1820 to 1830 period was decorated with dark, inky blue transfer prints. This rich hue was made from cobalt, which was perfect for this purpose because it was inexpensive, it covered up imperfections in the pottery itself, and it withstood the high heat of the kiln. In order to appeal to the sensibilities of their American customers, the Staffordshire potters often used American scenes, sometimes of a patriotic nature. There was the "Landing of General Lafayette," "Commodore MacDonnough's Victory," and one that showed the sea battle between the *Constitution* and the *Guerrière*. There were also more mundane views of "Boston State House," "City Hall New York," "Dam and Water Works Philadelphia," and many others. It should be noted that more generic views featuring images of such things as fruit, flowers, and pastoral scenes were also made as well as views of British landmarks and historical events. After about 1830, the blue started getting lighter (and by about 1850 it was very light indeed), and other hues, such as black, pink, red, green, and mulberry were introduced. American scenes disappeared and were replaced with Asian and classically inspired vistas.

TIP: American collectors tend to prefer American views, and items with images of flora and fauna are less expensive. A 7¼-inch plate, for example, with a picture of a large dog might sell for around $200, but a 10½-inch plate showing the sea battle between the ship they called *"Old Ironsides"* (actually the *Constitution*) and the *Guerrière* should bring around $2,000.

Imari This is a name given to porcelain wares made in and around the Japanese town of Arita since the seventeenth century. The porcelain was supposedly exported to the outside world through the port of Imari, hence the name. Unlike the Imari wares made in China for export, the Japanese appreciated their Imari, and much of the best Japanese ware was not exported to the West. The Imari that did make it to Europe greatly influenced the design of European pottery and porcelain. It should also be noted that Imari-style wares were probably first made in China, but Western collectors tend to associate it with Japan. Imari is typically decorated with images of flowers, fans, baskets of flowers, birds, and people that are often arranged in panels or geometric reserves. The first Imari was blue and white and is known as "sometsuke." At about the same time the Arita potters were making sometsuke, another famous Japanese potter, Kakiemon I (1596–1666), learned how to apply colored enamel over a glaze and to fire it at a relatively low temperature to make it permanent. The Arita potters followed suit and began adding red to the blue and white, and this became known as "aka-e" or, more commonly, "Sansai" Imari. By the middle of the seventeenth century a portion of the main street of Arita was called "Red Picture Street" because it was lined on both sides with the houses of enamelers putting red enamel on top of blue and white Imari. It was not long before other enameled colors were added, and this gave rise to Nishikide, or "brocade" Imari. (Brocade Imari has nothing to do with brocade fabric. To the Japanese, a brocade is any profusion of bright colors.) This type of Imari has cobalt blue under the glaze, and some combination of red, gold, green-yellow, and/or purple enamels over the glaze. The final type of Imari is called "Kinrande." It has a red background with gold designs.

> **TIP:** Late-nineteenth- and early-twentieth-century Imari wares can be very crude, and these low-quality examples are not highly regarded by most serious collectors. Care should be taken to buy quality Imari, not just any example that falls into the category.

Ironstone Patented in 1813 by Englishman Charles James Mason of Lane Delph, Staffordshire, this heavy, durable, cheap pottery was made by "pounding slag of ironstone in water" and then mixing it with flint, clay, Cornwall stone, and cobalt oxide (to aid in the whitening). Early wares were colorfully decorated in an Imari or quasi-Asian style, while later wares were often left completely white. This ware was so popular that many other companies made similar versions that were given designations such as Stone China, Opaque China, and Granite China.

> **TIP:** Examples of "Mason's patented Ironstone," brightly painted in the Oriental manner, can be quite expensive. A single circa 1815 soup bowl, for example, should be valued between $250 and $300.

Jasperware Many people consider this elegant pottery to be the crowning achievement of Josiah Wedgwood's career. After years of painstaking trial and error, he perfected this fine-grained stoneware in 1775. Typically, Jasperware has a solid-color background—usually light blue, dark blue, green, or tan—to which a separate, bas-relief decoration (usually white) has been applied, or "sprigged on." This produces a lovely, three-D, cameo-like decoration that ordinarily consisted of classical scenes; busts of monarchs and famous people; or leaves, flowers, and garlands. Pieces with rare colored backgrounds such as lilac do exist, and collectors are particularly fond of the very rare items that feature more than two colors in their designs. Wedgwood's original intent was for the Jasperware body to be a solid color throughout, but in practice some pieces are only tinted on their surface; these are called "Jasper-dip." Other companies besides Wedgwood also made a similar product, and these include such notable potters as William Adams and John Turner. Imitation Jasperware was also made in Germany by such companies as Schafer and Vater. These are commonly referred to as "German Jasperware."

> **TIP:** Jasperware is still being made by Wedgwood, and the modern product can be extremely expensive. A circa 1999, foot-long blue

plaque, for example, decorated with typical mythological figures, can retail for $2,000.

Limoges In 1768, an important deposit of kaolin was discovered near this French town, which is located some 230 miles southwest of Paris. Since kaolin is one of the chief materials for making porcelain, forty china factories were located there by the late nineteenth century. Among them was the famous Haviland concern, which was founded in 1865 by New York City china importer David Haviland. It is estimated that the various china-making companies located in Limoges turned out more than 60,000 different patterns of dinnerware.

> **TIP:** In addition to dinnerware, Haviland also made some very fine art pottery in the 1880s and '90s that greatly influenced American potters, such as those who worked at Rookwood. This ware was often on a terra-cotta-colored body or on stoneware and can be identified by the company's "H & Co." mark.

Lustre In the early nineteenth century, British potters started applying thin metallic films to ceramic bodies to produce what they called "lustre" decoration. The basic types were copper lustre, which was made from gold, and silver lustre, which was derived from platinum. Copper lustre was usually applied over a dark body, which gave the finished product a coppery or glistening gold finish. When the same copper lustre was put on a white background, the color became pink or purple, and when this pinkish/purplish lustre appears in spots and splatters, it is called "splash-lustre" or "Sunderland-lustre." Silver lustre was invented to provide a look-alike for real silver. Objects that were completely covered in silver lustre in order to make them look like metal teawares were made from 1840 to 1870, but the most desired silver lustre pieces are the "silver-resist" items. Substances that would "resist" the lustre when it was applied were used to make patterns on the item being decorated. After the lustering had taken place, the resist was removed, leaving a white pattern of such things as birds, flowers, people, and landscapes surrounded by a shimmering silver background.

> **TIP:** Wedgwood made a very rare variation of splash-lustre called "Moonlight-lustre." It is a marbleized glaze with spots of pink, gray, brown, purple, and sometimes ruby. It was made from about 1805 to 1820, and Josiah Wedgwood II called it "Holy-door marble." Other companies made a similar product, but the Wedgwood product should be marked with the company's name.

Majolica This Victorian earthenware is decorated with colorful lead glazes. Examples are often very fancifully shaped: an umbrella stand might resemble a stork among cattails, or a dish for game meat pies might look like a bird sitting on a nest. Some pitchers look like bunches of asparagus, covered boxes look like cauliflowers, and teapots may be shaped like monkeys with coconuts. Many pieces were unsigned, but Wedgwood, Minton, and George Jones made some of the best English pieces, and these generally carry company logos. The most sought-after American majolica was made by the Griffen, Smith and Hill Company of Phoenixville, Pennsylvania, and by Chesapeake Pottery in Baltimore, Maryland, both of which usually signed their products. Victorian majolica should not be confused with Italian and Spanish maiolica, which is a tin-glazed earthenware that originated during the Renaissance.

> **TIP:** Majolica can be very expensive. The Minton stork-and-cattail umbrella stand mentioned above is worth in excess of $20,000, and the Minton monkey-and-coconut pitcher more than $4,500. Even tiny butter pats by Griffen, Smith and Hill surpass the $125 level, and fancy oyster plates by Wedgwood with dolphins bring about $1,000 each.

Meissen Augustus the Strong, Elector of Saxony and King of Poland, almost bankrupted his various countries and provinces buying Asian porcelain, and it is said that he traded a company of soldiers for one Imari vase. When Augustus found a man whom he

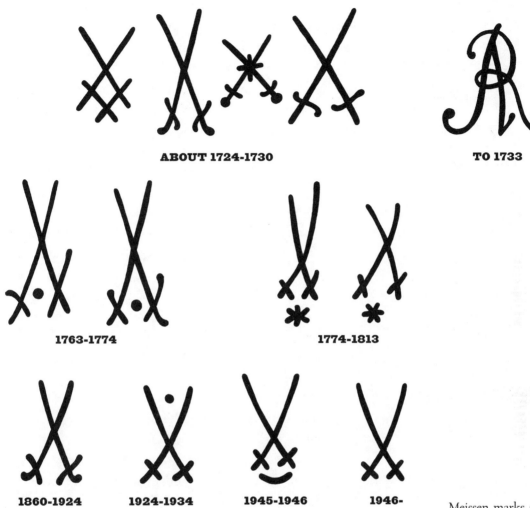

ABOUT 1724-1730

TO 1733

1763-1774

1774-1813

1860-1924   1924-1934   1945-1946   1946-

Meissen marks and the dates they were used.

thought could turn base metal into gold, he took him prisoner with the idea that the resultant gold would pay for his porcelain "habit." Johann Frederick Böttger never did make gold, but, with the assistance of E. W. von Tschirnhaus, he succeeded in making Chinese-style hard-paste porcelain about 1709. Porcelain made at Meissen is some of the finest and most valuable in the world, but collectors should beware of fakes. Meissen's famous mark of crossed swords has been appropriated by any number of other companies, including Bristol, Worcester, Samson, Gardiner, Coalport, and many

MEISSEN

While these marks say "Meissen," they are *not* marks used by the famous Meissen factory established by Augustus the Strong in the early eighteenth century. Instead, they are marks used by another maker located in the city of Meissen. Both of these logos were used by C. Teichert, and they constantly confuse new collectors.

more. So, when crossed swords are encountered, collectors should not automatically assume they are looking at something made in the Meissen factory.

TIP: Meissen porcelain came in five different qualities, each with its own mark. Pieces with a crossed-swords mark are first-quality, but when a single slash is cut across the blades, that means the item in question was deemed to be of only fair quality and was sold undecorated to be painted outside the factory. Swords with two slashes across the blades signify a second-quality piece, but one that was decorated in the factory. Three slashes across the blades and a perpendicular slash off to the side indicate third quality; these pieces were sold unpainted. Four slashes across the blade signify a piece so inferior that it was only sold to factory employees. Collectors should pay attention to these designations and not pay first-quality prices for inferior-quality porcelain. However, superior-quality decoration on second-quality pieces painted outside the factory can be quite valuable.

Nippon In 1890, the United States Congress passed the McKinley Tariff Act, which required that all items imported into the United States be marked with the country of origin. This law went into effect in 1891, and from that point forward, ceramics were marked "France," "Germany," "England," and so forth. The Japanese name for their country is "Nippon," so this was the designation that appeared on Japanese wares exported to this country between 1891 and 1921, when the United States Treasury Department required that Japan switch to "Made in Japan" or "Japan." Other countries started using the phrase "made in" in the years just before and just after World War I.

TIP: American collectors are very fond of Nippon wares, but be aware that their quality varies widely. Some examples are rather simplistic and are painted in a slapdash manner, but others have rich backgrounds with heavy gilding and intricately painted decorations of land-scapes and portraits. These latter items can cost thousands of dollars each. Most Japanese wares exported to this country before passage of the McKinley Act are completely unmarked and are called "pre-Nip-pon" by collectors.

Old Paris Starting about 1760, many small factories in and around Paris started making porcelain. Much of it was an imitation of the porcelain made in Sèvres, and much of it was completely unmarked. This often causes problems for modern collectors because a portion of this production was later fraudulently signed with the Sèvres' crossed *L*'s.

> **TIP:** Old Paris continued to be made into the Victorian era, but most collectors have less interest in the items made after about 1830.

Salt glaze This is a special glaze used on stoneware, whose process came to England from Germany in the late seventeenth century. It is produced by throwing a handful of salt into a kiln filled with stoneware. When the salt hits the heat, it vaporizes, and these vapors subsequently condense on the stoneware, leaving a clear, hard surface with pits, a texture something like the skin of an orange.

> **TIP:** The Germans used salt glaze on stoneware jugs, bottles, and mugs. Collectors are particularly interested in a special type of bottle called a "bellarmine," which is characterized by the incised portrait of a bearded man on the neck and shoulder of the bottle. These were first made about 1520 and continued in production for centuries. In Germany, they were originally called "Bartmann" (or "bearded man") jugs, and "Graybeards" in England. The name "Bellarmine" came from a Cardinal Bellarmino, who was hated by the Germans because he opposed the Reformation in Holland by force of arms. Ordinary bellarmines are now valued in the $800 to $1,200 range, with better examples going for somewhat more.

Satsuma Original Satsuma ware was made in Japan's Kagoshima Prefecture, which was under the control of the Lords of Satsuma. At the very end of the sixteenth century, one of the lords brought back twenty-two Korean potters who had been captured during a war. These potters created Satsuma, which is a semi-porcelain that is covered with a crackle glaze that ranges in color from beige to cream and ivory, and serves as a beautiful background for raised enamel painting. "Crackle glaze" refers to a glaze that has small cracks running through it. These cracks were created on purpose by applying a glaze that shrinks more than the body does. When this happens, the glaze cracks or crackles, and is said not to "fit" the body. Satsuma was very popular with the Japanese, and, when Europeans opened up the Japanese market in the mid-nineteenth century, Europeans and Americans liked it as well. To supply the demand, the Japanese set up kilns outside the Satsuma area to make Satsuma-style wares for foreigners. These were made in places such as Yokohama, Tokyo, Awaji, and Kyoto, and they were much more extensively painted and more brightly colored than the traditional Satsuma that appealed to Japanese tastes. By the 1920s and '30s, these Satsuma-style wares had become quite crude and were being exported to the United States by the boatload, where they were sold in 5 and 10 cent stores and other, similar outlets.

TIP: Artist-signed Satsuma from the late nineteenth and early twentieth centuries has become very expensive. The best objects signed by Kinkozan sell well above the $10,000 level, and other pieces signed "Kozan" are not far behind. Lesser examples by these artists start at about $500. Average pieces sell in the $1,000 to $2,000 range.

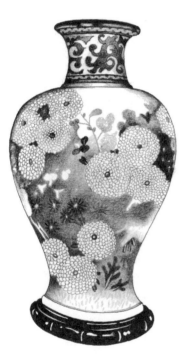

Early-twentieth-century Japanese Satsuma vase decorated with characteristic enameled flowers against a cream-colored background.

One of several marks used by Kinkozan.

造 山 光 錦 都 京 本 日

Sgraffito This term refers to a technique for decorating ceramics that involves scratching the surface with a sharp instrument to make a design or picture. Said to have originated in ancient times, this technique, which is also known as "incising," was often used on Pennsylvania Dutch wares from the late eighteenth and early nineteenth centuries to depict images of flowers and birds.

TIP: Weller, one of the premier makers of American art pottery, used sgraffito on one of its most artistic lines, known as "Second Line Dickensware." This pottery has intricately decorated scratched-in pictures of golfers, Indians, monks, animals, and scenes from Charles Dickens' novels. Prices for Weller's Second Line Dickensware start at about $1,000. The best pieces go for $2,500 or more.

Slip Slip is liquefied clay that is poured into a mold to form an object. This liquefied clay, which has the consistency of heavy cream, is also used as a medium to decorate a piece of pottery. Slip can be tinted and then applied to the surface of a piece by allowing it to flow through a funnel-shaped cup with a hole in the bottom, or by piping it through a device that is not unlike a pastry bag. The cup method is often employed to make line decorations, while the bag is used to make more involved designs. Slip can also be applied with a brush or a palette knife, and entire pots are sometimes dipped in it. This technique has been used for centuries, but it was brought to its highest level of perfection by French Barbotine artists and American art potters. Most of the lovely oil-painting-like decorations seen on Rookwood, early Roseville, and Weller were done with slip.

TIP: American art pottery that has floral decoration made with slip painting can be very beautiful but is very common. Images of people, animals, and landscapes are much rarer and make the pieces much more valuable. Despite this general rule, however, a 27-inch-tall, slip-painted vase with orchids by Mae Timberlake in Weller's Hudson line reportedly sold for approximately $22,000. This high price was due to the monumental size of the vase and the reputation of the artist, whose work is highly desired by serious collectors.

Spatterware From the late eighteenth century through the early nineteenth century, English Staffordshire potters decorated items (mainly tea wares) by dipping a brush in various colors of paint and then spattering the color onto the surface of the dish. Sometimes this spatter was only used as a border around the edge, and sometimes it was applied all over the surface. Sometimes it was in a single color, and sometimes it was in as many as four or five colors. In the center there was usually a decoration of a peacock, a star, a dove, a schoolhouse, a tulip, or another flower or fruit. Red and blue are the most commonly found colors. Yellow, green, and black are much rarer and much more sought after. Maroon, purple, and brown also can be found.

Early-nineteenth-century spatterware plate in the House pattern.

TIP: A simple cup and saucer with both a red-and-yellow rainbow and a red-and-green thistle should be valued around $2,500, while a similar cup and saucer with only a maroon spatter and a blue eagle and shield is worth about $250.

Spongeware Spongeware is similar to spatterware, but began to be produced at a somewhat later date, in the 1840s and beyond. Its speckled color was applied with a sponge that was sometimes cut into shapes, such as stars, flowers, angels, and eagles. The color range was wider than spatterware, but the basic colors were much the same: red, blue, green, yellow, black, and brown.

TIP: Spongeware is much less expensive than spatterware. A cup and saucer can generally be bought at auction for less than $100.

Staffordshire This is perhaps the most important of the several pottery-making districts in England. Name any type of English pottery and you will find that it was made here. American collectors tend to associate the name "Staffordshire" with transfer-printed blue and white wares, but this is far too narrow a definition. The Staffordshire district is located east of the Welsh border, between Liverpool and Coalport. Some of the district's most important pottery-producing towns include Tunstall, Longport, Burslem, Cobridge, Hanley, Stoke, Fenton, Longton, and Lane End. The most famous potteries located here are Davenport, Doulton, Ridgway, and Wedgwood.

> **TIP:** Be very careful when buying Staffordshire figures. The characteristic images of dogs and other animals, as well as depictions of people, have been widely reproduced, and collectors tend to dismiss examples that were made in the early twentieth century. They prefer the ones that were made in the early to mid-nineteenth century. Unfortunately, it is sometimes very hard for a novice to tell the difference. Buy only with a guarantee.

Stoneware Stoneware is a porcelaneous material that is fired in a very hot kiln. Like porcelain, it cannot be scratched with a steel knife, and it will hold water even when unglazed. The main difference between stoneware and porcelain is that the material used to make stoneware is less well refined and purified, and stoneware is never translucent. The color of a stoneware body is usually buff, gray, or red-brown.

> **TIP:** Americans often associate stoneware with gray-colored crockery with cobalt blue decoration. Nineteenth-century examples with simple floral designs can sell in the low hundreds of dollars, but large pieces with unusual, well-executed depictions of birds, animals, and people can bring prices ranging from around $2,500 to well over $10,000.

Terra-cotta An unglazed pottery, terra-cotta is generally reddish to yellowish buff in color, and very soft and porous. It is not suitable for making vessels intended to hold water. European sculptors often used it for busts and statues.

> **TIP:** Terra-cotta becomes "red ware" when a glaze is added to a red-clay terra-cotta vessel so that it will hold water. Often the glazes on red ware are brown, yellow, green, or brownish black in color, and they give the item an interesting, shiny outer coating.

Transfer print This process has been around since the middle of the eighteenth century, and it was an inexpensive way for potters to decorate large quantities of pottery and porcelain items in an elaborate manner. The process begins when a copper printing plate is engraved with a design. One plate has to be made for each form that the potter wants to decorate; when the plate is finished, it is "inked" with an oily ceramic pigment. After the excess is cleaned off, a piece of paper is pressed into the surface of the plate and the design is "transferred" to the paper. At this point, the paper is handed to a relatively unskilled person, who trims off the superfluous paper and passes the print to another person, who in turn applies it to the surface of the item to be decorated. Later, the paper is soaked off, and the ceramic item is fired to burn out the oil in the pigment. Lastly, the piece is glazed and given a final firing.

> **TIP:** It is not economically feasible to have copper plates engraved unless the resulting transfer prints are going to be used on a large number of items. This means that any transfer-printed item is almost certainly just one of many, and any transfer-printed pieces that are now rare are scarce because of loss and breakage, not because of the number initially produced. To detect a transfer print, examine the decoration with a magnifying glass: If little dots are part of the design, it is a transfer print.

Glass

Country auctioneers and antiques dealers sometimes call anything that is breakable "glass." This, of course, is incorrect.

Like ceramics, glass is made from natural materials taken from the earth. Ceramics are made from clay, but glass is made from silica, such as silicon dioxide, boric oxide, aluminum oxide, or phosphorus pentoxide. This silica, or "sand," is heated to a molten state, then cooled. In fact, scientists consider glass to be a supercooled liquid, not a solid.

The first glass is thought to have been made in the third millennium B.C., and initially appeared in the form of beads. Vessels appeared around 1600 B.C., and were made by wrapping hot loops of glass around a core (probably ceramic). Glassblowing probably originated in Syria, but not until the first century B.C.

Glass was a precious commodity in ancient times, and in modern times outstanding examples made by such great names as Tiffany, Gallé, and the Daum brothers can bring prices that would buy a modest house or, in a few rare cases, send a child through four years of an expensive college. Buyers should be wary, however, because it is very easy to fake a signature on glass.

A Tiffany signature, for example, can be placed on any piece of glass with the aid of a diamond-point pen. Literally thousands of pieces of glass in the Tiffany style that were legitimately made by such modern companies as Lundburg Studios and Orient and Flume have had fraudulent Tiffany signatures scratched onto their bottoms by forgers—and these pieces have been sold to unsuspecting consumers who thought that if it says "Tiffany" on the base, it must indeed be by Tiffany.

Some glass companies such as Steuben and Hawkes signed some of their wares by dipping a stamp with the company name or logo into hydrofluoric acid and then applying the stamp to the glass. This left an often-faint signature that is easily faked by anyone who is crooked enough to have a present-day stamp maker forge a similar stamp that can also be dipped into acid and pressed against a previously unsigned piece of glass.

The point here is that signatures on glass (or on paintings, ceramics, furniture, or anything else, for that matter) should not be taken at face value. Critical examination and evaluation should not stop with the discovery of a signature. Finding a mark on a piece of glass is only the beginning point for research, and it tells the collector to look at that maker's known work and see if the piece under consideration falls within the correct parameters.

With glass, one quick way to check out whether a particular piece is old or not is to check the bottom for wear. Everything that is old should have signs of wear in the places where it would have been handled or where it would have come into contact with a surface. Glass is particularly susceptible to wear on its base, and a piece that does not have scratches on the bottom is somewhat suspect. Unfortunately, scratches, like signatures, are not hard to fake on glass—but, mercifully, they are usually easy to detect. Genuine wear on old glass should be relatively short and scratches should intersect each other in a kind of cross-hatching pattern. Fake scratches—the kind you get when you take a piece of glass outside and rub it back and forth across a sidewalk or brick wall—are longer than real wear marks, and many will run parallel to one another.

Steuben acid-cutback vase in Fircone pattern. The branches and blossoms are in gold Aurene against a colored background.

With this said, it is time to examine some words and phrases relating to collecting vintage glass.

Acid cutback This is a decorating technique that usually requires two layers of differently colored glass, one placed on top of the other. In one method, a design was inked onto the glass, and then all the other areas were coated with a protective wax. When the vessel was immersed in acid, the inked areas were cut away and the waxed regions were spared. This left a two-color, cameo-like design with the top color slightly raised against the background color. This and similar methods were used by Tiffany, Mt. Washington, Steuben, Gallé, Durand, and Webb.

> **TIP:** A 12-inch-diameter Steuben calcite (an ivory white glass)- and-gold "Aurene" compote decorated with acid-cutback depictions of lilies is worth about $2,000 at retail.

Agata Agata is a type of glass developed by Joseph Locke at the New England Glass Company about 1887. A dark bluish mineral stain was placed over the surface of a New England Peachblow (also known as Wild Rose) base, which shades from a soft pink or dark raspberry to a white. This base was then splattered with a volatile chemical, leaving behind blue spots and mottles. A relatively low-heat firing fixed this decoration, but it was still fragile and easily worn.

> **TIP:** Agata was made for only one year and is very rare and expensive. The price depends on how deep the color of the New England Peachblow and how intact the mineral staining happens to be. A 7½-inch pitcher with great color and good mottling can sell for as much as $3,500.

Agate Several colors of glass are mingled together and then blown to create a vessel that has streaks and whorls of color that resemble semiprecious stones such as agate, chalcedony, malachite, jasper, and lapus lazuli. The most famous agate glass was made by Tiffany (sometimes called "laminated glass"), and by Bohemia's Frederick Egermann, who called his agate glass "Lithyalin." Lithyalin was made between 1828 and 1840.

> **TIP:** It is hard to imagine glass more expensive than Tiffany, but an outstanding 4¾-inch-tall Lithyalin beaker, reddish brown with cut green leaves, should be valued about $6,000. Simpler, more ordinary examples bring somewhat less.

Satin glass stick vase (so-called because it was meant to hold a single flowering branch, or "stick") with air-traps in the diamond-quilted pattern.

Air-Trap A "gather," or molten "blob" of glass, is blown into a mold with a pattern in it that leaves indentations in the outer surface of the glass. Although other, more unusual designs can be found, these indentations are usually diamond-shaped, round, teardrop-shaped, or arranged in a herringbone pattern. Next, the glass is encased in another layer of glass that traps air in the impressed design. The finished glass has a very nice, shimmering, almost underwater look. This type of decoration is most often associated with satin glass (a type of glass that has been dipped in acid to roughen up the surface and give it the look of satin), and is sometimes called "Mother-of-Pearl" satin glass.

TIP: A 6½-inch-tall satin glass pitcher with an air-trap diamond-quilted pattern in a single color such as blue, pink, yellow, or green is worth about $450.

Alexandrite First produced by Thomas Webb & Sons of England, this one-layered, multicolored art glass shades from pale yellow to rose to blue. Stevens & Williams, also of England, called another type of glass Alexandrite; it shaded from amber to rose to blue, but instead of being one layer, it was three, with amber being the base glass and rose and blue cased on top. Koloman Moser and Heisey both made a glass they called "Alexandrite," but theirs are not tri-colored wares. Instead, they tend to change colors when exposed to different kinds of light (such as incandescent and fluorescent).

TIP: A less than 3-inch-tall Webb Alexandrite toothpick holder with an underliner is valued in excess of $3,000.

Amberina There is a legend that Joseph Locke accidentally dropped his gold wedding ring into a batch of amber glass at the New England Glass Company. When the glass was finished and then reheated, the "accidental" gold in the glass mixture caused the reheated portion to turn red, while the unheated part stayed amber. The story is pure, romantic bunk. Joseph Locke did patent an amber-to-red, heat-shaded glass in 1883, called "Amberina," but it was made by deliberately adding a small amount of gold salts to transparent amber glass (the wedding ring would not have produced the same results). Many other glass companies in both Europe and America also made Amberina. Perhaps the most prized Amberina was the product of the Libbey Glass Company of Toledo, Ohio. Their Amberina can be distinguished by the company's signature and by the fact that it shades from amber to fuchsia—a kind of purplish red.

> **TIP:** In 1886, the New England Glass Company made a few Amberina pieces with a whitish lining that tends to look a bit chartreuse to the naked eye. This glass is called "Plated Amberina." All of these pieces are ribbed on the outer surface, and all are very valuable. A 7-inch-tall tankard pitcher, for example, can be worth over $12,000. Beware of reproductions that have dead-white, chalky-looking linings.

Ambrotype This is a one-of-a-kind photograph on glass. This process was a cheap substitute for the daguerreotype (a one-of-a-kind photograph on a copper plate). An ambrotype is actually a negative on glass backed with black paper or dark shellac to heighten the image and make the picture look like a positive. This process was widely used for portraits and was most popular from 1855 to 1860. Ambrotypes are generally found mounted in cases made of leather or *gutta percha* (a type of plastic made from tree resin).

> **TIP:** Ordinary ambrotype portraits are very common, and the smaller sizes (up to 2¾ by 3¼ inches) can be bought for less than $50 each. Pictures other than standard portraits—such as images of soldiers and individuals going about their occupations, landscapes, animals, and larger-sized pictures (up to 6½ by 8½ inches)—can bring much more.

Aurene Aurene is a trade name used by Steuben Glass Works, and it can be found scratched onto the bottom of some of their pieces. Aurene refers to an iridized, semi-opaque glass that can be found in shades of gold, blue, green, brown, and red. Gold Aurene is similar in appearance to Tiffany's gold Favrile, but the two glasses are made from different formulas. The name Aurene is derived from the first three letters of the Latin word for gold, *aurum,* and the Middle English form of sheen, *shene.* Thus "aurene" means "gold sheen." It was first manufactured about 1904. Gold Aurene is by far the most common of this type of glass, and green, brown, and red are the rarest and most expensive.

> **TIP:** After Steuben glass was made, it was sent to the stockroom to await being sold. Pieces were signed only before they were sent out, and, if it was a big order, or if the stock clerks were very busy, many pieces wound up not being signed. Although the word "Aurene" is found on many pieces, on many others it is not present, and this is to be expected.

Blown, or free-blown, glass These terms refer to handmade glass that is formed by gathering a quantity of molten glass on the end of a hollow pipe. Air is then huffed (blown) through the pipe to put a bubble into the glass. This glowing, hot mass is further expanded by continued blowing until it is the desired size. As the process continues, the glass is shaped and manipulated with tools to create the intended form.

> **TIP:** Blown glass can often be distinguished by the absence of mold lines and by a pontil, which is a coin-sized spot in the center of the base. This spot can be polished to leave a dime- to fifty-cent-piece-size ring, or left unpolished with jagged ridges.

Bohemian glass Bohemia is the name of a region that was once part of the Austro-Hungarian Empire. Many glass factories were located in Bohemia, and many different types of glassware were made there. American collectors, however, tend to associate the term "Bohemian glass" with a type of ware that has a thin layer of red, yellow, or blue glass cut through to a much thicker, clear layer. Forest scenes and castles are the most common decorations.

> **TIP:** The Bohemian glass described above is still being made today, so collectors need to look for wear on the bottoms of pieces they may be thinking about buying.

Boston & Sandwich Glass In 1826, Deming Jarves founded this famous glass company in Sandwich, which is on Cape Cod, Massachusetts. Among other products, this company was a pioneer in making American pressed glass. It closed in 1888.

> **TIP:** Most of the products of the Boston & Sandwich Glass Company were made in clear, colorless glass. Almost anything done in color—amethyst, canary, sapphire blue, cobalt blue, or emerald green—is rare and commands a premium.

Bristol glass The town of Bristol in England was a glass-making center by as early as the seventeenth century. Its glassmakers were renowned for the quality of their glass, especially their transparent blue-and-green; their cut and engraved pieces; and their opaque white glass. Somehow, this town's name has become associated with cheaper, opaque white glass primarily made in Bohemia, France, Italy, Germany, the United States, and in lesser British glasshouses. When modern American collectors say "Bristol," what they are referring to is a relatively inexpensive piece of glass made from semiopaque opaline glass that has been decorated with hand-painted depictions of flowers, landscapes, or portraits. Usually the background is tinted with an enamel that characteristically shades from a darker color at the top to a lighter, or white, color at the bottom. This glass is primarily mid- to late Victorian, although some was produced in the early twentieth century.

A typical Bristol-glass vase. The walls on these pieces are generally very thin and they almost always have rough pontils, if they have a pontil at all.

TIP: Bristol glass is very common and not highly regarded by most current collectors. Values for single pieces start at about $50 and seldom rise above the $300 mark. The price for large pairs of vases with above average, intricate decoration can be somewhat higher.

Burmese This term refers to an opaque, heat-shaded art glass that shades from yellow to pink. It was invented and patented by Frederick Shirley in 1885 and was manufactured by the Mt. Washington Glass Works of New Bedford, Massachusetts, and by England's Thomas Webb & Sons. There is a legend that when Shirley presented Queen Victoria with several pieces of this particular glassware, she exclaimed, "Oh! It looks just like a Burmese sunrise!" and that is how it supposedly got its name. Mt. Washington made Queen Victoria a tea set elaborately decorated with enameled flowers and beading done in gold and glass beads. The pattern became know as the "Queen's Pattern," and Webb called his product "Queen's Burmese." Remember, Burmese is a single layer of glass that is heat-shaded, which means that there should not be a clear demarcation between where the pink stops and the yellow begins. Glass that is merely pink on the top and yellow on the bottom is not necessarily true Burmese. If you see two layers of glass, or can clearly see where the two colors join in a line, it is not real Burmese. Beware: Burmese has been widely reproduced.

TIP: Burmese was made in both shiny and satin finishes, and most items were plain with no enameled decoration. Collectors, however, are most interested in the pieces with painted decoration, particularly ducks and Egyptian motifs. A small (3 to 4 inches tall) Burmese undecorated vase is worth only about $300, but a 12-inch vase embellished with pyramids, an oasis, and an ibis is worth closer to $4,000. Be wary; sometimes new decoration has been added to old glass.

Cameo glass Cameo jewelry is made by carving through the different-colored layers of a shell or stone to create an image in relief. Cameo glass is made by layering different colors of glass (called "casing") and then carving through them to make a picture or image. This technique was known in ancient times, but it was revived in France, England, Bohemia, and the United States in the nineteenth century. Most cameo glass has just two layers of glass, but the French sometimes used as many as eight (anything over three is extremely unusual). Multiple-layer cameo often commands a premium—but beware, sometimes multiple layering is simulated through the use of enamel.

> **TIP:** Cameo glass made by Emile Gallé, the Daum brothers, George and Thomas Woodall, and Thomas Webb & Sons is highly regarded and eagerly sought. Some very rare pieces have brought more than $100,000. Collectors are particularly interested in pieces that depict non-floral subjects. Unfortunately, recent years have seen the market flooded with reproduction pieces signed "Gallé" and "Daum Nancy" (Nancy is the city in which the Daum Brothers factory was located). Be careful when you buy. Make sure the dealer you are buying from is reputable and get a written guarantee that doesn't just say "signed Gallé" or "signed Daum Nancy," but also says something to the effect that the piece that you are buying is "by the artist" (or factory) and "of the period."

Carnival glass Made by any number of manufacturers from about 1905 to the present day, Carnival glass is an iridescent pressed glass that comes in a variety of colors such as marigold, blue, amethyst, green, white, red, smoke, and many others. Carnival glass was cheap in the early twentieth century, so cheap that it was often given away as a premium or prize, but now it is very collectible. Some of it is quite expensive. Value depends on its form, the color of the base glass, and the design.

This extremely rare example of Carnival glass was made by the Millersburg Glass Company of Millersburg, Ohio, founded by John Fenton in 1909 (John and his brother Frank Fenton founded the famous Fenton Art Glass Company in 1905, but they could not get along). This company was in business only until 1913. Millersburg Carnival glass is prized by collectors and some of it can be extremely expensive. This particular piece is called "Pipe Humidor" and is a mere 8 inches tall. In marigold this piece should be valued at $6,000, in green $7,500, and in amethyst $8,000.

TIP: Value varies widely in Carnival glass, and a good case in point might be the items found in the Cherry pattern (also known as Hanging Cherry) made by the Millersburg Glass Company of Millersburg, Ohio. A 4-inch-diameter bowl in this pattern is only worth about $60 if it is found in marigold. But the same bowl is worth $1,100 if the color of the base glass is blue. As was said above, form is also important, and while a cherry covered butter dish in amethyst is worth only about $400, a banana compote in that same color and pattern is worth more than $4,000.

Coralene Coralene is a type of decoration that involves affixing tiny beads of glass to the surface of a piece of glassware in order to create a pictorial design. The most common form of this type of ware features depictions of coral. Images of seaweed, fish, plants, and flowers can also be found.

TIP: If you rub your finger (gently) across a piece with old Coralene decoration, the beads will stay attached; but if you repeat the process across reproduction Coralene, some of the beads will come off.

Crystal There is a great deal of confusion about what exactly "crystal" is. Classically, the term refers to rock crystal, a clear quartz that was often carved into vessels or made into pendants for chandeliers. Today, however, the term is used to refer to any transparent glass that resembles rock crystal. Crystal is most often a high-quality glass that has a lead content of at least 24 percent. Glass with 24 percent lead is called "half-lead" crystal; with 30 percent, it is called "full-lead" crystal or "cristal superieur."

TIP: Lead glass is often called "flint glass" in England and the United States. This designation arose when the English started using ground or calcined flint as sources of silica for their glass. At about the same time, the manufacturers also started adding lead to their glass. The two ingredients became inexorably linked, even though they are not always used together.

Custard As the name implies, this opaque yellow/ivory glass-ware, first made in England in the 1880s, resembles the dessert of the same name. Some say that Harry Northwood, son of the renowned English glassmaker John Northwood, brought custard glass to America, but others claim the honor goes to the La Belle Glass Company of Bridgeport, Ohio. In any event, a number of manufacturers made pressed glass from custard, and objects in this color are generally the most expensive of all the pressed glass pieces. Beware: Numerous reproductions do exist.

> **TIP:** A Northwood Grape and Cable pressed glass butter dish in clear, colorless glass with red and gold accents is worth about $150, but a Grape and Cable butter dish in custard glass is worth a bit more than twice that figure, around $325.

Cut glass Glass objects decorated with facets, miter cuts, grooves, and/or panels placed there by a rotating wheel of iron or stone are called "cut glass." This method of decoration has been around since the eighth century B.C. American cut glass can be divided into three periods. The first was from approximately 1770 to 1830, and was characterized by engravings of swags, birds, flowers, or stars and such, alone or in combination with either simple flute cuts, the English strawberry diamond-and-fan pattern, sharp diamonds, or pillar cuts. The second period lasted from 1830 to around 1880, and was characterized by pieces with simple, broad panels of flute cuts. The best ware of this period is intricately engraved in patterns that are much more sophisticated than the engraved glass of the first period. This period is also associated with the first American cut glass done in color. The third and final period was from 1880 to 1910. It is known as the "Brilliant Period." This is the period in which cut glass became really popular and was *the* gift to give to brides or wives on their anniversaries or birthdays. This glass is distinguished by thick, heavy, high-quality lead glass that has been intricately and deeply cut with geometric patterns such as hobstars, fans, and notched prisms. Brilliant

Period cut glass is very prismatic, and the cuts tend to be sharp, although not as sharp as the modern laser-cut reproductions that are being made in various places around the world today. Colored and color-cut-to-clear American Brilliant Period cut glass was made, but it is very rare.

> **TIP:** Some pieces of American Brilliant Period cut glass were signed by the maker. These signatures greatly increase the value of the pieces on which they appear. Unfortunately, these signatures are often very hard to see because they were applied by a stamp dipped in acid. This leaves a very faint, grayish mark that is easier to spot if you huff your breath onto areas where such a mark might be found (on the inside bottom of bowls, on the underside of bases, and at the bottom of handles), or if you rotate the object so that the light hits its surface at a variety of different angles. When the light strikes the piece in just the right way, a signature will seem to pop out at you. As we said earlier, collectors need to be aware that it is an easy matter to put new signatures on old glass. All that is required is a rubber stamp, a bit of hydrofluoric acid, and no scruples.

End-of-Day glass There is a myth that at the end of the workday, glassblowers took the various colors of leftover glass, mixed them up, and blew objects from the resulting mixture—thus the name "End-of-Day" glass. Unfortunately, this story is just not true. End-of-Day is really a glassware identified by its streaks and spots of various colors, and it was a regular product of the glass factories that made it. End-of-Day is sometimes called "spatter glass."

> **TIP:** This glassware first appeared in the nineteenth century, but it continues to be made to this day.

Favrile This is a trade name used by Louis Comfort Tiffany for his glass. Some sources say the name was taken from the Latin word for "handmade"; others say it was taken from Old English for "belonging to a craftsman." Tiffany registered the name in 1894.

TIP: Sometimes the word "Favrile" is found incised on the underside of a piece of glass along with "L. C. T." or "L. C. Tiffany," but just because it is there, do not assume that the piece in question was actually made by Tiffany. There are more fake Tiffany and Favrile marks out there than genuine ones, and it is a very easy matter to incise the notations mentioned above into non-Tiffany glass with a diamond-point stylus.

Flashing When a piece of glass is dipped into a batch of differently colored molten glass and a thin layer of color is left on the outside, it is said to be flashed. This technique is often seen on Bohemian glass, where a thin layer of color—usually red, yellow, or blue—is flashed onto a clear, colorless blank, and then the color is cut away to form a design.

TIP: Flashing differs from casing in that flashing produces a much thinner layer of colored glass. Also, casing is blown into a vessel of contrasting color, while flashing is a dipped-on outer coating.

This late-nineteenth-century Mary Gregory vase depicts a little girl sitting on a rock playing with butterflies. Some say that the raised white decoration against a colored ground is an attempt to produce an inexpensive facsimile of English cameo glass.

Gregory, Mary According to legend, an artist at the Boston & Sandwich Glass Company named Mary Gregory enameled images of children onto glass. There was indeed an artist named Mary Gregory at Sandwich, but recent research has determined that she specialized in painting animals, not children. Still, her name is associated with this glassware, which depicts a boy or girl in silhouette, painted with white or pinkish white enamel. The background was usually clear, colorless glass, or it could be any of a variety of colors including red, amethyst, cranberry, green, amber, or blue. The best Mary Gregory pieces show the children in action doing such things as rolling a hoop, chasing butterflies, fishing, or perhaps on a swing. Mary Gregory glass is now thought to have

originated in the 1880s in Europe and it was popular through the turn of the twentieth century. Reproductions exist in large numbers.

> **TIP:** The most desired Mary Gregory colors are cranberry and amethyst. Pieces with clear and amber bases are the least desired and least expensive. An amethyst Mary Gregory water pitcher with an image of a swinging girl is worth about $650.

Iridescence Iridescence is a display of lustrous, pearl-like colors across the surface of a piece of glass. The colors seem to shift as the glass moves or as the light source changes. Natural iridescence occurs on glass that has been buried for hundreds, if not thousands, of years, and is created by chemicals in the earth reacting with the surface of the glass. J. and L. Lobmeyr of Vienna, Austria, introduced an artificially iridized ware in 1863.

> **TIP:** Loetz, Tiffany, and Steuben produced iridescent wares in the late nineteenth and early twentieth centuries, and it is now thought that Tiffany was inspired both by ancient glass and by Loetz.

Lacy glass This is pressed glass that is characterized by small, raised bumps of glass (called "stipples") that make up the background, while raised, unstippled designs of flowers, foliage, rosettes, birds, swags, and such appear here and there across the surface. This glass does look a bit like lace, and it is associated with the Boston & Sandwich Glass Company, which made it during the 1830s and '40s. French companies made similar products, as did glassmakers in the American Midwest.

> **TIP:** When collectors say "Midwestern" glass, they are talking about products made around Pittsburgh, Pennsylvania, and in Ohio and West Virginia. Color is very important to the value of lacy glass. For example, a lacy sugar bowl in the Gothic Arch pattern is worth only about $125 in clear, colorless glass, but in blue the same piece is worth more than $2,500.

Loetz This important glass company was established in 1840 in Klostermule, Austria. Among many other things, the company made iridized glassware that is sometimes said to resemble the work of Tiffany. There is some thought, however, that it was Loetz who influenced Tiffany, not the other way around. The company continued to work until World War II. They also made acid-cutback glass and threaded glass.

TIP: Most Loetz glass is unsigned, and many of the "Loetz" signatures that one encounters are fakes. It has also become a common practice to call any unsigned piece of iridized European art glass "Loetz." This is incorrect, and one way to detect some of this spuriously labeled glass is to know that almost all of Loetz's glass had a pontil. Many of the items incorrectly given Loetz's name do not have this telltale feature.

Millefiori This is Italian for "a thousand flowers." To create this glass, Venetian glassmakers started by making canes composed of long glass filaments. Small slices, which might poetically be said to resemble the heads of flowers, were cut from the ends of these canes and placed in close proximity to one another in a mold. These bits of multicolored canes were fused together with clear glass to form the finished piece of millefiori. This type of glass was made in ancient times, but the Venetians revived it in the 1500s, and it is still widely made today. Although this style of glass is closely associated with the Italians, its manufacture is not limited to that country.

Early- to mid-twentieth-century millefiori cup and saucer. Most of the pieces seen for sale today are fairly modern. Collectors should look for fine-quality canes and genuine signs of wear to distinguish old from relatively new examples.

TIP: Paperweights were often made using millefiori canes in the center of the weight, sometimes alone, and sometimes as a base for other decoration.

Murano Another name for Venetian glass. Geographically speaking, Murano is a group of small islands just off Venice. It is here that the Venetian glass industry settled to preserve its secrets from prying eyes and to keep the furnaces' flames from burning down Venice proper.

> **TIP:** Look for modern Murano glass signed "Venini," "Seguso," and "Barovier and Toso." Items made by these companies during the 1940s, '50s, and '60s can be quite valuable. Some artistically made objects go above the $10,000 level.

Opalescent glass Any colored or clear, colorless piece of pressed or blown glass with a milky white haze running through the body—generally around the top and the decoration—is opalescent glass. Opalescence is achieved by adding arsenic to a batch of glass. (No, the arsenic does not make the glass toxic.) It was first made in England about 1870 and was popular in the United States around 1900.

> **TIP:** Most opalescent pieces are valued in the $50 to $400 range, but a few pieces go much higher. A cranberry pitcher with an opalescent Daisy in Crisscross pattern is worth about $1,000.

Peachblow On March 8, 1886, a wealthy woman by the name of Mrs. Mary Morgan bought a Chinese porcelain vase of a kind known as Peach Bloom or Peach Blow. She paid the then-incredible sum of $18,000, and the press went wild. Mrs. Morgan's purchase was in all the newspapers, and soon the B. D. Baldwin Company of Chicago issued a line of "Peach Blow" cosmetics. Meanwhile, Hobbs, Brockunier and Company of Wheeling, West Virginia, decided to try to copy Mrs. Morgan's vase in glass to sell to the general public. They plated an opal glass body with a yellowish amber glass that had been infused with gold salts. When it was reheated, the top portion of the amber became ruby in color. The finished product has two layers, and shades from yellow/amber at the base to mahogany/ruby at the top. Hobbs, Brockunier called this ware "Coral"; today's collectors call it "Wheeling Peachblow." At about the same time, the Mt. Washington Glass company of New Bedford, Massachusetts, copyrighted the names "Peach Blow" and "Peach Skin"—but the products that they made were very different from the Hobbs, Brockunier ware, and looked nothing like Mary Morgan's expensive Chinese vase. Mt. Washington replaced the uranium oxide present in their Burmese glass with cobalt or copper oxide; the resulting heat-shaded, single-layer glassware shaded from a pale blue to a dusty rose pink. If Mt. Washington Burmese looks like a sunrise, Mt. Washington Peachblow looks like a sunset. The third nineteenth-century maker of a Peachblow glass was the New England Glass Company of Cambridge, Massachusetts. Theirs was called "Wild Rose," and it was a single-layered, heat-shaded glass that was white at the bottom and pink at the top.

> **TIP:** The Peachblow made by Mt. Washington is very rare and very valuable. An 8-inch vase decorated with enameled flowers should be valued about $3,800. As a comparative, a Wheeling Peachblow tumbler is worth about $500, while a New England Peachblow tumbler is worth about $200, and one by Mt. Washington has a value of about $1,500.

Pontil This is really the navel of a piece of blown glass. After the glassblower has gathered a glob of molten glass onto the end of his blowpipe and has huffed (and puffed) a bubble into its center, he attaches an iron rod on the other end of the now-hollow spheroid. This rod is called a "punty." After the blowpipe is removed, it serves as a handle while the glass mouth is opened, the handles are attached (if necessary), and the other finishing details are accomplished. When the punty is broken off, the jagged spot that remains is the pontil. Sometimes this pontil is left rough, like a scar, and sometimes it is polished to leave a smooth, mirror-like surface that ranges from about the size of a dime to the size of a half-dollar, or even larger. Pontils are important because they indicate that a given

The so-called "Morgan peachblow vase" with its griffin holder. Made by Hobbs, Brockunier and Company of Wheeling, West Virginia, in the late nineteenth century.

piece is handmade (which can be indicative of good quality), but it should be noted that sometimes the bottom of a piece of glass is completely polished so that no pontil mark is visible. Unpolished pontils sometimes suggest a European origin. This is not to say that all European glassware of the mid- to late nineteenth century has a rough pontil, because many of the better examples are in fact of the polished variety. It should also be noted that early American glass (pre-1876) often has a rough pontil.

The pattern on this pressed-glass piece is known as "Maple Leaf." It was made by the Gillinder Glass Company in the late 1880s. In addition, this pattern can be found on such items as tumblers, plates, compotes, platters, and trays.

TIP: Pontils can be a clue to age. A pontil with a frosted surface often indicates a twentieth-century reproduction.

Pressed glass When a blob of molten glass is pushed into a mold by a plunger, the resulting glassware is said to be "pressed glass." This cheap, quick method of making glass first appeared in the United States in 1827 and in Europe a bit earlier. One of the advantages of pressed glass is that any pattern on the inside of the mold is transferred (in reverse) to the outside of the glass as it is pushed into the mold. This allows inexpensive pressed glass to resemble very expensive cut glass, and it has also allowed for the creation of a huge variety of patterns that range from simple geometrics to elaborate pictorial representations.

TIP: The patterns on pressed glass tend to be very rounded and smooth, and objects that have been pressed have seam lines from the mold. On the other hand, patterns found on pre-1910 cut glass are sharper, and there should not be any mold lines.

Rubina "Rubina" is the name given to a type of blown glassware that shades from red to clear. It is not heat-shaded like

Amberina but rather is produced by flashing or die-casting on the color. Rubina was made by a number of different companies.

> **TIP:** A similar glassware called "Rubena Verde" shades from red to green. This was the invention of Hobbs, Brockunier and Company of Wheeling, West Virginia, and is a product of the late nineteenth century.

Satin glass This refers to glassware that has been dipped in hydrofluoric acid. This acid bath roughs up the surface, giving it a grainy, satin-like finish.

> **TIP:** We described Mother-of-Pearl satin glass earlier as a type of glass that has an air-trapped pattern and a satin finish. Rainbow Mother-of-Pearl satin glass is the same, only there are rainbow-like bands of color across the surface. The rather pale colors may be pink, blue, green, or yellow. Rainbow Mother-of-Pearl satin glass can be very expensive and a cruet with good coloring can be worth as much as $1,500.

Slag "Slag" is a type of marbleized opaque glass that has been made primarily in the United States and England from about 1870 to the present day. This glass can be found in a number of different colors, but caramel, chocolate, purple, and pink are collector favorites. The original production of slag glass ended in the first quarter of the twentieth century, but reproductions abound, and several modern companies—such as Imperial and Westmoreland— have reintroduced it.

> **TIP:** Pink and chocolate slag have the most potential value. For example, a pink slag cruet in the Inverted Fan and Feather pattern can be worth almost $2,000, and a chocolate slag butter dish in the File pattern should be valued at almost $3,000. Some people say that caramel slag and chocolate slag are the same glass, but to our minds caramel is lighter in color and shows more white marbleizing.

Vaseline This is a type of greenish yellow transparent glass that is said to resemble petroleum jelly. Made as early as the 1870s, it is still being manufactured, generally by pressing, today.

> **TIP:** Unless they are very special, vaseline glass items are fairly afford-able. A perfume bottle, for example, might fetch $200 to $250, and a celery dish in the Daisy and Button pattern might realize $150, or a bit less. Collectors should not confuse vaseline with an earlier glass called "Canary," which is very similar but lacks the slightly greenish tint.

Silver and Other Metals

Everyone knows what silver is—or at least they think they do. But silver can be a little tricky because it comes in so many different grades and purities. Silver is a very soft precious metal, and, like gold, it is almost never used without being alloyed with another metal to make it less soft. Flatware, for instance, is never made from pure silver because a fork would bend when it was stabbed into a steak. Similarly, a bowl is not made from pure silver because it would warp from the least pressure, and any decoration on it would be worn away from even a light polishing.

By custom and by law, different countries in different parts of the world have dealt with the problem of silver content differently. In continental Europe, for example, silversmiths often used an alloy that was 80 percent pure silver and 20 percent base metal. This is called "800" silver (meaning that for every 1,000 parts of metal, 800 are silver). This purity is often marked on the silver itself with a stamped "800." In Scandinavia and Germany, silver with an 83 per-cent purity was popular, and the number "830" often appears on these wares.

The English adopted a sterling standard in 1300, and this provided for silver that was to be 92.5 percent pure (925 parts silver to 75 parts base metal). However, not until 1560, during the reign of Elizabeth I, was the sterling standard firmly set at 92.5 percent pure silver.

It is interesting to note that the word "sterling" was derived from the name of a group of German people whom King John had brought to England to refine silver for coinage purposes around the year 1300. They called themselves "Easterlings" because that is the direction from which they came. In a statute of 1343, the first two letters of this term were dropped, and the word "sterling" was applied to silver for the first time.

Oddly enough, Americans, who adopted most things English, did not adopt the sterling standard for their silver. Until 1861, most American silver was "coin" silver, which was approximately 90 percent pure silver, and was usually made from melted-down Spanish coins. It is said that it was the Tiffanys who pushed to have the United States adopt the British sterling standard in 1861.

The melting of coins to make silverware was a real problem in seventeenth-century England. To stop this practice, a new law was passed in 1697 requiring that makers of wrought silver conform to a new standard of 95.84 percent pure silver. This was called the "Britannia" standard, and it lasted only until 1719, because the silver made with this grade of silver was very soft and could not hold up to domestic use.

Collectors are interested in items made from a wide variety of metals other than silver. Art objects made from bronze can have great value, and utilitarian pieces made from brass, copper, and pewter attract the attention of many. We hope that the words and phrases that follow will take some of the mystery out of these metalwares.

Aftercast When a cast is made of an original bronze and then used to make duplicates, or when an old mold is used by someone other than the original artist (or manufacturer) to make new bronzes, the resulting pieces are said to be "aftercasts." Sometimes these copies are difficult to spot, but usually aftercasts lack the original's foundry marks and the sharp detail, or are slightly smaller than the originals.

TIP: Beware of bronzes marked "Remington"; there are far more after-casts of this artist's work than originals.

Alloy When two or more metals are combined to make a different metal, or to change the physical properties of the primary metal, an alloy has been created. Brass, for example, is an alloy of copper and zinc, and silver is usually alloyed with copper to make it harder.

TIP: Alloyed metals often take on different colors depending on the proportions of the metals used. Eighteen-karat gold, for example, looks richer and has a subtly different color than 14-karat gold since there is less alloy in the finished metal.

Bleeding This is a condition on Sheffield silver plate in which portions of the silver have worn off, leaving the copper under-layer exposed.

TIP: Unless it is really unsightly, collectors prefer that bleeding not be repaired. If bleeding has occurred on pre-1836 Sheffield plate, resilvering is absolutely, positively out of the question and will dramatically lower the value of the piece.

Brass As stated above, brass is an alloy of copper and zinc. Generally, brass has a very golden color, but with the addition of more zinc than normal, the color can be almost white—thus the term "white brass."

TIP: Brass can be both very utilitarian and very decorative. It might be used to make a bucket, a ladle, a tabletop, or a vase. Currently, collectors are avoiding pieces marked "India."

Bright-cut engraving This type of decoration was popular from about 1770 to 1810, and again from 1870 to 1890. It is produced by engraving the surface of a piece of metal with a special tool so that beveled cuts are left behind where slivers of metal are gouged out. These beveled cuts reflect light very nicely—thus the name "bright-cut."

> **TIP:** Bright-cut decorations often consist of garlands and swags with flowers and leaves.

Britannia We have already mentioned the Britannia standard, and said that it refers to silver that is 95.84 pure, but the term "Britannia" also refers to a pewter-like alloy made of tin, copper, and antimony. This alloy was often used as a base for electroplated silver.

> **TIP:** The mark "EPBM" means "Electroplated Britannia Metal." "EPNS" refers to "Electroplated Nickel Silver." An alloy of nickel, copper, and zinc, nickel silver is also called "Argentine," "German Silver," and "Paktong."

Bronze This is the reddish brown alloy of copper and tin. In ancient times it was used to make weapons, and because it is easily cast, it has long been used in the casting of bells and the making of statuary.

> **TIP:** In the late nineteenth and early twentieth centuries, statuary was often cast in cheap pot metal and then coated with bronze to make it look more expensive than it really was. These ersatz pieces are usually lighter in weight than solid bronze pieces, and the fraud can be unmasked by making a small scratch in an unseen place, perhaps underneath. If, when the scratch is made, a silvery streak appears, it is a "bronzed" statue, not a bronze statue.

Champlevé Champlevé is a decorative technique in which grooves are gouged into a metal's surface and then filled with colored enamel (powdered glass). After the piece is heated and the enamel fuses, the surface is polished. Although similar to cloisonné, the finished product tends to be a little cruder, and the decoration appears in bands or shaped reserves.

TIP: A 16-inch-tall Chinese brass-covered urn decorated with Champlevé enamels from the late nineteenth century should be valued approximately $1,800, if it is in good condition and has good-quality work.

Chasing "Chasing" is a decorative technique that involves taking a tool known as a punch and pushing it across a metal surface so that an indented line is formed, but no metal is removed. This technique can be used by metalsmiths to produce very elaborate designs, including leaves, vines, and scrolls.

TIP: Beware of chasing that is a later addition. Often silver pieces made in the mid- to late eighteenth century were very plain, but in the Victorian period elaborate chased designs were added to "update" the look. Collectors are horrified by these defaced pieces.

Cloisonné Although cloisonné work can be found on ceramics, wood, and lacquer, this decorative technique is usually associated with metalware. Cloisonné is created by soldering metal wires onto a metal body, filling the resulting little pockets—or "cells" ("cloison" is French for cell)—with colored enamel, and then firing the piece to fuse the enamels. The final step involves polishing the surface until it is smooth and the enamels are of uniform height. On ceramics, wood, and lacquer, the wires that make up the cells are only held on with glue, and this makes them very easy to damage.

TIP: Chinese cloisonné has been made since the sixteenth century, but most pieces found on today's market are post-1850. Pieces marked "China" were made after 1891, and examples marked "Made in China" were manufactured after 1921. Cloisonné is still being extensively made in Asia.

Coin silver "Coin silver" is an eighteenth- and nineteenth-century American silver standard that varied between 89.2 and 90 percent pure silver. Pieces are occasionally marked with the words "Coin," "Pure Coin," "Standard," "Premium," or "Dollar," or with a "C" or "D."

TIP: American coin silver can easily be overlooked because it is often marked with only the name of an obscure maker. Joe remembers buying a lovely coin silver basket for $28 that was marked with a maker's name that was not familiar to the dealer who owned the piece. This $28 find was worth well over $1,000 to those either "in the know" or willing to do just a little quick research.

Daguerreotype A one-of-a-kind photograph on a silver-coated copper plate is called a "daguerreotype." The process was introduced in 1839 by Louis Jacques Daguerre, and these photographs were popular from the early 1840s through the late 1850s.

TIP: Daguerreotypes can be distinguished by their mirror-like surface, which requires the viewer to hold the picture at an angle to get the best view of the image. These photographs are often found in leather or *gutta percha* cases, and their prices start at about $50 and can go up into the multiple thousands for rare views of famous people, interesting landscapes, and other unusual subjects. As with ambrotypes, large pictures are more desirable. Please be careful with them. Daguerreotypes are very sensitive to the sun and can fade away to oblivion, so keep them in a cool, dark, dry place.

Electroplated silver The English firm of G. R. & H. Elkington is usually credited with the invention of the process that allowed a thin coating of silver to be deposited on a base metal using electrolysis. The process was invented in 1838, but Elkington did not take out its first patent until 1840, and, for a time, it licensed the right to use the process to other companies such as Christofle in Paris, France. American companies—primarily located in Connecticut—started making electroplated silver in the 1850s or a bit before.

Three typical marks found on American coin silver. Many coin silver pieces are marked with only the maker's name or initials. A reference to the fact that the metal is silver is made only occasionally. The mark "L. Fueter N. York" refers to Lewis Fueter, who worked in New York City about 1775. "G & H 1847" is the mark of Gale and Hayden of New York City and Charleston, South Carolina. They worked in the mid-1840s. "D. Goddard & Son" refers to Worcester, Massachusetts, silversmiths in business in the 1840s.

TIP: On electroplated silver items, marks such as "A1," "Standard," "Triple plate," and "Quadruple plate" often appear. These refer to the amount of silver that was originally applied to the piece. For A1 plate, just 2 troy ounces of silver were used to plate 144 teaspoons. Triple plate had 6 troy ounces on the same number of spoons, and Quadruple pieces had 8 troy ounces on them. Incidentally, a "troy ounce" weighs just a bit more than a regular, or "avoirdupois," ounce. One troy ounce equals 1.0971 ounces avoirdupois. The weights of items made of silver and gold are always measured by the troy system.

Ferrotype More commonly called a "tintype," a ferrotype is a photograph on a sheet of japanned iron. Ferrotypes were less expensive than either ambrotypes or daguerreotypes, and this made them more available to people of the middle and lower classes. They were popular between about 1860 and 1890.

TIP: Tintypes are very available and most can be bought for only a few dollars. Particularly interesting to collectors are the examples that depict Civil War–era soldiers. Some of the more valuable of these show Confederate soldiers, soldiers with a plethora of weapons, and children dressed as drummer boys.

Hallmark In its earliest use, the term "hallmark" signified the punch that was put on at Britain's Guild of Goldsmiths to signify that this governing body had tested a given piece of silver and the metal content was of the proper purity. Today, however, the term is generally applied to any mark punched into silver or gold to denote purity of metal, date of manufacture, maker, or place of manufacture. In some cases, a hallmark might indicate whether or not an object was exported or imported, and whether or not proper taxes had been paid. Perhaps the most famous hallmarks are those used by the English since the year 1300, but, because few of us will ever encounter silver or gold of that date, we will limit our discussion to marks as they have appeared from the eighteenth century to today. Hallmarks are also sometimes called "touch-marks," because the right to affix hallmarks was called "the power of touch." The five types of symbols customarily found on English silver and their meanings are:

The Lion Passant, first used to denote the sterling standard in England in 1544.

The Lion Passant or standard mark

The first symbol that was used to denote that a metal was of the sterling standard (92.5 percent pure) was a depiction of a leopard's head, but in 1544 a lion with his tail curved over his back—called a "Lion Passant"—replaced this first symbol. When this important emblem is spotted, the words "English sterling silver" should immediately leap to mind. For pieces of silver that are composed of metal with a purity of 95.84 percent, a representation of the seated figure of Britannia was used. The Britannia standard was used for only a short time (1699 to 1720).

The maker's mark

By law, every maker of English sterling silver had to have a mark that was his, and his alone. The first marks were often symbols such as bells, grasshoppers, birds, fish, crosses, or hearts, but initials did occur. By the turn of the eighteenth century, initials had com-

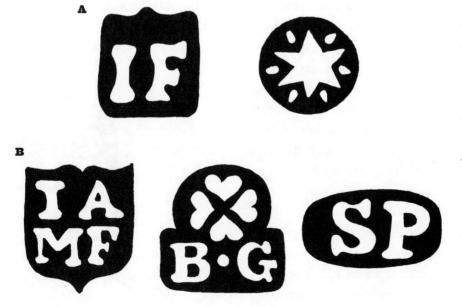

A: Early makers' marks used in the sixteenth century by London silversmiths. Many smiths used symbols instead of letters because they were illiterate.

B: Eighteenth-century makers' marks used by London silversmith Joseph Allen and Company ("IAMF," circa 1735) and Benjamin Gignac ("BG," circa 1770). The "SP" mark is from an untraced London silversmith from the late 1790s.

Four different styles of the letter *L* used as date or assay marks in London. The first was used in 1826–27, the second in 1846–47, the third in 1866–67, and the fourth, 1886–87.

The crowned leopard head was used as the London town mark starting in 1478. Over the years, this mark has changed frequently. Sometimes the tongue is out, sometimes not. The crown disappeared in 1821.

pletely replaced symbols. It should be noted that the reason maker's marks were affixed to silver was because if any piece was found to be less than sterling, the penalties were harsh, and the authorities wanted to know whom to punish.

The date mark or assay mark

This mark signified that the silver in an object had been tested for purity, and consisted of a single letter inside a specially shaped punch. The first twenty letters of the alphabet were used, excluding the letter *J*, and after each nineteen-year cycle was completed, the style of the letters was changed, along with the shape of the punch in which they appeared. It should be understood that the London assay office had one cycle of date (or assay) letters, while the assay offices at other centers such as Birmingham, Sheffield, York, and Newcastle used different cycles of letters and punches for the same dates. This means that in 1796/97 the London assay office used a capital *A*, that same year in Exeter it was a lowercase *y*, and in Sheffield it was a *z*. This may sound confusing, but most reference books on English silver provide charts that make the year-by-year and city-by-city progression quite simple to follow.

Early London leopard-head mark. This one was used around the year 1400.

Town marks

As we said above, a leopard's head was the original sterling standard mark, but when the Lion Passant replaced it, a leopard with a crown on its head became the symbol that a piece had been made in London. When assay offices opened around the country, each was assigned a particular punch, its "town mark." Birmingham was an anchor; Sheffield was a crown. York was originally half

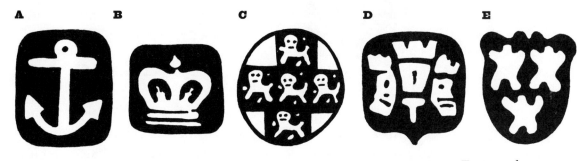

leopard and half *fleur-de-lis;* then, in 1700, it became a cross with five lions inside. From the beginning of the eighteenth century, Exeter used a castle, but Newcastle used three castles. American collectors see the marks for London, Birmingham, and Sheffield most often.

Town marks on English silver:
A: Birmingham
B: Sheffield
C: York (1700 to 1857)
D: Exeter
E: Newcastle

The Sovereign's Head mark

Silver was and is one of those commodities that makes a nice target for taxation. In 1784, a new tax went into effect on silver; and to show that the tax had been paid, a stamp featuring the head of the king was affixed to the silver. The first king depicted was George III; the last, in 1890 (106 years later), was the young Queen Victoria. Collectors have a special affinity for pieces with the head of a bewigged king, and these pieces are often included in the category of "Georgian" silver.

Sovereign's-head mark. Used from 1784 until 1890, with some variation.

> **TIP:** Do not treat a hallmark as if it were a guarantee. Fakers have been known to remove the marks of a famous maker from a badly damaged or insignificant example of his work (such as a spoon) and place them on a large piece made by a lesser maker to raise the piece's value. This is not as hard to do as it sounds. To detect a fraud, huff your breath around the hallmarks. If faint seam lines appear around the symbols, the piece is in all likelihood a fake.

Niello A craftsman begins this decorative technique by engraving a design onto a piece of gold or silver. These grooves are then filled with a mixture of copper, lead, and sulfur in borax, which, after it is fired, forms a black enamel.

> **TIP:** Niello is often associated with Russian silver, and while it was indeed a popular decorative technique in that country, silversmiths have used it elsewhere as well.

Oxidizing To accent the beauty of certain decorative elements on silver, an oxidizing agent is sometimes applied to darken the metal in strategic areas, giving a design shadows and highlights.

> **TIP:** Overzealous polishing can remove this oxidation, and this can seriously reduce the value of the piece of silver. Overpolishing should be avoided on all silver.

Pewter Pewter is not just one metal. It is an alloy of tin and copper with a bit of bismuth or antimony, and sometimes a little lead. The formula has varied a great deal, but, in general, the more tin, the better the pewter. One type of this metal, called "Trifle" pewter, has up to 40 percent lead in it, and is very dark and heavy. Its makers were called "triflers," and they used this pewter to fabricate small items (trifles) such as buttons, buckles, and writing equipment. For the most part, pewter with significant lead content was not used to make products that would be used for food or drink, because even in the late eighteenth century, it was known that lead was a poison.

> **TIP:** American pewter seldom has lead in it, and good-quality pewter has an almost silvery sheen. Eighteenth-century American pewter is fairly rare, because much of it was melted down to make bullets during the Revolutionary War.

Pinchbeck An alloy of copper and zinc, pinchbeck was invented by Christopher Pinchbeck and was used to imitate gold.

TIP: Pinchbeck is also called "Chapman's gold" or "Mannheim gold."

Plique-à-jour This is cloisonné that had its metal back removed after the enamel was fired. The result is a wonderful stained-glass effect that is as fragile as it is lovely.

TIP: Pieces of plique-à-jour are usually very small. Spoon handles and small bowls are the most commonly found objects.

Repoussé This is a technique in which the decoration is formed by hammering from the underside, thereby creating a raised design on the outer surface. This design is often accentuated by chased or engraved details. The technique has been used since ancient times, but it was introduced to this country by Baltimore's Samuel Kirk in the 1820s.

Kirk's Repoussé is one of the most popular patterns ever made.

TIP: Kirk's famous Repoussé pattern sterling silver flatware is still being made and is one of America's most popular wares.

Sheffield Plate In 1742, in a Sheffield, England, garret, Thomas Boulsover was trying to repair a knife. During the process, he managed to fuse a piece of silver to a piece of copper, and it occurred to him that this process might have commercial possibilities. Boulsover started making small items such as buttons and boxes from this new sheet metal, but he was not a good businessman and was soon out of business. Subsequently, his salesman, Josiah Hancock, made a fortune manufacturing large pieces of Sheffield Plate that looked exactly like real sterling silver, but could be sold for a fraction of the cost. Initially, Sheffield Plate appealed to the rich and the noble, and they often had pieces engraved with their crests. This frequently required that a plug of solid silver be inserted into the tray or vessel where the crest would be placed so that when the engraving was done, its copper underlayer was not revealed. These plugs can be detected by huffing breath onto the crest. If a faint line appears around the decoration, it is a plug, and the piece is Sheffield Plate. True Sheffield Plate was made until 1838, when electroplating was invented. After that, electroplating was often done on copper and coupled with the name "Sheffield," but it is not true Sheffield Plate.

> **TIP:** Many pre-1838 pieces of Sheffield Plate are unmarked. This is true in part because there was a period when stamping a mark on these pieces was forbidden. In the early days of the making of Sheffield Plate, some makers applied marks that were a little too similar to the ones being used on real sterling silver. When the silversmiths complained to their guild, the marking of Sheffield Plate was forbidden. This edict was in effect until 1784. Even after that date, many pieces of fine Sheffield Plate went unmarked.

Toleware The term "tole" is taken from the French phrase "tôle peintée," or "painted tin." From the late eighteenth through the mid-nineteenth century, coffeepots, trays, boxes, candlesticks, urns, wine coolers, jardinières, and the like were made from tin and then painted with a background color that was often embellished with geometric, floral, or pictorial designs. The background colors were usually black, red, blue, cream, or a mustardy yellow. Black is the most common hue seen by far. Pre-1850 tole has an unvarnished background and a "dull" (that is, not shiny) look. Post-1850 painted tin may be stenciled and may have gold trim.

> **TIP:** Tole painting became a popular hobby for ladies in the early to mid-twentieth century, and it is easy to be fooled by pieces made by the more talented of the amateurs. Some of these artists were trying to

produce authentic-looking copies of items made a century before, and in many cases they succeeded well enough to fool most people not familiar with the older wares.

Furniture

When Joe first started being interested in antiques, he was surprised by how many people wanted to take shortcuts. One man swore that he could tell the age of a piece of furniture just by looking at the dovetails, another was impressed if pegs were used in the construction, and one woman was sure she had found the key to understanding the age of furniture when she found a book on the history of nails.

No one wanted to hear that modern craftspeople can make perfectly good handmade dovetails, that pegs can be used to secure a contemporary mortise-and-tenon joint, or that furniture repairers routinely keep a supply of genuine old nails that they have removed from old furniture to reuse as needed.

Knowing about antique furniture is not hard, but it does take time and study. Go to museums and visit fine antiques shows and shops. Get as much "hands-on" experience with real antiques and fakes as possible. Because of all her experience, Helaine can tell fake paint on a piece of furniture from across a room, and Joe can spot refinishing and replaced parts at a glance.

In sum, what you need is common sense, trained observation skills, and knowledge of what "old" construction looks like. An understanding of these terms will help you on your way.

Apron A horizontal piece of wood located below the seat of a chair, below the top on a table, or below the case on a desk, bookcase, or other piece of "case furniture." Aprons are sometimes also referred to as "skirts," and they generally run between the legs of a piece of furniture for support.

TIP: Sometimes aprons can be an indication of age, as reproductions often have skimpier, narrower aprons than those that appear on pre-1830 originals.

Banister-back or baluster-back chair Backs on these chairs are made of turned posts called "banisters," or splats in the shape of "balusters." These run vertically from a cross rail just above the seat to a crest rail at the top of the chair.

An eighteenth-century bat-wing drawer pull.

TIP: This was a very popular form during the seventeenth and eighteenth centuries.

Bat-wing This often refers to the shape of drawer pulls or hardware favored on many eighteenth-century case pieces such as chests, desks, and secretaries. These have wing-like protrusions on each side and an element in the middle that resembles a bat's head. There is also a "bat-wing apron" that has graceful, wing-like curves on either side and a protrusion in the middle that looks like the silhouette of a bat with its wings spread.

TIP: Having the original bat-wing pull on a period Queen Anne or Chippendale-style piece of furniture is a big plus. Be sure to look inside the drawers to make sure that there are no extra holes, which generally indicate replacement hardware has been used.

Early-nineteenth-century German or Austrian Biedermeier cabinet. The wheel-shaped mullion is a Neoclassical design element characteristic of this style.

Biedermeier Biedermeier is a style of furniture that was popular from about 1815 to

1860. Its design elements were borrowed from the French Empire and Directoire, English Regency, and Sheraton styles, and its name was derived from a German political cartoon character who represented a well-to-do but cultureless individual. Generally associated with Germanic countries, this style features curved lines in chair backs and legs. Dolphin, swan, and griffin-shaped legs were often used. Cabinet pieces, however, were generally fairly rectangular and blocky. Mahogany, cherry, pear, and birch were some of the more commonly used woods.

> **TIP:** During this time period, writing long, florid letters was in fashion, and, because of this, one of the primary forms of Biedermeier furniture was writing furniture, such as desks and secretaries.

Birdcage Of course some birdcages are for our feathered friends, but the "birdcage" related to antique furniture is found under the top of a tilt-top table. This device is composed of two blocks and four columns and it enables the tabletop to tilt and pivot.

> **TIP:** Birdcages that do not actually perform any function are sometimes found on fakes and reproductions.

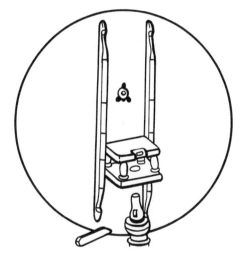

The underside of an eighteenth-century American tilt-top table showing the construction of a "birdcage."

Block front This type of furniture is one of the few eighteenth-century styles that is truly American in origin. A block front is found on case pieces (desks, chests, secretaries, etc.), and consists of three vertical sections. The section in the center is recessed or concave, and the two flanking sections on the sides are convex or raised in relation to the center. This configuration creates a front that seems to be made up of three undulating blocks, and it is associated with the Goddard and Townsend workshop of Newport, Rhode Island.

American eighteenth-century block-front chest of drawers with shell carvings. These block and shell pieces are associated primarily with Rhode Island, but examples were also made in Massachusetts and Connecticut.

TIP: Not all block-front pieces were made by Goddard and Townsend, and not all were made in Newport. Other craftsmen made pieces with this form, and examples from Boston are also known. Most pieces date from the 1760 to 1780 era. Drawer fronts in this style should be carved from one piece of wood.

Bombé A shape found on case pieces such as commodes and cabinets in which the fronts and sides swell or bulge outward is referred to as a "bombé." This fashion originated in Continental Europe.

TIP: During the Chippendale era (1750–1780), bombé-shaped pieces were a popular form in Boston.

Borax This refers to a type of cheap furniture made during the 1920s and '30s. Borax furniture was usually made from inexpensive hardwoods such as gum, and then decorated with router lines and painted, or stamped-on, wood grain. The finished product was very showy when new, but normal wear almost always ruined the fragile finish in just a few years, leaving a piece for which the only possible description is "unsightly."

Cabriole leg. Note the out-curved "knee" at the top and the in-curved "ankle" at the bottom.

TIP: Avoid pieces of furniture with "veneerite." This is paper with a printed wood-grain pattern on it that approximates the look of real wood veneer. Any attempt to "strip" a piece of furniture with veneerite on it will end in disaster.

Cabriole leg This is a leg composed of two curves, the upper one out-curving, or convex; and the lower curve in-curving, or concave. The result is an inverted S curve that often ends in a ball-and-claw or pad foot.

> **TIP:** The out-curved portion of the leg is know as the "knee," while the in-curved portion is called the "ankle."

Chippendale Thomas Chippendale the elder (1717–1779) was an English cabinetmaker, and the first of his profession to publish a book of design. Entitled *The Gentleman and Cabinet Maker's Director*, it appeared in 1754 and was very influential on both sides of the Atlantic Ocean. Chippendale's designs incorporated elements of the Rococo blended with Gothic and Chinese motifs. Forms tended to be very fluid, naturalistic, and irregular. Starting in the nineteenth century, the term "Chippendale" was applied to furniture made by any number of cabinetmakers who had been inspired by *The Gentleman and Cabinet Maker's Director*.

> **TIP:** Furniture that is often called "Chippendale" in the United States is called "George II" or "George III" in England, after the English monarch who was on the throne at the time these pieces were created.

A   **B**

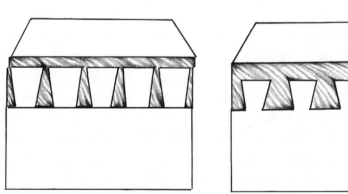

A: Drawing of a hand-cut dovetail. On hand-cut dovetails, there should be slight differences in shapes and spacing. Also, there should be a "gauge line" at the bottom of the dovetail (large end of the triangle) that assisted the craftsman in cutting the joints to the right depth.

B: Drawing of a machine-cut dovetail. On machine-cut dovetails, the dovetails and recesses are uniform and have exactly the same dimensions. There is no gauge line.

Dovetail A dovetail joint resembles a dove's tail, and is formed when flared, triangular tenons (protrusions) are fitted into corresponding slots. This type of construction originated in the seventeenth century, and it is most often seen as the method that connected drawer sides to drawer fronts and backs.

> **TIP:** Early dovetails are often very large and wide. Single dovetails are often found on early-eighteenth-century drawers, and a higher number generally indicates a later date. Very precisely cut dovetails suggest that they were manufactured and not handmade. Examine a chest of drawers by pulling out all the drawers just a bit and lining up the dovetails in each drawer vertically. All the dovetails should appear to be made the same way, and the drawer construction should be consistent. If there are differences, either repairs have been made, entire drawers have been replaced, or the piece under examination was assembled from several different chests.

Eastlake style In 1868 Charles Locke Eastlake wrote a book entitled *Hints on Household Taste* in which he opposed the heavily ornamented Victorian furniture then in fashion. Eastlake wanted to see a return to simpler furniture with joined construction and without heavily carved ornamentation. The illustrations in his book created a fashion for the revival of so-called medieval construction and the development of "Modern Gothic."

> **TIP:** The Eastlake style was far more popular in the United States than it was in England. In the United States the term was applied to very rectangular furniture with spare decoration that usually consisted of very shallow line carvings in geometric and floral patterns. American Aesthetic movement furniture is an outgrowth of Eastlake, but this furniture is much more ornamented and much more highly desired on the current antiques market. Aesthetic movement furniture is heavily influenced by Japanese art and can often be identified by the floral inlays and use of Japanese motifs such as fans and flowers.

Empire In the United States, "Empire" refers to furniture made during the second part of Neoclassicism (the first being the Federal period, from about 1790 to 1815). Empire furniture incorporated design elements taken from archeological findings, and it was in vogue from about 1815 to 1840. American Empire furniture is characterized by heavy forms that are often mahogany-veneered. Animal-paw feet, acanthus-leaf carvings, ormolu mounts, and chairs modeled on the Greek "klismos"—with a concavely curved back and sabre legs—are also typical.

TIP: English Empire furniture is quite different and is referred to as "English Regency." This was popular during the first ten years of the nineteenth century and was derived from Greek Revival and Egyptian themes. Mahogany and rosewood were favored, and many pieces were japanned black. Brass mounts and inlays are typical as are ebony inlays.

Federal An American style popular between 1790 and 1815, the Federal style was inspired by the French Directoire style and by illustrations found in George Hepplewhite's *The Cabinet-Maker and Upholsterer's Guide* (1788) and Thomas Sheraton's *The Cabinet-Maker and Upholsterer's Drawing Book* (1791–94). The basis for both of these books was Robert and James Adam's *The Works in Architecture of Robert and James Adam* (1773), which promoted a very neoclassic aesthetic based on what the English brothers Adam had observed in Italy. American Federal is very geometric and symmetrical and often features carved decorative elements such as urns, eagles, ribbons, swags, and garlands. Inlay is a fairly common element and can be found in the form of bellflowers, stringing, paterae (oval or round shapes arranged in a radiating pattern), and more urns, eagles, ribbons, swags, and garlands. Lines are often straight, and the favorite woods are mahogany, satinwood, maple, and birch.

A Federal sewing table with bag made in New England, circa 1790–1810.

TIP: First-phase American Neoclassical furniture is called "Federal"; similar English furniture is more properly called "Hepplewhite" or "Sheraton."

Victorian Gothic chair, mid-nineteenth century. Note the back, which is very reminiscent of a church window. The four-lobed design at the top of the chair is called a "quatrefoil."

Gothic Gothic furniture draws its inspiration and design elements from Gothic architecture. Eighteenth-century furniture of this style is associated with the designs of Thomas Chippendale; but applied to furniture of the nineteenth century, the term denotes a substyle of Victorian furniture that features pointed arches, trefoils, quatrefoils, and tracery. Chairs are probably the most common Gothic form, and the chair backs often remind collectors of church windows.

TIP: Victorian Gothic was mainly made in the 1840s. It was more popular with designers and architects than with the general public, and original pieces are fairly uncommon.

Inlay To make inlay decoration, pieces of contrasting colored woods, metals, or other substances (such as ivory and mother-of-pearl) are inset into an otherwise solid wooden surface.

TIP: There are many different kinds of inlay. "String" inlay (or "stringing") refers to bands or lines of inlay; "marquetry" refers to inlay that is arranged to make a pictorial image; and the term "parquetry" is attached to inlay laid down in a geometric format.

Japanning Japanning is a method used by European and American craftsmen to imitate Oriental lacquerwork. This finishing technique originated in the second half of the seventeenth century and involved applying layers of paint and varnish to create a surface that would often be painted with Western interpretations of Asian scenes (called "chinoiserie"), or with raised plaster or gesso designs in an Asian mode. The basic coloring of japanning is black, but other colors such as red were also used.

TIP: Japanning was popular in the mid-eighteenth century; in the United States, it was particularly favored in Boston. Japanning also can be found on metal.

Lamination Lamination, as related to furniture construction, is the process of taking a number of thin sheets of veneer and then pressing and gluing them together to made a strong, solid sheet. This process is associated with the mid-nineteenth-century work of John Henry Belter, who made some of the most desired Victorian Rococo Revival furniture. Belter was known for laminating rosewood, then shaping it in a mold to form contours that lent themselves to the curves and naturalistic forms of the Rococo.

> **TIP:** John Henry Belter did not invent the laminating process, nor was he the only Victorian furniture maker to use it. The arms and legs of Belter sofas and chairs are carved from single pieces of wood and generally only the back is laminated. One clue to look for is the hairline seam that appears on the back of laminated items.

Married As the term implies, "married" means that parts of two or more pieces of furniture have been put together to make one piece. A desk might be mated with a bookshelf to make an ersatz secretary, or a lowboy coupled with a chest to make a spurious highboy.

> **TIP:** Married pieces are often sold at auctions, and they can usually be discovered just by looking at the back. The boards of different origin will not match, and the assemblage will stick out like the proverbial sore thumb.

Mortise-and-tenon joint. The "mortise" is the recess into which the "tenon," or peg, is inserted. Often, this joint is held together by inserting a wooden pin through both components.

Mortise-and-tenon A system of construction that involves fitting a tenon, or tongue-like protrusion on the end of one piece of wood, into a hole, or mortise, cut into another piece of wood. A peg is then often inserted through this arrangement to hold the tenon securely in the mortise.

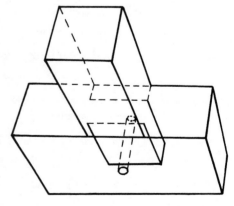

> **TIP:** As the surrounding wood continues to dry and shrink, the pegs will be slightly pushed out

from their original, flush position. Collectors call this "backing-out," and it is a good sign of age.

Oxidation Oxidation is the process whereby oxygen in the atmosphere darkens the exposed surface of wood over time.

> **TIP:** Oxidation provides a useful clue as to whether or not a given piece of furniture is old, and whether or not all its parts are original. Collectors like to pull out drawers and examine the interiors of pieces because these areas were often not exposed to oxygen, and they should be relatively clean and light-colored. If the interior region has inexplicably darkened, has had stain applied, or has light and dark areas in close proximity, warning flags should go up. Also, backs of pieces should be uniformly dark from oxidation, and inconsistencies in this coloration are suspicious.

Patina The texture and color given to wood by years of oxidation, accumulated wax and dirt, and the fine scratching caused by countless acts of touching and rubbing.

> **TIP:** Patina is critical to the value of a piece of old furniture. When a pre-1830 piece has had its patina removed by stripping or refinishing, its monetary value can be cut by half or more.

Queen Anne "Queen Anne" is the name given to a style of furniture popular in America from around 1720 to 1755. It is distinguished by the introduction of the cabriole leg and by S shapes. The carving is generally very restrained; a chair's back splat is solid, not pierced; and hoop-shaped seats are common.

> **TIP:** Be very careful when buying pieces that purport to be Queen Anne, because this is said to be the most commonly faked type of American furniture.

Renaissance Revival "Renaissance Revival" is a subcategory of Victorian furniture popular from about 1865 to 1885. The term is usually applied to massive, large-scale furniture based on Renaissance architectural forms. An individual piece would often be elaborately carved with everything from fruit and vegetables to heads of beautiful women. Marble tops were used extensively on tables, chests, and sideboards, and the beds tended to be huge and to have imposing rectangular headboards. Often, burl walnut accents were set against walnut backgrounds. Greek, Roman, and sometimes Egyptian influences can be seen in these pieces.

> **TIP:** Some of the more important furniture makers who worked in the Renaissance Revival style were Kimbel and Cabus, George Hunzinger, John Jeliff, Mitchells and Rammesberg, and Alexander Roux.

A John Henry Belter Victorian Rococo Revival chair. Note the elaborately pierced back.

Rococo This is a furniture style developed in France. Its name is derived from the French word *rocaille,* which means "rock-work," a term originally used to describe the grottos and fountains located in the gardens at the Palace of Versailles. In French furniture, it is associated with the reign of Louis XV, but by the mid-eighteenth century, the style had reached England, where it influenced the work of Thomas Chippendale and others. Rococo is characterized by the use of the cabriole leg and by naturalistic forms such as carved depictions of rocks, shells, fruit, and flowers. Scrolls, ribbons, and acanthus leaves were also employed as decorative elements, and pieces have a light, airy feeling. The Rococo style was reinterpreted and revived in Victorian times and was very popular from about 1840 to 1870. The proportions on these revival pieces are larger, and the feeling is much more ponderous.

> **TIP:** Some of the most desired Victorian furniture is in the Rococo Revival substyle. John Henry Belter worked in this form, as did Charles Boudoine, J. and J. Meeks, and Pru-

dence Millard. The best pieces were generally made from rosewood, and had elaborate pierced carvings that involved cutting completely through the wooden background to create a three-dimensional shape.

Veneer "Veneering" is the process of cutting thin strips of wood—or other materials such as ivory or tortoiseshell—and applying them to the outside surface of a piece of furniture. This is done for decorative effect and also for more economical use of exotic woods and substances.

> **TIP:** When the word "veneer" is mentioned, many people have a negative reaction, and think that veneered pieces are less desirable than objects made from "solid" pieces of wood. Although this may have some validity for many modern pieces, for antiques, the use of veneer often suggests a very labor-intensive process that amounted almost to an art form. It should be remembered that the materials that were used were often quite rare and precious, and veneer was a way to utilize their beauty without being profligate with the rare or expensive substance. One thing to remember: Veneers from before the mid-nineteenth century are generally thicker than veneers used later.

Paper

That this area of collecting exists at all surprises many homeowners who find themselves having to clear out an estate. They cannot imagine that a single postcard might be worth more than $8,000, or that the first issue of *Playboy* magazine with its cover picture of Marilyn Monroe is worth around $4,000 in pristine condition.

Joe remembers helping to organize and sell the estate of author Alex Haley, and that the sale of two paper items shocked everyone who attended the auction. The first was a simple paper napkin, the kind once kept in metal holders on restaurant tables. On it were some handwritten musings by Malcolm X that he had penned just after he was released from prison. The note was unsigned, but the napkin sold for $29,000! The other memorable piece was a postcard with a monkey on the front. On the back, Malcolm X reflected on how the monkey was more highly regarded by society than he was. The postcard was signed and sent to Haley during the time when the two men were collaborating on *The Autobiography of Malcolm X*. It sold for $7,500, which is probably a world record for a modern postcard.

The list of paper items that are collectible is practically endless. It includes such diverse items as paper dolls, posters, stock certificates, valentines, magazines, trade cards, fruit-crate labels, advertising items, newspaper headlines, fans, sheet music, and on and on and on. It should also be understood that, while many of these paper items are valued at less than $10 each, many others are worth $100 or more—up to the $10,000-plus level.

Condition of paper items is very important. Tears, stains, and other damage is repugnant to paper collectors, and they will avoid items that have been water-damaged, prints that have had their margins trimmed, photographs that have faded in the sun, and children's books that have extensive crayoning on their pages.

Always keep in mind that paper items of every description may be much more valuable than they appear to be, and if paper pieces are a puzzle, here are a few words and phrases that should help.

Advertising cards Also called "trade cards," these originated in the eighteenth century, but the height of their popularity was in the 1880s and '90s. Usually measuring somewhere between 2 by 3 inches to 4 by 6 inches, these were brightly colored advertisements that pushed everything from liniment and soap to sewing thread and Levi's jeans. Victorians received these cards from store owners, who often stamped their business addresses on the back. In many cases, the trade cards that have survived are found glued into albums, and if they cannot be removed in perfect condition, they are greatly devalued. Four special categories of trade cards that interest collectors are: "mechanicals," which have moving parts; "hold-to-light cards," which reveal their designs when they are placed in front of a light source; "die-cut" cards, which are cut in the shapes of such things as animals, people, and boxes; and "metamorphic" cards, which are transformed when a flap of some sort is folded down.

> **TIP:** Most late-nineteenth-century trade cards can be bought for $10 or a bit less, but prices can range into the hundreds of dollars for rarer examples. Collectors are particularly interested in such items as the cards put out by Levi Strauss, and cards featuring Palmer Cox's Brownies, Santa Claus, and unusual machinery or forms of transportation.

Albumens "Albumens" are photographs made by coating paper with a mixture of egg white and silver salts. These photographs were popular from about 1855 to 1890, and they can be recognized by their thick, gelatin-like surface, a faint orangish discoloration, and fading around the edges.

> **TIP:** Some of the most famous photographers of the nineteenth century made this kind of photograph. Original albumen prints either signed by or attributed to artists such as Julia Margaret Cameron, Oscar Gustav Rejlander, Nadar, or Roger Fenton can fetch thousands of dollars each at auction, depending on condition and subject matter.

Big Little Books First published in 1933 by the Whitman Publishing Company of Racine, Wisconsin, Big Little Books became so popular that many companies such as Saalfield, Goldsmith, and World Syndicate published very similar books for young people. These thick, hand-sized tomes featured heroes such as Dick Tracy (the first character featured), Flash Gordon, Buck Rogers, Tarzan, G-Men, and Red Ryder, and cartoon characters including Blondie, Donald Duck, Betty Boop, Little Orphan Annie, and Mickey Mouse. Comic books pushed them from favor in the 1950s.

> **TIP:** Although these have survived in great numbers, they did not usually survive in good condition. Big Little Book collectors want their

books to be intact, with all their pages, and with as little wear as possible. Even so, many examples are worth less than $20 each, but some rare titles can command prices into the mid- to high hundreds. Collectors are particularly interested in Disney characters, superhero and space adventures, and books packaged as premiums by the Cocomalt Company in their cereals.

Broadside Technically, any large sheet of paper that has been printed on only one side is a broadside; but to collectors, a broadside is a piece of paper printed on one side that dispenses information, such as public notices and advertisements. Few measure more than 24 inches long. Widths vary from about 8 inches to as much as 18.

> **TIP:** Broadsides relating to wars (mainly the Revolutionary and Civil), theatrical events, transportation, or historical incidents are the most desired. Examples with fancy borders, interesting illustrations, and portraits are also in demand. Prices for specimens in good condition start about $50 and only occasionally rise above the $1,500 level.

Brush-stroked prints This term refers to prints that have had a clear coating applied over their surface. The texture of this coating resembles the brush strokes found on real oil paintings.

> **TIP:** These are real foolers for some people, and we get hundreds of phone calls every year from people who are convinced that their prints are original works of art because they can feel "brush strokes" when they run their fingers across the surface. It is sometimes very difficult to convince these individuals that if the piece in question is on paper or ordinary cardboard, it is, in all likelihood, an inexpensive print with a textured surface.

Cartes de visite Sometimes called "CDVs," these small "visiting card" photographs usually measure 3½ by 2¼ inches, and are customarily pasted on 4- by 2½-inch cards. The process that produced these photographs was patented in 1854 by André Adolphe Disderi, but they did not become popular until 1859 when Disderi distributed pictures of Napoleon III throughout France as a tribute to the emperor on the occasion of his leading troops into battle against Italy. The fad spread to England when Edwin Mayall published an album featuring fourteen cartes de visite portraits of Queen Victoria and her family; in the United States, the leading proponent of the carte de visite was Napoléon Sarony, who specialized in photographs of entertainers and literary figures. Soon, people were collecting cartes de visite of famous people, as well as having these photographs made of themselves. They were often left as visiting cards in the homes of friends, and it was not unusual for families to have large albums of cartes de visite that included photographs of family and friends, as well as images of politicians, entertainers, circus performers, military heroes, and so-called freaks of nature. Cartes de visite were very popular, and it has been estimated that in the mid- to late 1860s as many as 400 million of these were printed each year.

> **TIP:** Most cartes de visite of ordinary people are very inexpensive, but examples featuring Abraham Lincoln, James Buchanan, Kit Carson, and Mark Twain (among others) can be very pricey. A Mathew Brady carte de visite of Abraham Lincoln, for example, should be valued at $1,500 or a bit more if it is in good condition. Images of Lincoln by other photographers are generally somewhat less expensive, and some specimens (especially those not taken from life, such as those derived from paintings and engravings) can be bought for as little as $100. Also, keep in mind that a carte de visite of Robert E. Lee is worth as much as $7,500 if it was personally autographed by the general.

Chromolithograph This is a lithograph that was printed with more than two colors. It is a process associated with the mid- to late nineteenth century (the first one appeared in 1858) and the early twentieth century.

TIP: One of the leading makers of chromolithographs in the United States was Louis Prang, and many of his prints—such as "Siege of Atlanta" and "Battle of Shiloh"—are available in the $300 to $450 range in excellent condition.

Cigarette cards These pictorial cards were placed in cigarette packages as premiums. Similar cards have also been given away with candy, tea, soap, cheese, and even dog food. They were popular during the late nineteenth century, and featured images of such people and things as actors, sports figures, celebrities, Native Americans, cars, airplanes, national flags (often carried by pretty women), and images taken from nature. They were made well into the twentieth century, and some are quite modern. Cigarette cards were also printed on fabric; these are called "silks."

TIP: Cigarette cards are usually collected in series of multiple cards with related subjects. Single cards often have a very modest value, but it must be mentioned that the most valuable baseball card of all time is really a cigarette card. It features Honus Wagner, and it is rare because Wagner disapproved of smoking and had all but a few of these cards destroyed.

Currier & Ives Nathaniel Currier went into the printmaking business with a man named Stodart in 1834. Stodart did not last long, however, and Currier went it alone until about 1847, when he was joined in the business by his brother, Charles. How long Charles was around seems to be open to conjecture, but in 1857, Currier went into partnership with James Merritt Ives. This firm continued to operate, eventually under the direction of their sons, until 1907. It is said that the firm made more than 7,000 different prints, and a mind-boggling number of them were sold on the streets of New York City, the way they sell hot dogs and pretzels today. Currier & Ives' work covered the gamut of American life, from pictures of presidential deathbeds to boat races, and burning buildings to sweet depictions of small children.

TIP: Currier & Ives prints have been widely reproduced, but there are a few clues that might help separate the real from the spurious. Real Currier & Ives prints are hand-colored lithographs, and oftentimes the colors go outside the lines. Also, under inspection with a magnifying glass, the designs on a real Currier & Ives print will be made up of short lines; on fakes, the presence of little dots can often be detected. Original Currier & Ives prints came in a variety of sizes, but the most prevalent were 7 by 9 inches, 8.8 by 12.8 inches, 9 by 14 inches, and 14 by 20 inches. Reproductions often come in sizes that do not conform to the known dimensions of originals. The most valuable Currier & Ives prints tend to be of the so-called large folio size, which is larger than the 14- by 20-inch size. Pictures of children, beautiful women, flowers, still lifes, and religious scenes are the least desired of the Currier & Ives prints, while the nautical, countryside, sporting, and political specimens command the most interest. Examples such as the large-folio "Husking," "Mink Trapping, Prime," "Trolling for Bluefish," and "Lightning Express, Leaving the Station" can bring in excess of $10,000 if they are in pristine condition (margins still intact, no tears, no foxing, no water stains, colors still bright).

Ephemera A term that applies to paper items that were meant to last for only a short time, ephemera includes such things as newspapers; ticket stubs to sporting events, the theater, and rock concerts; sales pamphlets; and magazines. All are now very collectible.

TIP: The April 5, 1882, *Chicago Tribune* announcing the death of Jesse James is valued at $600 if it is in good condition.

Etching In this process, a metal plate is coated with an acid-resisting substance. An artist then uses a tool to draw lines through this coating to expose the metal underneath. The plate is then given an acid bath, and the lines are "bitten" into the metal itself. Having served its purpose, the acid-resisting substance is removed, and the plate is inked for printing. Most etchings are black and white.

TIP: Etching was very popular as an artist's medium from the late nineteenth century through the 1930s. Many artists did etchings, and often their signatures can be seen written in pencil in the margins of the finished products. Unfortunately, the majority of these works are fairly inexpensive and can be bought for $500 or less. Etchings by a famous artist such as Childe Hassam start about $1,000 and go up to the $20,000 range for his best work, while etchings by Winslow Homer start about $10,000 and go above the $30,000 mark. Etchings by James Abbott McNeill Whistler start about $500 and rise above the $30,000 mark.

Foxing The name given to unsightly brown spots or pale patches of discoloration found on paper, particularly prints, is "foxing." This is generally caused by mold, mildew, or impurities in the paper.

TIP: Foxing is not uncommon on antique prints, but its presence will hurt the value of a piece greatly. Luckily, professionals can restore prints that have been affected by foxing, but it is not a job that should be attempted by an amateur.

Fraktur Classically, this word refers to a category of German block-letter type used in the printing of documents and manuscripts, but to collectors it is a hand-lettered or hand-embellished document created by people of Germanic origin who lived in Pennsylvania, the Carolinas, New Jersey, Ohio, Kentucky, Virginia, and in the Ontario province of Canada during the eighteenth and nineteenth centuries. The document in question is generally a birth, baptismal, or wedding certificate, but sometimes the term "Fraktur" is used to describe a decorated bookplate or an illustrated family history. Frakturs often start out with a preprinted form (although some may be drawn by hand with pen and ink) that is then hand-decorated around the border and in other blank spaces with colorful depictions of angels, hearts, birds, flowers, and animals. Later, less-desirable frakturs often had printed-on decoration and these were generally just embellished with hand-applied color enhancements. The best frakturs were generally made before 1820, and the custom was fading from general practice by the 1830s.

> **TIP:** Frakturs fall into the category of folk art, and the best of the hand-drawn ones can bring prices well above the $20,000 mark. Ordinary specimens, however, start about $150 or even a bit less.

Lithograph This process was discovered in 1792 by Alois Senefelder, and it was based on the principle that grease and water do not mix. To make a lithograph, a design is drawn with a greasy crayon on a stone, zinc, or linoleum surface. Water is applied to the surface, and then the ink, usually black, is applied. The ink sticks to the crayon, but does not adhere to the other wet areas. When a piece of paper is pressed against the stone in a press, the ink is transferred to the paper, leaving an image. If color is to be added, a different stone is needed for each hue.

> **TIP:** Most nineteenth-century lithographs started out black and white, and on a print with varying colors, the final image with all its colors had to fit together just right, but they seldom did. Usually, the color either did not entirely fill the spaces allotted to it, or it slightly slopped over the edges. This is usually very subtle, but it is a good clue to age and authenticity.

Margins The blank area or outer border found around the outside of a print is the "margin." The phrase "full margin" usually refers to a wide border that has not been cut, while the term "thread margin" indicates that the margin is so slight that its width is only that of a thread.

> **TIP:** Collectors often find prints with margins that have been cut so that the pieces of paper would fit into frames. This practice horrifies enthusiasts, and it greatly devalues the print—it is not unlike cutting

up $100 bills so they will fit better into your wallet. It is money thrown away.

Original print This phrase refers to a print that has been produced by or made under the supervision of the artist who created the original image. These prints are customarily signed in pencil on the right side of the bottom margin and the size of the edition and the number of the particular print is written as a fraction, such as "10/25" (i.e., this print is number 10 from an edition of 25).

> **TIP:** The size of the edition of an original print is very important. Traditionally, an edition with more than fifty prints has been considered to be too large. Original prints made in editions of 500, 1,000, 1,500, or more are just too plentiful for the tastes of most serious collectors, and, in the short term, prices on these tend to rise very slowly, if at all.

Silhouette There is a wonderful legend about the origins of these cut-out paper pictures. It maintains that these images got their name from Étienne de Silhouette, who was finance minister to Louis XV. The taxes levied by Silhouette were so notoriously high that wealthy people felt that they had been reduced to a shadow of their former financial selves, and, over time, Silhouette's name became attached to these "shadow" portraits. Whether this story is true or not is open to debate, but silhouettes as we know them are made by placing a subject in front of a bright light and projecting a shadow of his or her profile onto a white piece of paper. The image is then traced and cut out of black paper and mounted on a white card. "Hollow-cut" silhouettes are just the reverse, in that after the image is cut out of the white paper, the paper with the profile-shaped hole in it is mounted over a black card. Gifted artists were able to depict families and room settings in this way as well as ships, "scenics," and even railroad cars (all done freehand). These were popular in the eighteenth and nineteenth centuries until about 1860, when photography made them obsolete.

TIP: There was a revival of silhouette-making in the 1920s that lasted until the 1950s—but collectors are only now becoming interested in these later efforts. Signed silhouettes are in great demand and specimens by Edouart and the Peale family are especially desirable. Examples marked "Peale Museum" or "Peale's Museum" are a good find.

Stereoscopic views During the span of time between the early 1850s and the Eisenhower administration of the late 1950s, millions of stereoscopic photographs were taken. These dual photographs were made with a special camera, and when they were mounted on cards, they could be viewed through a device called a "stereoscope." The two images were slightly different from one another, and when they were placed in the stereoscope, the viewer's eye perceived a three-dimensional image. It should be mentioned that stereoscopic views also were made using the daguerreotype process, which produced one of these dual pictures on a copper plate. These are now rare and can be very valuable. Glass "stereoviews" were made, and these too can be rare and valuable.

TIP: There was a time when nobody wanted stereoviews and they could be bought for just a few dollars. Now, prices can range above the $1,000 level for rare views. Early stereoviews should have square corners; the ones made after the late 1870s have rounded corners. Subject matter to look for includes photographs of Native Americans; Civil War scenes; Western mining; aviation and unusual transportation; records of expeditions and surveys; nudes; ships; and personages (such as Mark Twain, Abraham Lincoln, Dwight Eisenhower, George Custer, Babe Ruth, and Robert E. Lee).

Textiles and Needlework

To most collectors, the term "textile" brings to mind quilts, coverlets, and table linens. But this term also includes such diverse items as carpets, tapestries, samplers, and vintage clothing.

As a general rule, collectors evaluate textiles by three standards: the quality of the craftsmanship; the appeal of the design or the charisma of the "graphics"; and the overall condition. The skill level of the maker is critical to the monetary and aesthetic values of almost any textile, and talented fingers guided by artistic eyes are a must for the creation of first-rate specimens.

Textiles are of great interest to many modern collectors. Here are a few words and phrases that should help to illuminate this subject.

Aniline dye Before the mid-nineteenth century, dyes were made from naturally occurring substances and vegetable matter. Every American household once seemed to have an iron pot on the hearth that was used for boiling plants to extract their color—iron pots, in particular, were used because it was found that they made the colors (particularly indigo) deeper and cleaner. Then, in 1856, the first aniline dye was made from coal tar. Mauve in color, the dye formed the basis of many of the synthetic colors available today.

> **TIP:** Vegetable dyes made at home tend to be fairly drab, and early names for them included "lead," "sad-color," "slate," and "liver." Aniline dyes, on the other hand, were bright, but they tended to fade. Mauve, for example, usually faded to gray.

Appliqué quilt In this variety of quilt, the design elements were cut out and their edges turned under and hemmed. Then, the device—be it a heart, a bird, a building, a vase, or whatever—was sewn or applied to a solid-color background. The trick was to cut out designs that were interesting and then arrange them to form a harmonious and beautiful whole. These quilts were most popular between 1775 and 1885.

> **TIP:** Two famous types of appliqué quilts are the "Hawaiian" and the "album" quilt. Missionaries

Hawaiian appliqué quilt, circa 1850. Looking closely, it is possible to pick out the tropical leaves and fruit that were the inspiration for the design.

brought washable cloth to the Hawaiian islands in the 1820s, and they also taught the women of the royal court to sew and quilt. Later, this skill was taught to the children in the missionary schools. For the most part, Hawaiian quilts have two colors—one brilliant hue against a white background—and the appliqués are traditionally one piece (like a giant paper cutout) that covers the entire surface of the quilt. The inspiration for a Hawaiian quilt was usually tropical leaves and fruit. The leaves are often rather jagged, even thorny looking, in outline, and the resulting pattern can be rather abstract. These are mainly products of the early to mid-nineteenth century, but modern ones are also being produced. The album quilt is a mainland American classic that often incorporates trapunto (raised designs stuffed with cotton) and embroidery as well as appliqué. The main portion of the design is made up of squares that are like pages in an album, each one with its own decoration. Such a quilt might feature the various flowers in a lady's garden, with one flower depicted on each "album page" (or square). It might also feature the quilter's favorite birds, or perhaps scenes from family history or buildings in town. Often different women made each album page, and they were then sewn together to form the friendship album. The most famous and valuable album quilts are associated with Baltimore, Maryland, and are called "Baltimore Album" quilts.

Bobbin lace Also called pillow lace or bone lace, bobbin lace is made by laying out a pattern on a firm pillow and then executing the design by weaving, twisting, or braiding the threads that are held on bobbins, which were originally made of bone. Two types of pillows are used—one mushroom-shaped for making "free" laces, and the other bolster-shaped for making "straight" laces.

TIP: The legend is that bobbin lace originated in medieval times when a Flemish woman noticed a spider weaving a web on her black apron, and decided to imitate the work of this eight-legged creature. To facilitate the process, her boyfriend made some small wooden bobbins to hold the threads so that they would not get tangled. Some famous types of bobbin laces are Chantilly, Mechlin, and Valenciennes.

Crazy quilt Popular from 1870 to 1890, crazy quilts were generally made from oddly shaped pieces of silk, satin, or velvet, with an occasional piece of wool or cotton thrown in every now and then. They were often "memory" quilts with bits and pieces assembled from meaningful textiles, such as old wedding dresses, men's ties, neighbors' and relatives' clothing, plus graduation and prize ribbons and fragments from other cloth items with sentimental resonance. These scavenged fragments were often attached in a haphazard fashion with large embroidery stitches that were a part of the overall design. The stitches might take the form of zigzags, or V shapes, or be in a form suggesting some sort of vegetation. The best crazy quilts were then embroidered with names, dates, and intricate depictions of flowers, birds, people, and such. The resulting design is very quirky and has an abstract quality that borders on Cubism in some instances. Because of their very personal nature, these were parlor pieces kept on display for company to see and admire.

Central design for a coverlet embroidered with crewelwork, circa 1820. The pattern was first drawn freehand, and the flowers show a distinctly Asian influence.

TIP: Not too many years ago, crazy quilts were not highly regarded, but by the late 1990s they began to be more appreciated. Now, prices have moved well above the $5,000 mark for better examples in good condition.

Crewel Crewel is a type of embroidery that some say originated in India, while others maintain that it was first done in England in the early seventeenth century. Crewel designs typically feature a profusion of birds, flowers, fruit, trees, and animals—images drawn from Persian, Indian, Chinese, and, less exotically, English motifs—rendered in brightly colored wool or yarn sewn on coarse linen homespun. Crewelwork was used to upholster chairs and to decorate draperies, bed hangings, and bed coverings.

TIP: English crewelwork was often very dark and busy with the entire background of a piece covered in embroidery, sometimes including heraldic devices and family crests. These are usually lacking on American pieces, which tend to be much lighter and brighter in color and which normally have less embroidery arranged in more free-flowing patterns. English examples usually have borders worked with geometric designs, but most American specimens do not have borders.

Flax wheel Also called a Saxony wheel, this small spinning wheel was designed to spin flax. It was introduced into England in the sixteenth century and came to this country with the first settlers. Do not confuse it with a quill-and-bobbin winder, which has much the same configuration, but is lighter and does not have distaff fittings at the back. A distaff is a "stick" or staff-like device that fits on the back of a flax wheel and holds the tow, wool, or flax in its cleft upper end. Fibers are taken from the distaff and spun on the wheel to make thread. Between the distaff and the wheel is a spindle or bobbin that collects the thread after it is spun.

TIP: Some flax wheels are very old but, for the most part, they are not monetarily valuable. Most are valued in the $500 to $750 range.

Hooked rugs Starting in the 1830s, thrifty American women began making small area rugs by pulling strips of fabric through a mesh backing with a hook—thus the name "hooked rug." The fabric strips used in these rugs were often harvested from the household "rag bag" because they were either too small or too worn to have any other use. The first backing materials were either cotton or linen, but jute burlap replaced them in the 1850s. Early on, the more skillful makers created their own patterns for their rugs. These patterns might be geometric, floral, or pictorial. Later, patterns began appearing in ladies' magazines and sewing manuals, and still later, pieces of burlap with designs printed on them were produced commercially. These later rugs were generally made using yarn instead of strips of fabric, and their designs might imitate Oriental or Aubusson carpets as well as the more traditional motifs.

> **TIP:** Collectors should be aware that there was a great revival of rug hooking in the 1920s, during the period known as "Colonial Revival." This is something of a contradiction in terms since hooked rugs were not a colonial American product.

Jacquard In about 1820, a new type of loom was brought to the United States. Invented by Frenchman Joseph Jacquard, it was actually an attachment for the looms that made double-woven coverlets. Into this attachment was fed a punch card that looked something like a piano roll, and this punch card guided the loom's operation to produce a predetermined pattern that was far more intricate and sophisticated than any weaver could produce on his or her own. Surviving Jacquard coverlets are generally wool, and they are known for their elaborate patterns and intricate borders that often include a block in the corners that might give the weaver's name, the place of manufacture (town, county, and state, in some cases), the date of manufacture, and sometimes the owner's name. Jacquard coverlets without these name blocks are said to be prison-made, but this is highly speculative.

Jacquard coverlet with Double Rose and Bird border at the foot, and Grapevine border on the side. The center motif is called "Sunburst."

> **TIP:** The value of a Jacquard coverlet depends upon its condition, its color, and the patterns used for both the border and the center. Most Jacquard coverlets are blue and white, and deviations from this color scheme are interesting to collectors. Two colors are the norm for this type of coverlet, and examples with three or more hues can command a premium. Elaborate pictorial center designs, such as the Boston Town design, which shows the city and harbor of Boston complete with ships, are much desired, as are examples that have borders with images of trains, ships, houses, eagles, and other birds, such as roosters.

Linsey-woolsey This term is applied to coarse fabrics made from a combination of either linen and wool or cotton and wool. It is interesting to note that the word "Linsey" does not refer to linen, but to the English town of Lindsay, where it is thought that this type of fabric was first made. Traditionally, linsey-woolsey was quilted for extra warmth, and was originally made into clothing. The petticoats of our female Pilgrim forebears, for example, were often made from linsey-woolsey. In the United States, this term has come to be applied most commonly to a type of quilted bedcovering that was popular in the eighteenth and early nineteenth centuries. These bedcoverings can be quite large, but they are short and wide, and often the lower corners were cut so that the spread would fit around a bed's lower posts and would reach to the floor. They were made extra wide because many early American beds slept three to five people, and the warm linsey-woolsey had to cover all of them.

> **TIP:** It is thought that Europeans learned to quilt during the Crusades after they noticed that the Turks wore quilted garments under their armor for warmth. These garments consisted of two layers of fabric with a layer of wool in between. This three-layer "sandwich" was sewn together—or quilted—to keep the various components together.

Needlepoint lace Lace made with a needle and thread is called "point" or "needlepoint" lace. The process starts with a pattern pricked into a piece of paper that is sewn onto a backing fabric. Then, using loop and buttonhole stitches, the pattern is outlined and filled in with joining bars.

> **TIP:** Needlepoint is usually the most expensive lace. Two famous varieties are point de Venise and point d'Alençon.

Overshot "Overshot" is the name applied to a type of home-made coverlet of wool and linen made by rural and many urban families on their looms. These are normally pre-1850, and the process of making them started with the growing of the fiber, and continued on through the making of the thread, the dyeing of the yarn, and the looming of the spread using patterns called "drafts." The patterns commonly consisted of diamonds, squares, and stripes, and carried names such as Snail's Trail, Lover's Chain, Double Chariot Wheel, and Nine Snowballs. Since home looms were rather narrow, overshot coverlets are always seamed down the middle to join two lengths of fabric to yield a coverlet wide enough to cover a bed.

> **TIP:** When coverlets were seamed together, care was not always exercised to match the patterns precisely. In some parts of the country this was done on purpose because it was believed that a broken line deflected evil, and, therefore, a coverlet with the pattern slightly askew in the middle brought good luck to those who slept under it.

Patchwork quilt "Patchwork" refers to the process of sewing small patches of varying kinds of fabric together to make a bedcovering with a regular and distinct pattern. In its simplest form, all this requires is fragments of cloth cut into squares, diamonds, hexagons, or triangles, and the ability to sew an even, straight stitch. Young girls began making a basic quilt as soon as they could sew. The goal was for each young woman to sew thirteen patchwork quilts before she got married—proceeding from the first, simple one to the thirteenth, which would be her most elaborate, and this final quilt was called her "Bridal Quilt." Along the way, she learned how to save and cut the patches, how to design a pleasing pattern, and how to make the more elaborate stitches used in the actual quilting process. It was said that the young lady who did not have her quilts done by her twenty-first birthday would never be married. The classic period for American patchwork quilt making was 1775 to 1875, but interesting examples were made during the early twentieth century and through the years of the Great Depression. Many modern quilters view the patchwork-quilt-making process as an art form.

> **TIP:** As a general rule, eighteenth-century patchwork quilts have no borders; nineteenth-century examples usually do. Early-nineteenth-century quilts often have large central designs, but by 1860 the large central motif had been replaced by smaller designs.

Sampler The first known samplers are from the late sixteenth century. At that time, a sampler was often a long strip of cloth worked with vertical rows of stitches that the young seamstress had mastered. These early pieces were called "examplers" or "samplaires," and they were customarily rolled on an ivory rod and kept in a drawer for easy reference when a how-to refresher was needed. There are all kinds of samplers. Some samplers are just compilations of mending and darning stitches that a home-maker had to know to keep her family clothed, and there are also simple specimens called "alphabet" samplers that consist of an embroidered alphabet and the numbers 1 to 10. Throughout their history, samplers have been used to showcase the domestic skills of young needleworkers, but they are also often expressions of the maker's piety and sense of family pride. Better samplers characteristically have a stitched verse of scripture or inspirational poetry, and still better ones might depict scenes from the girl's life, including houses, trees, and animals. Sometimes samplers detailed a family's history or depicted a map of some kind. The best American samplers were made from about 1790 to 1840.

> **TIP:** Many people are surprised to learn that nineteenth-century alphabet samplers can be very inexpensive. These can be purchased for as little as $100 if they are plain and uninspired.

Stevengraphs Thomas Stevens of Coventry, England, made small pictures of woven silk that he matted and framed or sold as bookmarks. Many of these carried an advertisement on the mountings or on the back. When they first appeared in the 1860s, Stevens sold them mainly as souvenirs and as patriotic tokens. Such titles as "Declaration of Independence" (woven at the Columbian Exposition), "Death of Nelson," and "Crystal Palace" are much desired by collectors.

> **TIP:** Collectors prefer Stevengraphs in their original mats and frames. The vast majority of these little framed pictures are available at retail for less than $400, and bookmarks generally bring less than $100.

Tongue rug Said to be the first sewn rugs made in America, these floor covers were made from numerous "tongue" or elongated D-shaped pieces of fabric sewn onto a backing. Classically, these are pre-1820, but later examples do exist.

> **TIP:** Tongue rugs were replaced in popularity by button rugs in the early nineteenth century. Button rugs were made of round pieces of cloth or round pieces of braided material sewn onto a backing. The tongues on a tongue rug always cover the background completely, while the buttons on a button rug do not entirely cover the canvas or other backing material, which peeks out around the various components. Button rugs are also called "Penny" rugs.

Trapunto This form of needlework is said to have started in Italy and worked its way to England. It came from there to the American colonies. To make trapunto, two pieces of cloth—usually a top cloth of fine cotton and a bottom cloth of homespun linen or cotton—are sewn together with very fine stitches in a design that often features such elements as a cornucopia, baskets of flowers, feather wreaths, plumes, roping, vines, and bunches of grapes. After the stitching is done, the design is stuffed from the back with small wads of cotton that are pushed through the holes in the homespun. This stuffing causes the pattern to take on a three-dimensional, sculptural quality that is quite pleasing to the eye if done well. Trapunto was popular in the eighteenth century, but fine nineteenth-century examples are also much prized.

> **TIP:** Trapunto is sometimes called "white work" because it is normally done with white cloth and white thread. It requires such fine and precise stitches that, in days gone by, it was the last skill that a young woman mastered before her wedding. Do not confuse trapunto with Sicilian cable work, which consists of geometric lines stuffed with cording.

Walking wheel A "walking wheel" is a large spinning wheel that is at least 46 inches in diameter. These devices were used to spin coarse fibers such as wool. On small flax or Saxony wheels, the person doing the spinning sat, but to use these larger wheels the person stood and "walked" as the fibers were twisted into thread or yarn.

> **TIP:** The walking wheel usually has either no groove or one groove that accommodates a belt; a flax wheel normally has two grooves in the wheel. Oftentimes the individual doing the spinning on a walking wheel would not turn the wheel by hand, but would use a "wool finger," which was shaped something like a small, old-time policeman's nightstick or "billy club."

Catchall

Some words do not fit into neat categories. In this section we will be discussing auction terms that you need to know when you go to sales, names of important styles that apply to a broad range of decorative arts, and other words that are heard every day in the collecting world.

Absolute auction This is an auction at which the seller guarantees that everything will be sold to the highest bidders with no reserves. A reserve is a minimum price set by the owner of a given object, and it represents the smallest amount of money the owner will accept for the merchandise (for example, a $2,000 reserve on a corner cupboard means that the piece will sell for no less than that amount). Auctioneers may or may not be willing to disclose the amount of the reserve. It never hurts to ask.

> **TIP:** Learn the auction laws in your state. In some states, if an object is brought to the block during an absolute auction, it must be sold no matter what it brings. In other states, the auctioneer must accept a first bid, and once that bid is accepted, the piece must be sold.

Antique This is a term that is widely misused and abused. According to the United States Customs Service, any item more than one hundred years old is an "antique." Some purists, however, doggedly persist in saying that the Victorian era was just a nasty aberration that should be ignored, and insist that to be truly an "antique" an object needs to have been made before 1830. They choose this cutoff point because they say that is when furniture and most other items stopped being made by hand. In the early days of the twenty-first century, this attitude has all but disappeared, and the word "antique" has come to mean anything that originated in an earlier day or generation. It should also be noted that in recent years glassware that is over fifty years old has begun to be referred to as "antique."

> **TIP:** Do not focus on whether or not an object is called an antique. This is far too slippery a concept. What should concern you are the issues of authenticity and desirability of an object to collectors.

Art Deco This is a real "can of worms," because no one seems to agree exactly on what Art Deco is, when it started, or when it ended. It is critical to understand that the term "Art Deco" was not in wide use until the late 1960s, and in the 1920s, when the style was flourishing, few would have associated this term with the bold

This bronze statue by French artist R. Philippe is the embodiment of the active and elegant Art Deco woman who is often seen in art and illustrations. With her bobbed hair, she is often depicted dancing with a moon-like orb, or with long skirts or flowing scarves à la Isadora Duncan.

colors, the zigzagging and parallel lines, the geometric florals, and the dancing flappers that say "Art Deco" to us. There is some thought that the roots of Art Deco go back to 1909 and the first appearance of Sergei Pavlovich Diaghilev's Ballet Russe in Paris, France, which had scenery that was vividly colored and bold. This "modern" look supplanted the sensuous tendrils and curves of Art Nouveau, which had been the height of French fashion since the 1890s. Fashion designers took up this new look and created clothing, jewelry, and accessories, and soon sculptors, architects, interior designers, and makers of everything from furniture to glass followed suit. Actually, there were two components of the Art Deco style. The first was a voluptuous look that featured lush depictions of geometrically stylized fruit and flowers; its icon was the bobbed-hair flapper attired in scant clothing, dancing with the moon as if it were a beach ball, or elegantly posed with a wolfhound. The second branch emerged from a desire to create a design revolution and took its inspiration from industry and the machine. It espoused straight, clean lines; squares and rectangles; chrome; glass; and no nonsense. World War I interrupted the development of Art Deco, but it achieved its most impressive showcase at the 1925 Paris Exposition Internationale des Arts Décoratifs et Industriels Modernes. Soon after that, the style began to decline, and by the mid- to late 1930s, it had more to do with commercial production than with artistic expression. Today, Art Deco encompasses the decorative expressions of several artistic movements including Cubism, Futurism, and African art.

TIP: Do not be misled when shopping on the Internet. Many, many items from the 1940s, '50s, '60s, and '70s are described as Art Deco that are not.

Art Nouveau The roots of Art Nouveau can be traced to the 1880s (sometimes called "proto-Art Nouveau"), but this movement did not really flourish until the 1890s. Art Nouveau's creators were revolting against Victorian eclecticism and mass-produced decoration, and were attempting to return to the tenets of good craftsmanship. Based on natural forms and the curved lines found in flowering plants, Art Nouveau banished the straight line and replaced it with twisting, curving, undulating lines that seem to go on endlessly. Art Nouveau designs often feature overblown blossoms coupled with twining vines, or a woman with sensuously curling hair. In contrast to the Art Deco woman who was often depicted dancing with the moon, the Art Nouveau woman was generally shown in profile staring wistfully at the moon or just reclining. Some of the leading artists associated with Art Nouveau are Louis Comfort Tiffany, Emile Gallé, Alphonse Mucha, and Charles Rennie Mackintosh.

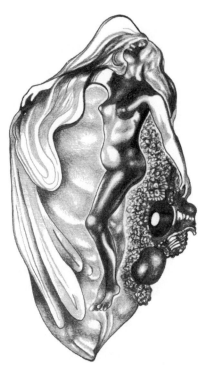

The Art Nouveau woman, as seen on this circa 1900 inkwell, was depicted in period decorations as being more languid than the Art Deco woman. The Art Nouveau woman usually had long, flowing hair that fell in sensuous curves, and she was more likely to be shown gazing at the moon than dancing with it.

> **TIP:** Art Nouveau was really somewhat out of fashion by the 1910s, but Tiffany and other companies kept it alive until the 1920s.

Arts and Crafts Like Art Nouveau, this nineteenth-century movement started out as a reaction against Victorian eclecticism and against the era's abandonment of craftsmanship in favor of industrial production. Beginning in the last quarter of the nineteenth century, English tastemakers such as author John Ruskin and poet-craftsman William Morris (of "Morris chair" fame) advocated a return to medieval standards of handicraft, and promoted the establishment of craft guilds whereby artists, designers, and craftsmen could cooperate on the creation of all sorts of objects—both decorative and useful. The furniture was generally made of oak; and, while some of it was spare with very rectangular lines, other pieces were much more elaborate, with long strap hinges that sometimes ended in areas of pierced metalwork, or had elaborated inlays that depicted naturalistic forms rendered in a very stylized manner. Arts and Crafts came to the United States about the turn of the twentieth century. Elbert Hubbard founded his Roycroft community in East Aurora, New York, in 1895, and Gustav Stickley opened his Craftsman Workshops in Eastwood, New York, in the late 1890s. Both the Roycrofters and Stickley were inspired by English precedents (particularly William Morris), and made sturdy furniture with simple rectangular lines from quartersawn oak. "Quartersawn" refers to the practice of sawing an oak log into quarters before slicing it into lumber. This allowed the "tiger-stripe" grain to show to its best advantage. Ornamentation on this furniture was limited to the metal hardware (usually hand-hammered copper), and to exposed mortise-and-tenon joints, but some early Stickley pieces did have a small amount of simple inlay.

> **TIP:** Arts and Crafts pottery is also very important to collectors and realizing very high prices right now. Look for examples by Newcomb College, Grueby, Teco, Fulper, Saturday Evening Girls (Paul Revere), Overbeck, Pewabic, and Clewell.

As is where is This phrase is used by auctioneers at the beginning of auctions. The first part of the phrase means that all objects are sold as they are, with no guarantee as to their authenticity or condition. The second part of this phrase means that all items are sold where they are, and it is the buyer's responsibility either to remove them the day of the sale or to make arrangements beforehand for taking their purchases later. This phrase is not just talk on the auctioneer's part—it is a legal contract that exists between buyer and seller, and it is binding.

> **TIP:** When you buy something at auction, it becomes your property the instant the gavel falls. If an item is stored after it is bought and it becomes lost, stolen, or damaged, it is the responsibility of the buyer, not of the auction house.

Bakelite Not all plastic is created equal. Invented by Dr. Leo Hendrik Baekeland in 1907, Bakelite was originally designed to be used for electrical applications, particularly as an insulator. It is an opaque substance that can be laminated, molded, and stretched into filaments, and it can be found in colors of red, yellow, gold, white, blue, green, orange, brown, and black. Among other things, it was used extensively to make radio cases, costume jewelry, and handles and knobs for household items. "Catalin" and "Marbalin" are names used by other companies for plastics with the same chemical formula as Bakelite. Bakelite kitchen items date after 1927.

> **TIP:** To tell if a plastic is Bakelite, first check to make sure it is opaque. Transparent plastics are probably Lucite (which is also collectible). Next, rub the plastic in question with your finger until the friction makes the piece and your finger hot. Then sniff the object. If you detect a fairly unpleasant, rubbery odor, it is probably Bakelite.

Buyer's premium To collectors, a "premium" once meant a small gift you received either when you did something (such as listen to a radio program) or when you purchased a product (such as Cracker Jack). Today, a "buyer's premium" is something collectors pay for the privilege of buying at auction, and it is a percentage of the purchase price that is added to the highest bid. Originally, buyer's premiums were generally 10 percent, but in recent years these premiums have escalated to 15 percent, and now premiums of 20 percent and higher have appeared at some auction houses. Under the buyer's premium system, if the premium is 10 percent and a purchaser is the high bidder at $1,000, the cost of the piece is actually $1,100. Buyer's premiums are designed to transfer the bulk of the cost of selling merchandise at auction from the owner of the merchandise being sold (who usually pays a commission to the auctioneer) to the purchaser. Theoretically, a buyer's premium allows the auctioneer to reduce significantly the amount of commission charged to the owner of the item being sold, or to eliminate the commission altogether, and this helps attract merchandise.

> **TIP:** There are some who say that if you want to pay $100 for an item and there is a buyer's premium of 10 percent, you should plan to bid only $90. That is perfectly sensible, but it seldom works.

Chinoiserie "Chinoiserie" is a name that is applied to Chinese-style decoration on items made in the West, particularly in Western Europe or the United States. These items were particularly popular during the eighteenth century, but the style persisted well into the nineteenth century. The term is most often applied to porcelain objects, but textiles, furniture, and other small decorative objects can also have chinoiserie decoration.

> **TIP:** Early English makers of soft-paste porcelain sometimes marked their chinoiserie products with pseudo-Chinese marks, and these can be confusing.

Composition doll Dolls have been made from a variety of substances—wax, wood, cloth, porcelain, rubber, and plastic—as well as from composition, which is usually a mixture of such substances as sawdust, flour, rags, or wood pulp bound together with glue. Composition bodies were commonly made for dolls with bisque porcelain heads in the late nineteenth century, but to be a "composition doll" *per se,* both the head and the body must be made from this material. Composition dolls are twentieth-century, and even though the sawdust and glue mixture tends to crack and flake, these dolls are rapidly gaining favor with collectors.

> **TIP:** Composition dolls featuring the images of Ty Cobb, Jackie Robinson, the Lone Ranger, or the Dionne Quintuplets are all prized by collectors, but the all-composition Shirley Temple by Ideal is probably the most famous. First made in 1934, an 11-inch example in excellent condition sells for around $900, and a 27-inch version, also in excellent condition, brings around $2,000.

Estate auction This is the sale of the contents of an entire home belonging to someone who is deceased. It may be held "on premises," which means at the house where the person lived, or at an auction gallery. "On premises" sales often bring the most money. Estates may be sold at auction, or the executors (sometimes called "personal representatives" these days) may choose to have an estate tag sale in which all items are pre-priced, and the public is invited in to buy.

> **TIP:** Be careful. Sometimes estate auctions and estate sales are "salted," meaning that goods not belonging to the house are brought in for sale. Although this can be to the buyer's benefit (because it provides a wider range of merchandise to buy), the "salted" items can be of lesser quality, and they may have condition or authenticity problems.

"Grandfather clock" If you want to wind Joe up and send him into orbit, call a "longcase" or "tall-case" clock a "grandfather clock." This last appellation was given to floor clocks in tall cases with pendulums and hanging weights because of a sentimental song about a "Grandfather's clock" that "stopped short, never to go again when the old man died." This designation is now in common use, but it is incorrect.

> **TIP:** On a clock's dial, the circle with the numbers in it that start with 12 on the top and 6 on the bottom is called a "chapter ring."

Half-doll Also called a "pincushion doll," a "half-doll" usually depicts a female figure from the waist up, but representations of men and children are known to exist. Popular from about 1900 to 1935, these often had skirts attached at their waists that served as lamp shades, pillow tops, and pincushions. Half-dolls also adorned the tops of dresser jars, jewelry boxes, and clothes brushes. Most of these were porcelain, but papier-mâché and composition examples can be found.

TIP: Most half-dolls' arms were molded close to their bodies, and these are not as desirable as the examples that have arms held away from the body. Look for examples with elaborate hats or unusual hairdos, or ones holding an object such as a letter or a flower. Also, bigger is better, and pieces signed by the maker—or numbered—demand a premium.

Jugate A "jugate" is any piece of political memorabilia that depicts two candidates—usually the presidential and vice-presidential candidates. It may be a pin, a button, a poster, or a fan.

TIP: Jugates are prized by collectors of political memorabilia. Currently, the most expensive political pinback button is a rare jugate featuring Cox and Roosevelt from the 1920 presidential campaign. Recent reports, however, say that a Davis and Bryan jugate from the 1924 election has sold privately in the $100,000 range. This is unconfirmed, but from a reliable source.

Left bid At an auction, when a potential buyer cannot attend the actual sale, a bid is sometimes left for the auctioneer to execute. A deposit is often required.

TIP: Left bids can sometimes be tricky. Some auctioneers will use a left bid as an opening, and this can mean that the buyer pays more than necessary, or loses the bid altogether. If there is only one left bid, what the auctioneer is supposed to do is open the bidding on the floor, and then bid the left bid in normal increments ($5, $10, $100, depending on what increments he or she is asking for from the floor) until there is no more competition. If the high bid on the floor is more than the left bid, the person actually at the auction prevails. If the high bid is the left bid, the absentee bidder wins. If there is more than one left bid, the auctioneer may open the bidding with the one that is second highest. Customs, however, differ from auction house to auction house, and bidders should find out what the exact procedure is before leaving a bid.

Limited edition Any item made in a way that is somehow limited in number is called a "limited-edition" collectible. This practice most often occurs in connection with prints; plates; figurines of people, animals, and cottages; Christmas ornaments; and bells. Sometimes limited-edition collectibles are issued in series, and the first year is usually the most valuable.

> **TIP:** Serious collectors of prints feel that any edition over fifty is too many. It should also be mentioned that plates and other ceramic items are often limited to a given number of "firing days," which can be as many as one hundred and fifty. With modern automated kilns, tens of thousands of items can be made in one hundred and fifty days, and this means that the item is "limited" only by the number the company can sell.

McKinley Tariff Passed in 1890, this law required that all items exported to the United States from foreign countries be marked with their country of origin. The McKinley Tariff went into effect in 1891 and from that date on, items from France were marked "France," items from England were marked "England," and so on. This lasted until 1914, when the law was changed to require that "Made in" be placed before the country of origin. After 1921, the country of origin had to be written in English, and that is when "Nippon" became "Japan," or "Made in Japan." Collectors find this an invaluable aid in dating items, particularly ceramics.

> **TIP:** The McKinley Tariff Act is not a foolproof guide. Some English companies, for example, put "England" on their wares before 1891, and Chinese exported some early-nineteenth-century wares that they marked "China" to comply with the statute.

Ming Dynasty This Chinese dynasty ruled from 1368 to 1644, when it was replaced by the Qing (Ch'ing) Dynasty. During this period, there were seventeen different emperors, some known for their patronage of the arts, others not.

> **TIP:** The Ming Dynasty has become synonymous with great works of art, and some people believe that anything that is "Ming Dynasty" is

very valuable. This is simply not true. Many, if not most, of the items made in this period can be bought for anywhere from a few hundred to a few thousand dollars each. Only the fine-art objects bring huge prices, and these are in the minority.

Pyrography   Also known as "wood-burning" or "poker work," "pyrography" is the art of burning designs into wood or leather. It was something of a fad in the late nineteenth and early twentieth centuries, and companies such as The Flemish Art Company of New York City and Thayer and Chandler of Chicago sold kits that contained the wood, the pattern, and sometimes the tools to create a box, a plaque, a book rack, or some other novelty item. Pyrography enthusiasts soon went beyond these "burn by the numbers" sort of kits and began either creating pyrography freehand or elaborately embellishing the designs supplied by the manufactures. Collectors are becoming more and more interested in these spontaneously created pieces.

> **TIP:** Not too many years ago, pyrographic items did not make a blip on most collectors' radar screens, and outstanding pieces could be bought for just a few dollars. Now, there is a growing interest in pyrography, and large pieces such as tables and chests are selling in the $750-plus range. Many large, well-done plaques are also pushing above the $500 mark.

Scrimshaw   "Scrimshaw" is the art of engraving or incising fine-line designs on the bones and teeth of marine mammals such as whales and walruses. Scrimshaw decorations can also be found on other natural materials, such as elephant ivory, bone, seashells, and ostrich eggs. It is most often associated with sailors on whaling ships and with the Inuit people (Eskimos), who often borrowed motifs from the sailors. The best scrimshaw was made in the early nineteenth century, but examples were made on whale teeth well into the twentieth century, and scrimshaw on ivory and other materials is still being done in the early years of the twenty-first century. Some of the most prized examples of scrimshaw are on whale's teeth, and feature images of ships, whales, and small boats laden with harpooners. In addition to whale's teeth, collectors find scrimshaw items in the form of such things as corset busks, pie crimpers, yarn winders, small boxes, spoons, bodkins (a sharp tool for making holes in fabric or leather), and cane handles. Many of these items were made by sailors as love tokens for their wives and sweethearts back home.

> **TIP:** Reproductions of whale's teeth decorated with scrimshaw-like decorations are very abundant. The fakes are basically made from plastic and fiberglass, and tend to be decorated elaborately with lots of whaling activity, plus names and dates. This is a case of "If it looks too good to be true, it probably is."

Union cases "Union" is the name of a material invented by Samuel Peck in the mid-1850s. It is a mixture of wood fibers and shellac, and its main purpose was to be molded into cases that held metal or glass photographs. These Union cases were originally manufactured by the Scoville Company, of which Peck was part-owner, but the process was soon copied by a number of other companies. Scoville also made photograph cases in leather and papier-mâché. Union cases came in a variety of sizes, from $9^{1}/_{8}$ by 7 inches to 2 by $1^{3}/_{4}$ inches, and with a variety of embossed designs that range from a representation of crossed cannons with a "liberty hat," to simpler geometric designs. As a general rule, the bigger the case and more intricate the design, the rarer and more expensive the piece. An example of this is a Union case in the largest size (called a "full plate") with the "Landing of Columbus" depicted on the front. It should be valued at more than $2,000. Union cases start at about $20 for small pieces with geometrics and go up from there, with most falling in the $50 to $450 range.

> **TIP:** Many people erroneously refer to Union cases as having been made from *gutta percha*, a rubbery substance made from the latex sap of certain kinds of Far Eastern trees. While collectible photographic cases were made from this material, they are not true Union cases.

Part Two: The Treasure Hunt

Now that you have the lingo down, it is time to take a room-by-room stroll through a typical American home and see what we discover. We will start in the kitchen, where unexpected riches can often be found, and from there we will move on to the pantry, looking for that $1,000 coffee can or $3,000 fruit jar.

Next, we will be exploring the dining room and discussing whether or not Grandmother's Limoges china has any great value. From there we will progress to the living room, the bathroom, the children's bedrooms, and the master bedroom. Then we will start investigating all of the out-of-the-way places, such as the hall closet, the garage, the garden, and, yes, the attic.

In short, we will be looking for antiques and collectibles in all the right places. Will we find them? Let us hope so!

CHAPTER THREE

The Kitchen

Surprisingly, the kitchen can be one of the most fertile fields in the whole house for successful treasure-hunting. The driving forces behind what makes kitchen items collectible tend to be nostalgia and obsolescence. Some people also have the desire to decorate their otherwise antiseptic modern kitchens with inviting objects from the past.

A good example of this latter motivation comes from the producer of our television show, *Treasures in Your Attic*, who goes "nutty" over what Joe, at least, considers to be the oddest things. It may be a turquoise-colored electric stand mixer from the 1950s, a wire bread rack with the name of a company printed on a metal plaque, or what are, again according to Joe, "ratty" old flour sifters and wooden-handled utensils.

These items are displayed in great profusion in every nook and cranny of our producer's kitchen. It is impossible to look at even the tiniest section of the room without seeing rolling pins, yellow ware mixing bowls, juicers, Fiesta ware, and every imaginable kitchen gadget made between the 1920s and the 1960s. Strangely, even Joe is impressed with this colorful profusion, and thinks it is a "pretty darn good-looking" display.

As for the role of nostalgia, our producer is also very fond of a Planters Peanuts jar that once did duty in her grandfather's general store in Elkhart, Indiana. This is a family piece, and as such is precious and beyond price, but sometimes family pieces disappear and similar items that bring back good memories are purchased as reminders of days gone by.

So many wonderful memories are associated with kitchens: tantalizing smells wafting from the oven; the soft bang and scrape of a spoon against a pottery bowl as batter is stirred for cakes; Grand-mother reaching into a cookie jar for treats; and long talks with friends and family as meals are prepared. The kitchen is a special place and it is not hard to understand why objects associated with this room are often regarded with great affection.

Let's start our prowl around this "heart of the home" by looking into some cabinets.

Bottle Openers

Open a drawer and you might find a figural bottle opener shaped like a skunk worth $150, or one with the enticing form of a grass-skirted hula dancer that could fetch $250 at retail.

Some of the most expensive of these devices feature collegiate themes, such as Paddy the Pledgemaster ($300), Freddie Frosh ($325), and Patty Pep ($425). Most of these were made in the late 1940s through the 1960s, and many of the best ones were made by Wilton Products, John Wright and Company, L. & L. Favors, and Gadzik (usually the signature of this last firm reads "Gadzik Phila").

To keep things in perspective, it should be noted that the items listed above are some of the most expensive figural bottle openers around, and other models in the shape of bears, cowboys, ele-phants, goats, ducks, roosters, sailors, and dogs generally retail for less than $100 each. On a more upbeat note, even the so-called church keys with beer advertisements on their handles are worth money and are sought after in some quarters.

To be sure, most of these fall under the $3 range, but a few of the better examples—such as those with wooden handles, those with bottle-shaped handles, and those with an opener section that slides out of the handle—can go up to about $30. Wall-mounted units are highly desired as well; and, because of its rarity, if you have one shaped like a skull, you can value it at about $525!

Corkscrews

As the search through that catchall drawer continues, a corkscrew worth $5,000 or more might turn up—but we all know that is highly unlikely. Still, a vintage piece with a handle made of stag horn or an unusual device from the nineteenth century could be lurking there, and these often sell in the $100 to $500 range.

The corkscrew originated in the mid-seventeenth century when wine makers started storing their best vintages in either glass or stoneware bottles. To seal them, they inserted tight-fitting corks into the necks, which left those who wanted to quaff some *vino* with just two choices: Break the neck off the bottle, or remove the cork.

Since the latter was far preferable (at least in polite company), it is said that oenophiles employed the rods from their flintlock guns, which conveniently had spiral ends, to remove the pesky obstructions from the containers' throats. Since then, all kinds of corkscrews have been invented, and the fancy early ones can be quite expensive.

Late-eighteenth-century English sterling silver corkscrew. It should be valued at $5,000.

For example, a sterling silver piece made in London in the first quarter of the nineteenth century, with a simple wing-nut-like turning device at the top, is likely to sell for as much as $4,500. But in our drawer, we are more likely to find humbler later examples. As a general rule, these bring in the $10 to $250 range, and some of them can be quite interesting.

Surprisingly, some 150-year-old corkscrews from the early nineteenth century with ivory handles, and complete with obligatory brushes sprouting out of one end, can be relatively inexpensive. One famous variety made according to the design of Sir Edward Thompson, for instance, falls into this category, and most of these fetch less than $300 each at retail, with only the fancier, more unusual ones going into the $500 to $750 range.

Cookie Cutters

Continuing our rummage through the kitchen catchall drawer, we turn up some plastic cookie cutters, which bring back a rush of nostalgic memories of afternoons spent making cute, sweet treats for family and friends. A set of four cutters featuring "Peanuts" characters with a Christmas theme is worth about $20, as is a set of two featuring Planters' Mr. Peanut.

Most plastic cookie cutters from the 1940s, '50s, and '60s are worth less than $1 each, but those in the shape of popular characters, or those that carry advertising, are much more desirable and much more valuable. A set of eight cutters from Robin Hood flour, for example, brings $30 to $35, which is not bad for something that probably came free inside a bag of flour or through the mail after sending in a few proofs of purchase.

It has been said that the first metal cookie cutters in America were made by itinerant tinkers from scraps of tin, and it is not hard to visualize that traveling craftsman setting up at a frontier back door and making a cutter to tickle some little boy's or girl's fancy. Often, these early cookie cutters can be distinguished by their very deep flanges, or cutting strips, which run as wide as 1½ inches.

Also, the edge of an early cutter's back tended to follow the shape of the design itself. In the late nineteenth century and beyond, the backs tended to be round, oval, square, or rectangular. In addition, it might be helpful to note that early cutters tended to be welded together in spots, while later metal cookie cutters were put together with a fairly continuous line of solder.

Some of the fancier eighteenth- and early-nineteenth-century cutters are horrifically expensive today, with prices that can run upward into the thousands of dollars each for the best examples— but these seldom turn up in kitchen drawers. However, pieces from the late nineteenth and early twentieth century do, and one in the shape of a horse that is approximately 6 inches square in size might bring $75 to $100 if it is fairly run-of-the-mill, and $225 to $275 if it is ornate and detailed.

A reindeer that is approximately the same size and intricately detailed might sell for as much as $550, and a well-made peacock of about the same size should fetch about $250. Smaller, more commonly found tin cookie cutters in the shape of hearts, tulips, and fish are usually priced in the $15 to $25 range, while the harder-to-find figurals such as deer, rabbits, men, and lovebirds start at just a little below $100 and go up to just below $1,000 for the best pieces.

Many of the cookie cutters we find in our drawer are going to be made out of aluminum, and most of these are not terribly valuable. A Minnie Mouse might bring $12 to $15, and a Santa Claus $8 to $10, but for the most part these run in the $1 to $6 range.

All kinds of other kitchen tools and devices from the 1960s and earlier litter our catchall drawer. Like us, you probably have rolling pins, meat forks, spatulas, turners, graters, and all the usual clutter that collects in such places, and, believe it or not, much of it has at least some value to collectors.

Eggbeaters

Of prime interest is the eggbeater, and you may be surprised to learn that a few of these can be worth in excess of $2,000 each! To be sure, the vintage EKCO eggbeaters that most of us have in our kitchens are worth somewhere in the $5 to $10 range, but a Jacquette (patent #3) brings a hefty $700 to $800, and a wall-mounted Keystone Manufacturing Company ("patented Dec 15, 1885") with wire whip blades brings close to $500 if it is in excellent condition. Please be cautious, however, because other Keystone eggbeaters of about this same vintage only sell in the $75 to $125 range.

Some eggbeaters were made to be used in conjunction with glass containers. These beaters usually had a wide disk between the handle and the blades that was meant to serve as a lid in order to prevent splatters and flying goo while the device was in use.

Oftentimes these glass receptacles had measuring graduations on the side, and sometimes they had pouring spouts and handles that made them look like measuring cups—which, of course, they were.

The value of these is determined by the color of the glass, and the most common and least desired is the clear, colorless glass variety, which usually commands prices between $25 and $45.

Clear, green glass is a little better, but the most desirable are the containers in opaque colors such as Jadeite green, Delphite or medium blue, Chalaine or light blue, and black. Clear, cobalt (dark) blue is also very desirable, and these pieces often run in the $65 to $150 range. Four-cup-size measuring pitchers or cups in Delphite and Chalaine blue have now pushed beyond the $450 mark, and one Chalaine measuring cup with no handle in this size has reportedly sold for $1,500.

Earlier we mentioned the existence of a $2,000 eggbeater, and this brings up a good point about how tricky pricing can be. Not too long ago, the Globe Cream Beater with its cast-iron rotary crank, wire dasher, and patent date of June 11, 1907, sold in an Internet auction for a few hundred dollars above the $2,000 mark.

Fewer than eight of these little beauties are known to exist, but most of the specialists in the field feel very strongly that the retail value of this particular item did not exceed $700 in the year 2000. It is speculated that this record price was achieved because two people who just *had* to have this Globe Cream Beater got into a bidding war and the price went up, and up, and up—through the ceiling, through the roof, and all the way to the moon.

It also has been reported that attempts to resell this eggbeater have been unsuccessful, and this further supports the contention that this piece is worth approximately $700, not $2,000 plus. Helaine disagrees and points out that this was the actual price paid, and that there must have been at least two people who were willing to pay this price. It's called "auction fever"!

Helaine also points out that if she were doing an insurance replacement value appraisal on this eggbeater, she would have to choose the $2,000-plus value because it is an actual price. Joe, on the other hand, feels that in order for the price to be "real," it has to be repeatable—in other words, if the same piece were to be sold again, it would have to bring the $2,000-plus price (or more), and indications are that it would not.

This pricing debate is an interesting problem, and we both hope that it gives some insight into how complicated antiques and collectibles pricing can be. Most of these problems occur with very rare, and/or very fine and desirable objects, but, for the most part, we do not have to worry too much about these as we explore the contents of typical American kitchen drawers or typical American homes.

Other things of a more easily quantifiable value that we might find hiding in those cluttered storage drawers are:

Rolling pins

Wooden pins with painted handles bring $10 to $30, depending on the color of the handles. Black is good, as is green, but red is a little less valuable. Aluminum examples bring about $30, but the most prized ones are made of glass. Crystal and white glass examples are the least expensive, commanding anywhere from $10 to $50 each, but ones in Delphite and Chalaine blue can run between $350 and $500 each. Recent prices, however, indicate that a Chalaine blue rolling pin with a shaker built into one of the handles should be valued at just a bit less than $2,000, and a similar one in Delphite blue at about $1,750! The rare Chalaine shaker-end rolling pins were made by the McKee Glass Company, and the Delphite ones by the Jeanette Glass Company.

Potato mashers

The value of potato mashers with painted wooden handles depends on the condition of the paint on the handle and on the style of the metal masher, with prices starting at about $8 and going up to $20 to $25 for unusual examples with great, unworn paint. Examples with Bakelite handles start at about $20 and go up to as much as $35 each. (See the "Catchall" section of chapter 2 for more information about Bakelite.)

Scoops

When they have painted wooden handles, scoops bring $10 to $15. Those with Bakelite handles are a little harder to find and bring as much as $75. Ice cream scoops with wooden handles fetch about $25 to $35, while those with Bakelite sell from around $45 to more than $100 each.

Meat tenderizers or mallets
With painted wooden handles, they bring $12 to $20 depending on style and condition.

We could go on and on and on about the collectibility of such things as slotted spoons, meat forks, melon ballers, spatulas, and wire whips. All are collectible; all generally bring in the $5 to $35 range, with the Bakelite-handled varieties usually being the most expensive. Prices depend on condition, color, and type of handle, and the style of the particular piece in question.

Remember, rust and peeling paint are your enemies, and any damage on these items is a kiss of death, since perfect pieces are not all that hard to find. For those of you interested in these types of objects, estate sales are great places to find bargains, and nice examples can often be found for very little. This is because the seller either is more interested in bigger-ticket items, or is unaware that these objects might actually be worth money.

We think it is time to slam shut the drawer that we have been so diligently rifling through and move on to a quick examination of the flatware stored in yet another kitchen drawer. We all know that the sterling silver flatware that we save for special occasions is valuable, but how about the stainless steel and everyday flatware with colorful Bakelite handles?

Stainless Steel Flatware

Recently we spoke with an antiques dealer whom we knew as a specialist in providing replacement pieces for old sets of sterling silver dinnerware. Imagine our surprise when she told us that she had switched her emphasis from silver to stainless steel! It took all the restraint we had not to blurt out in unison, "Have you lost your cotton-pickin' mind?!"

After doing a little research and seeing some advertisements for this kind of flatware in antiques trade journals, we found that this lady was not as crazy as we had supposed; and in fact, certain stainless steel flatware sets from the 1940s, '50s, and '60s are sought after by a growing number of collectors. Mainly, these are the high-quality sets designed by talented artists and crafted by noted companies.

One of the most desired of these patterns is Highlight, which was designed by the famous American Industrial designer Russel Wright, in 1952. Highlight is easy to identify because each piece carries Wright's name. If you happen to have examples of this pattern, take care of them, because each piece is worth between $35 and $50 if they have neither been through the garbage disposal nor been used to pry open pickle jars.

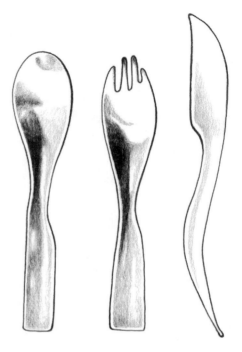

Stainless steel flatware pattern #7000 by Amboss is now very hard to find. Its sculptural quality is very appealing to many collectors.

Another stainless steel pattern to look for is 2720 by Paul Voss, which was manufactured by the German company Pott. Prices for this pattern average $15 to $30 per piece, with the teaspoon being the least expensive, and the dinner knife the most. There are any number of other stainless steel designs to look for, including the wide, sensually curved 7000 pattern made in about 1955 by Amboss.

Prices in this grouping range from $15 to $25, and this time the butter knife is the most expensive item. It needs to be kept in mind that some of these stylish designs—such as the aforementioned 2720 pattern by Voss and the Caravel pattern by Georg Jensen (with a price range of $25 to $50 per piece)—are still being made.

In general, if stainless steel flatware with a very '50s modern or streamlined designer look turns up in a kitchen drawer, it needs to be checked out carefully because it may be valuable. Lastly, keep in mind that this is not yet a widely collected area, and it may be hard to find someone who can evaluate pieces with authority. Look for a specialist who understands the potential.

Bakelite-Handled Flatware

Years ago, we took some women from New York City through the antique malls in Nashville, Tennessee, and we were totally flummoxed by what they were buying—Bakelite-handled flatware. It was colorful and all, but we found it hard to understand why these fairly sophisticated women were squealing with delight every time they found a fork, knife, or spoon, and it was hard for us to take these items seriously. Now we know better, and we also know (as those women did) that some of these pieces have serious values attached to them.

This Bakelite-handled flatware was intended for use at card parties. Complete sets are rare, and collectors are happy to find single pieces.

Run-of-the-mill four-piece place settings with single-color handles bring $25 to $30, but unusual pieces with colored Bakelite inlaid into a contrasting color can be amazingly dear. A good example of this is a twelve-piece bridge set made up of four three-piece place settings, each consisting of a small fork, spoon, and spreader knife. Each three-some's handle is inset with the symbol of a different card suit—heart, diamond, club, or spade—and a complete set in perfect condition can command a price as high as $1,000!

While this seems very expensive, if a Bakelite-handled fork, knife, or spoon turns up with inlaid polka dots on the handle, each piece is worth more than $200, and handles with an inlaid checkerboard design bring almost as much, with a price tag just under $200 each. Flatware with striped Bakelite handles, or alternating segments of clear Lucite and opaque Bakelite, are also quite desirable, and each piece fetches anywhere from $25 to $75.

As we have seen, kitchen drawers can be fascinating places to search for hidden treasure, but now let's take a look at some of the things that might be sitting on the countertop. Earlier, we looked at cookie cutters, and perhaps now we should start this portion of our investigation with cookie jars. After all, if we spot cookie cutters, there should also be one or more cookie jars.

Cookie Jars

When artist Andy Warhol's cookie jar collection was sold for such a fantastically high price in the 1980s, there was a huge surge of public interest in these cute containers. This mania lasted through the late '80s and early '90s, but in the waning years of the twentieth century, interest and prices subsided, and there is some thought that they will not recover for some time.

Reproductions have also taken their toll on cookie jar prices, and the shameless remaking of jars using old molds has left collectors confused and wary. One hint: Beware of any cookie jar that is signed "Brush-McCoy." Any such jar is a fake, because all the originals made by this company were completely unsigned.

Evaluating cookie jars can be very confusing, and some recent models can be surprisingly high-priced. A good case in point might be the Betty Boop jar issued in 1985 under the auspices of King Features Syndicate that is now worth about $800. Another Betty Boop—this one by Vandor—sells for only about $50.

Fitz & Floyd is a name that is often associated with current department-store stock, but some of their cookie jars such as Santa on a Motorcycle ($800) and Sock Hoppers ($475) can be quite pricey on the secondary or resale market. Others, such as their Scarlett O'Hara, Old MacDonald's Cow, Rio Rita, and Santa in a Chair, only bring in the neighborhood of $85 to $165 each.

Three categories that seem to encompass the largest concentration of valuable cookie jars are cartoon characters, "mammies," and space-oriented items. California Originals' colorful circa 1980 cookie jar featuring Woody Woodpecker coming out of a tree trunk and

"Mammy" cookie jar by Pearl China. Both the pocket on her dress and her lips are bright red, and her dress is yellow.

offering a cookie to a squirrel sells for around $1,000, and a 1953 Beany and Cecil by Kellams of Pasadena fetches about $550 to $600.

Mammy cookie jars and those depicting chefs, butlers, and Santas as African Americans often bring considerable money. Pearl China's mammy, with a yellow dress accented with a bright red pocket, is valued at about $850, while the companion chef sells for approximately $250 less. Another mammy in a yellow dress—this one made by the Mosaic Tile Company—commands approximately $500.

Both of these are likely to be unmarked, but the Mosaic Tile version is much more detailed and the yellow-kerchiefed woman is clasping her wrists across her ample tummy. The Pearl China one, on the other hand, is wearing a red kerchief, and has a darker, less detailed face.

Space-related items are perhaps best exemplified by NAPCO's jar called "Spaceship—Cookies out of this World." NAPCO is a Japanese company, and this particular piece, which features a nose-cone-shaped jar with fins and a bug-eyed astronaut sticking his head out of the top, sells for about $600.

Along these same lines, a *Star Wars* C-3PO jar from about 1977 is worth around $300 and an R2-D2 about the same. The Sierra Vista Spaceship is interesting because in brown it brings about $400, but in yellow the price goes up a bit, to around $450.

There are hundreds of different types of cookie jars out there right now, and it must be kept in mind that the earliest figural examples only go back to the mid-1930s, with most of the ones found on today's market dating from the 1940s or later. Quite modern ones, a category which includes limited editions and jars designed by artists, can be very desirable; but it should be understood that for every $500 to $1,000 cookie jar, there are probably thousands that sell for less than $50 each.

Canister Sets

On the counter, next to the cookie jar, there is probably a canister set, and that too may be very collectible. Joe fondly remembers the copper canister set that his favorite aunt had on her counter. It was by West Bend and consisted of flour, sugar, coffee, and tea containers with a matching salt and pepper. The set was from the late 1950s or early 1960s (if Joe's memory serves), and it was just part of the background. Today, this set is worth $40 to $50 if it is in good condition, and if you happen to have the matching covered cake container, the price goes up by $20.

Other metal or plastic four-piece canister sets from the 1950s or '60s can be worth money, too; the value generally depends on the graphics (or how well the images portray the era), and on the condition. Good ones sell in the $25 to $45 range, lesser ones start at $10 and go up to $20.

Glass canister sets from the Depression and a bit later can be much more valuable than their metal counterparts. Large ones in a kind of custardy yellow color that are embossed with names such as "Flour," "Cereal," "Tea," "Coffee," or "Sugar" might bring as much as $75 to $100 each, and the price for sets with four or five matching items would be in the neighborhood of $500 plus.

Canister pieces in amber, white, clear colorless, fired-on orange red, transparent and opaque green, and blue glass are also available. Most of these are mid-range items, but the price leaders are the Delphite medium opaque blue, the Chalaine light opaque blue, and the clear cobalt. In the 40-ounce size, the Delphite should be valued in the $200 to $375 range, as should the larger size in the Chalaine blue.

The 20-ounce size in the Delphite should be approximately 25 percent less costly than its larger cousin. There is also another color called "peacock blue," and the canisters in this hue are just a tad less expensive than those in Delphite and Chalaine, but in this color the 5-pound round sugar canister is the real find, and it should be valued at $400 on its own.

Range Sets

Near these canister sets were often glass shakers that were meant to sit on the back of the gas or electric range, where they would be right at hand for seasoning. These were usually marked "Flour," "Salt," "Pepper," "Sugar," "Paprika," or "Nutmeg"—and many times a matching grease jar went with them. As with the canister sets, color is absolutely vital, and we recently saw a Delphite blue salt and pepper in an antiques show priced at $250.

Range sets basically came in two silhouettes—rectangular, or rounded, almost moon-shaped, in profile. The rounded variety came in white glass with various colorful designs applied to the front, such as tulips, circles, and flowers in pots, and they are not as highly desired as some of the rectangular examples in the opaque colors.

Prices for the rounded shakers generally run in the $5 to $10 range, with grease jars bringing nearly double that price. The values for the rectangular examples are higher because these are the ones that came in the most desired opaque colors—but they do not, at this time, reach the $250 per pair price that was talked about earlier.

The most expensive of the opaques are probably those in a highly sought-after color with a rare painted—as opposed to paper—label with "Nutmeg" or "Soap Powder" on it. These fetch double or even triple the sums received for the more commonly seen "Salt," "Pepper," "Flour," and "Sugar." In shades such as Chalaine and Delphite blue, the more available ones sell for as little as $25 and rarer examples can escalate to about $100.

Salt and Pepper Shakers

While the salt and pepper shakers are the least desired items in range sets, other salt and pepper shakers found around the kitchen can be very hotly sought after. The variety is seemingly infinite, and we are mainly talking about the figural types made between the 1930s and today.

Some of these are really cute, and it is hard to resist the Shmoos of "Li'l Abner" comic strip fame ($275), or the legendary "sailorman" and his main squeeze, Popeye and Olive Oyl (early ones, $300; later ones—and that means 1960s to 1980s—$85 to $125). A Garfield and Odie can bring almost $100. Disney characters are also hotly collected, and a pair of dwarfs from *Snow White* brings $275, a *Pinocchio* duo fetches $175, and a Winnie the Pooh and Rabbit on a tray can sell for a little over $300.

Pieces such as a pair of Texaco gas-station pumps ($50 without the original box) are fun, and a toaster with one slice of white bread for salt and a piece of dark bread for pepper ($12) is fairly common, as the price suggests, but charming nonetheless. A cowboy and cowgirl set may sell for close to $100, a pair of mermaids bought in Florida as a souvenir might bring $50, and chocolate and strawberry ice cream cones set in a wire frame should sell for $15.

As you see, prices vary wildly, but almost any pair of novelty figural salt and pepper shakers is collectible—no matter their age. Keep in mind that it is necessary to have both the salt and the pepper—singles are not welcome—and that prices start as low as $5 and go up, up, up from there.

Leaving the countertop behind, it is time to start opening the cabinets and seeing what goodies might be hiding inside. This can be very exciting because you never know what you may find. Joe remembers going into a house and opening the cabinet under a sink and finding a $2,000 Royal Doulton vase that the lady of the house had used to hold cut flowers, while Helaine vividly recalls the $5,000 Tiffany bowl under the sink catching the drips from a water pipe. These kinds of startling discoveries are very rare, but they do happen.

Juice Reamers

One of the things that might be behind one of those cabinet doors is a glass juice reamer from the first half of the twentieth century. Most of the ones you will find will be in clear, colorless glass, and they are generally worth less than $35 each, but if you happen to find a cobalt blue one marked with a "c" inside a triangle (the trademark of the Cambridge Glass Company) and embossed with "pat. Jan 6, 1909," you have a treasure worth about $3,000!

Other rare reamers include three similar pieces with a pitcher bottom made by the Fenton Art Glass Company of Williamstown, West Virginia. The only difference among these items is the color; one is red and sells for approximately $1,250, another is black and sells for about the same price, and the third is an opaque medium blue that sells for around $1,800.

Most colored glass juice reamers sell in the $25 to $750 range, and many of the costlier examples occur in shades of black, transparent pink, Crown Tuscan (an opaque pink), cobalt blue, cornflower blue, emerald green, or amber. As with almost any collectible item we discuss, the condition is very important. Many of the reamers that turn up in kitchens have seen heavy use and may be in less than perfect shape.

Unless the piece is the rarest of the rare and simply not available anywhere in perfect condition, collectors are not interested in owning these bruised goods. An important lesson is not to make excuses for damage. Do not even *think* things like "If you were that old, you would have a little damage too!" There is no such thing as a small chip, and calling it a "flea bite" does not turn it into something else. After all, a "hairline crack" is still a crack, and if a person who is trying to sell you something starts using euphemistic terms such as these, it is time to run for your economic life.

Toasters

Many current collectors are also avidly looking for toasters and almost any other old appliance. Most of the gadgets designed to toast bread in the 1920s, '30s, and '40s sell in the $35 to $75 range, with a few pushing into the $100 to $150 level.

Imagine our surprise, then, when we opened the December 30,

1998, issue of *Antique Trader* and discovered Susan Eberman's report from Toast-In II, the convention of the Upper Crust collectors club, which contained the startling information that a single rare toaster might be worth as much as $12,000! This singular toaster is the General Electric model D-20, made about 1910, and it holds six pieces of toast all in a row like little soldiers.

Only one is known to exist, and Eberman quoted a price of $6,000 to $12,000. The interesting part about this is that since this is the only D-20 known, the collector who owns this singularity sets the price, and until that person actually sells it, there will always be a question as to whether or not someone will really pay this price for a toaster.

This unimpressive-looking toaster is the extremely valuable General Electric D-20.

Such a sum may be right on the money, but until actual dollars change hands, there is some doubt if this is a real price or one from the land of wishful thinking. The high value may be absolutely realistic, but if one or more D-20s were to show up in your or our kitchen, we fear that lofty price might drop like a barrel going over Niagara Falls!

The D-20 is actually a fairly ungainly device—there is nothing decorative about it—but the Pan Electric Toastrite Company's porcelain-front toaster decorated with the famous Blue Willow pattern is really charming and beautiful. Eberman noted that one of these rare beauties was on display at Toast-In II, priced at a not inconsiderable $3,500 to $4,000.

Toaster enthusiasts are sometimes interested in other vintage electrical appliances, such as waffle irons, coffee urns, and mixers. Waffle irons in particular seem to have a devoted following, and most of these fall into the same $35 to $75 price range as the toasters. Some of the more unusual of these push the $100 level, but we have not discovered a "home-run" waffle iron like the D-20 toaster.

The most desired coffee urns seem to be those that come complete with a matching tray, creamer, and sugar. Sets such as the Marie Antoinette with its drop handles and cameo-type silhouettes and the Louis XIV with its classical lines are pushing above the $200 mark, and prices seem to be rising.

Everyday Dinnerware

While we are still talking about the contents of kitchen cabinets, we should note that one of the first things we expect to find inside them is everyday dinnerware. The premier brand here is Fiesta by Homer Laughlin. Few noncollectors realize just how valuable and desirable these pieces can be.

Please keep in mind that common items such as a small plate can have a rather modest value. For example, 6- and 7-inch plates in the original late-1930s colors of red orange, cobalt blue, light green, turquoise, yellow, and ivory sell for less than $10 each, with the red and the cobalt bringing a bit of a premium. Similar items in 1950s colors, such as rose, gray, chartreuse, and forest and medium green, sell in the $10 to $15 range, with the medium green (a kind of bright Christmas green) commanding the premium.

One of the marks used by Homer Laughlin on its famous Fiesta dinnerware.

To illustrate the role color plays in the value of Fiesta ware, consider the disk-shaped water pitcher. In original 1930s colors, its value does not exceed $150, but in most of the 1950s colors, that price jumps to around $300—and in medium green, it leaps to around $1,250 or a bit more. In the juice size, the differential is even more dramatic: In the majority of the original colors, the value is about $50, but in red the price jumps ten times to $500, and in gray it multiplies almost sixty times—to almost $3,000!

It is hard for us to fathom a simple juice pitcher being worth that much money, but other Fiesta items garner incredible sums. Such items as the covered onion-soup bowl, the French casserole, and the lid for the #4 mixing bowl command serious attention from collectors, and serious dollars if the color happens to be right.

Things such as tripod candleholders in red, cobalt, or ivory (ivory is a real coming color in Fiesta) sell in the $650 to $700 range, a 12-inch vase in red, cobalt, or ivory might bring $1,500, and a simple soup bowl in medium green has reportedly brought more than $2,000! Those of you who have Fiesta may have a fortune in your cupboard, but remember, condition is everything, and chips, cracks, or staining will devalue Fiesta dramatically.

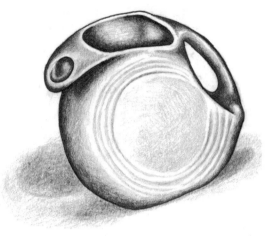

A Fiesta disk-shaped pitcher—the value depends on color and size.

Among American everyday dinnerware brands, Fiesta is unquestionably the champ, but there are other contenders that should not be overlooked. Items in Hall's Autumn Leaf pattern, which were made to be given away as premiums by the Jewel Tea Company, are certainly favorites, and some of these pieces are by no means cheap—although they generally do not attain the price level of Fiesta.

Still, a one-handled bean pot can cost over $1,000, a ¼-pound, square-topped butter dish can bring $1,400, and a candy dish with a metal base $500. One of the interesting things about Autumn Leaf is that the pattern was also used on accessory pieces, and items such as a tablecloth can bring anywhere from about $175 to $350 depending on the size and the material (plastic, sailcloth, or muslin) from which it was made.

Autumn Leaf canisters with metal lids sell in the $300 to $550 range for sets of three or four, but the ones with plastic lids only bring about $15 to $20 each. Waste cans command $450 if they are in excellent condition, and a square holder meant to hold a can of cleanser brings a whopping $1,500!

American everyday dinnerware (that is, earthenware, not fine china or porcelain) is a very wide area of collecting, and enthusiasts are looking for patterns made by an enormous number of companies. Gladding, McBean and Company's Franciscan ware in patterns of Apple, Desert Rose, and Ivy certainly has a large following, as do the patterns of Metlox Pottery (famous for their Poppytrail mark), such as Red Rooster, Pintoria, California Contempora, Free Form, and Mobile.

From 1938 to 1957, Southern Potteries of Erwin, Tennessee, made Blue Ridge dinnerware that was completely hand-painted under the glaze. There were approximately two thousand Blue Ridge patterns, most of which incorporated flowers, but depictions of trees, houses, people, fruit, and animals do occur, as do geometric designs.

This decoration was colorful, spontaneous, and perhaps a little unsophisticated. Dinner-size plates start about $20 each and go up to around $50. Cups and saucers start about $15 and go up to $60 for the better patterns. Intricate designs are more highly desired than the simple florals and geometrics, and a pattern featuring images of French peasants called "Normandy" commands prices that average 25 to 50 percent higher.

Blue Ridge specialty items can bring fairly high prices, and they often go unappreciated. An artist-signed turkey platter, for example, should be valued in the neighborhood of $1,200 to $1,500, while a lazy Susan currently fetches $750 or more. There is also a small hexagonal box with the image of a dancing nude on the lid that is valued at $1,000.

The hand-painted representation of a French peasant on this Blue Ridge plate by Southern Potteries reminds many of the Breton peasant found on French Quimper pottery.

Another company that has really captured the imagination of collectors over the last decade or so is the Watt Pottery Company of Crooksville, Ohio, which turned out a variety of hand-painted dinnerware patterns in the 1950s and '60s. The plant burned down in 1965. Their concentration seems to have been kitchenwares (mixing bowls, canisters, baking dishes, etc.), not dinnerware, which means that today the dinnerware tends to be somewhat uncommon and fairly expensive.

Some of the patterns include their famous Apple design, plus Autumn Foliage, Rooster, Starflower, Dutch Tulip, and so on. A 10-inch Apple plate, for example, is now worth in excess of $650, and a teapot or a coffeepot in the same design can go for more than $3,200. In Dutch Tulip, a 10½-inch chop plate, which was designed to be used for serving such things as pork and lamb chops, is worth just a little less than $1,000, but not every Watt dinnerware item is this valuable.

Two good cases in point are the 8½-inch plate in Rio Rose (some call this "Pansy"), which sells for about $50, and a salad bowl in Eagle, which only brings about $150. Still, any piece of Watt pottery is worth checking out, and almost any Watt canister or cheese crock is a real find that will run in the $500 to $1,200 range, depending on the pattern.

The list of American dinnerware makers is seemingly endless—stretching alphabetically from the American Chinaware Company all the way to the Wellsville Pottery Company—and most produced at least a few items that are sought after by collectors. We have covered a few of the more valuable of these, but in reality most of the vintage dinnerware pieces found in your or our cupboards are probably worth somewhere in the neighborhood of $3 to $15 each.

Just keep in mind that the plate from the 1930s, '40s, or '50s that you are still serving "baloney" sandwiches on may have a bit more monetary value than you think. So be careful with those items from Blue Ridge (Southern Potteries), Stangl, Iroquois, Paden City, Royal China, Salem China, and so forth—they are not necessarily disposable.

As an aside, it should also be mentioned that there seems to be a growing interest in the plastic dinnerware that goes by the generic name "melmac." Right now, a service for four in perfect condition sells in the $50 to $75 range, and there is every indication that its prices are increasing!

Jadeite Dinnerware

Not all everyday dinnerware was made from pottery or melmac. Dinnerware has also been made from glass. Most vintage glass dinnerware was either clear, red, white, blue, or ivory in color, but some of it was in opaque Jadeite green. (One maker, Anchor Hocking, spelled it "Jade-ite.") In recent years, this has become very popular and expensive due to its relentless promotion by a television icon.

Jadeite glass dinnerware was made for home use and restaurant use and, surprisingly, some of the most eagerly sought-after pieces are from the restaurant line. One pattern intended for home use was called "Laurel," and it was introduced by the McKee Glass Company in 1931. This pattern has a band of raised laurel leaves around the rims, and an 11-inch-diameter bowl is worth $80, a 9-inch dinner plate is worth $30, and a wine goblet can approach $175.

Keep an eye out for children's sets consisting of four cups, four saucers, four plates, a creamer, and a sugar in the Laurel pattern, because the set is worth about $1,250 if the pieces have pictures of Scottie dogs on them. Without the dogs, the set sells for about $400.

A glass creamer and sugar decorated with Scotties from the Laurel pattern child's set. These two pieces were made of Jadeite and are worth $350.

We vividly remember when this stuff could not be given away for more than a few dollars apiece, but times have definitely changed.

Other patterns in Jadeite include an Anchor Hocking design called "Banded," which is decorated with either one, two, or three scalloped bands. This deceptively simple pattern is very rare, and a three-band dinner plate reportedly sells in the $2,000 region!

Among the restaurant pieces, the 10⅜-inch plate marked "Fire-King Oven Ware" is worth around $600, and a handled soup bowl and saucer shaped like a regular cup and saucer, but larger, should be valued around $1,250. The ball pitcher in this line sells for around $850 if it is in perfect condition, and the gravy boat is pushing its way toward $3,000.

Ordinary pieces in the restaurant line bring much less money. A 9-inch dinner plate is just $35, a 6¾-inch salad plate $15, and a regular cup and saucer about $20.

Everyday Drinking Glasses

Many kitchen cupboards across America are crowded with so-called jelly glasses that once held gobs of grape or some other kind of jelly. These were washed out after they were emptied so that they could be used as everyday glasses.

In some cases the product they had held was not jelly but Kraft cheese spread. These juice-glass-sized containers are called "swankyswigs," and they were first made in the 1930s and continued in production until the mid-1970s. Today, most of them are worth between $2 and $8 each, but a few rise well above that level.

Among the more valuable are the green ($30) and the blue-and-red ($26) checkerboard, the West Virginia Centennial ($28), the Atlantic City ($26), and the #2 Tulip in red, green, and black ($30). Please be careful, because there are a lot of juice glasses out there with cute pictures of foxes, sailboats, stars, daisies, and forget-me-nots that originally contained things other than Kraft cheese, and they are not swankyswigs. Large numbers of these imitation wares came out in the 1970s and '80s. Like the jelly glasses, which have a

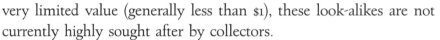

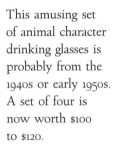

This amusing set of animal character drinking glasses is probably from the 1940s or early 1950s. A set of four is now worth $100 to $120.

very limited value (generally less than $1), these look-alikes are not currently highly sought after by collectors.

Starting in the 1940s, colorful sets of glasses with enamel-like pictures of everything from racehorses to birds, flowers, stripes, and geometric shapes were fashionable. Often, these had a matching pitcher, and most of the glasses held either $9\frac{1}{2}$ ounces or $13\frac{1}{2}$ ounces (for iced tea), while the pitchers were generally in an 80-ounce size.

Prices for these glasses start at about $10 each for the $9\frac{1}{2}$-ounce size with ordinary flowers on them, and go up to about $30 for rarer representations, such as animal characters or a Mexican street scene. The $13\frac{1}{2}$-ounce size starts at about the same level and goes up to $40 for the more uncommon representations like the ones mentioned above. Surprisingly, the pitchers are not much more expensive than the glasses and start at about $20 for one with very simple stripes on it and go up to about $50 for an example such as Mexican Garden.

Other drinking vessels that have found their way into our everyday kitchen cabinets are the ones that were (and are) given away by fast-food restaurants such as McDonald's and Burger King. Right now, the McDonald's variety is attracting the most attention, but any glass from this source that has a cartoon, movie, or sports image should neither be thrown away nor dismissed lightly.

The minimum value on a full-sized glass (as opposed to a juice-glass-sized tumbler) is about $5, and, unless an item was part of a special issue not widely available to the public, prices go up to about $25 for the pieces called "BigMac Languages" (which had "Big-Mac" and "twoallbeefpatties" written in five different languages) or the 1993 editions that read "I'm Speedy," "The Original Shake, Burger and Fries," and "McDonald's Restaurant circa 1957."

Special-edition glasses sent to restaurants but not distributed to the general public fetch somewhat higher prices, as high as $100 each. These include Muppet Caper Glasses Are Coming from 1982 and Camp Snoopy Glasses Are Coming from 1983.

On the upper end of the everyday glassware scale is the American pattern by Fostoria. This cubic-block design originated in 1916 and was made until 1986. It is generally found in clear, colorless glass, but pieces were also made in very limited quantities in red, amber, blue, canary yellow, green, milk glass, opaque aqua, and opaque peach.

The prices we are going to quote are for clear, colorless examples, but if you have one of the pieces in color, its price can be at least double or triple those mentioned. But be very careful. This pattern has been widely reproduced in recent years by both Viking and Lancaster Colony, and much of this production was in color.

Also, Indiana Glass has a pattern called "Whitehall" that looks like Fostoria's American, but Whitehall was not hand-finished by fire-polishing, and therefore its edges tend to be less rounded and somewhat sharper than the edges on real American pieces. So, be sure you know what you have before you get too excited by the prices.

American is one of the most sought-after patterns of everyday glassware, and some rarities have pushed considerably above the $3,000 level! True, top-dollar items such as hotel crushed-ice containers, porch vases, and dresser trays and jars are not easily found, but if you do find examples of these treasures, you will be happy to know that they are worth at least $2,000 each!

Objects that are more likely to turn up in a cabinet are a banana-split dish at $375, a round butter dish with cover at $145, a water bottle at $400, an appetizer tray with six insert dishes at $250, or a four-part square relish dish at $175. As for actual drinking glasses (which is what we were talking about in the first place), ice teas start at $18 and go up to almost $200 for an uncommon variety with a handle.

Tumblers, on the other hand, start at $10 and go up to $20 for a footed example. The rarity here is a 3-inch-tall "baby" tumbler with a value that can exceed $300. American pattern cocktail glasses run in the $15 to $18 range, while cups bring $6 to $10, and a beer mug should be valued at $45.

The drinking-glass cupboard might also hold party glasses with colorful and gilded decoration signed by Georges Briard, the trade name used by designer Jascha Brojdo. This glassware was made from the late 1950s until very recent times, and it was basically intended to be elegant barware decorated with stylish designs that ran the gamut from the bull and the bear of Wall Street to a high-ball glass that had a big "Arsenic" label on it, as in "What's your poison?"

There are literally hundreds of Briard designs and, in many cases, they coordinate with ice buckets, trays, and other related items. During his career Brojdo designed everything from tables to dinnerware, and consequently his name is just as likely to appear on a clock or an ashtray as it is on a drinking glass.

Today, these very contemporary glasses are beginning to be collected, and their prices are rising. Once upon a time, and not so long ago, it was possible to go through an antiques mall or second-hand shop and pick up a Georges Briard piece for next to nothing, but now that is becoming more and more difficult to do, and most of his drinking glasses are selling in the $5 to $12 range, depending on their size and decoration.

Although he was probably the most prolific, Brojdo was not the only designer putting his name on upscale glassware during this period of time. Other signatures include "Couroc" (a Monterey, California, company owned by Guthrie Courvoisier), Ned Harris, Fred Press, and Bob Wallack. Items by most of these designers are very reminiscent of Georges Briard's creations, but the prices are more in the $3 to $8 range. Unsigned glassware in this style may be Japanese knockoffs and worth still less.

Mixing Bowls and Food Molds

In a cupboard near the cabinets where the dinnerware and glasses are stored, there might very well be a mixing bowl with a surprising value. One of the most attractive and valued types is called "yellow ware," a kind of utilitarian pottery that ranges from a buff color all the way to a mustardy yellow.

This ware was first made in the United States in the mid-nineteenth century, but it was popular right up until the 1930s—and it is not all that unusual to see a piece still in use in a modern kitchen. In the early years, yellow ware was primarily made in Pennsylvania, Vermont, and New York, but later on the potteries of East Liverpool, Ohio, became its principal manufacturers.

Some of these bowls are really very attractive—almost too pretty to use for whipping up cakes or batches of cookies. If, for example, a nice, "old," 14-inch-diameter bowl turns up with an allover slip decoration (in this case, "slip" does not refer to a convenient place to keep a boat but to a kind of colored liquid clay) of cobalt-blue-and-white stripes and bands, it might be worth as much as $450.

Lesser bowls with molded rather than painted decoration, and later bowls with stripes only around the middle or near the top, often bring less, with the larger-size bowls selling in the $45 to $75 range. It should also be noted that sometimes the manufacturers of these bowls converted them to colanders by punching holes in the base and modifying the foot rim so that the pieces could more easily be rocked from side to side.

These pieces are very prone to damage, so collectors will accept a hairline or two between the holes or a chip on the foot. Older, rarer, and better decorated examples can bring prices in the $1,400 range, but plain examples and twentieth-century items usually start at $150 and go up to $450 or a tad less.

Companies such as Watt and Harker also made mixing bowls that are desired by collectors. Harker, which was located in both East Liverpool, Ohio, and Chester, West Virginia, and in business from 1889 to 1972, made some attractive mixing bowls with decal decorations on them. These are beginning to find favor with collectors and generally sell in the $20 to $30 range.

We spoke about Watt Pottery in the everyday dinnerware section, and their mixing bowls are surprisingly inexpensive when compared to their other products. A piece in the Apple pattern, for instance, generally brings $50 to $75, but bowls in patterns such as Tulip, Rooster, Morning Glory, and Dutch Tulip bring a bit more, with prices that top out in the vicinity of $200.

Many companies made mixing bowls in addition to dinnerware, and most of these sell in the rather modest $20 to $75 range. Nested sets of bowls are always desirable, and a nested set of Fiesta bowls is a real find indeed.

Yellow ware, copper, and tin were also popular materials for making food molds. All of these are collectible, and all of them can be quite expensive, depending upon their vintage and the design that they impart to the food placed inside them. An English copper food mold shaped like a crown with the initials *V* and *R* for Victoria Regina at the apex is valued at $4,000, but plainer specimens range in the low to mid-hundreds.

Find a yellow ware mold in your kitchen with an image of a rabbit or with a hen and her chicks in the bottom, and it might be worth $600. If the design features bouquets of flowers, a large, single flower blossom, a pineapple, or a fish, the price would be closer to $500, while more common images such as ears of corn bring a little less than $200 each.

Now, let's turn to metalware found in kitchens—items such as cast iron skillets, aluminum trays, enamelware (often called "graniteware"), and, yes, even those old muffin pans and flour sifters. The key to understanding the first two items is that knowing who made the piece in question is very important.

Griswold Cast Iron

In the case of cast iron skillets, the name to look for is Griswold, with Wagner following close behind. Griswold traces its origins back to the mid-nineteenth century and, until 1957, when they went out of business, they called Erie, Pennsylvania, home.

We have heard it said that at auctions in certain parts of the country, Griswold products are treated the same way Tiffany items are treated at auctions in other parts of the country. Imagine, if you will, a tiny, size 1 Griswold skillet selling for more than $1,000!

Once again, details are very important. Griswold skillets marked with size designation "#1" and "#0" are the same size, but a #1 is earlier, rarer, and many times more valuable. While the #1 sells for fairly big bucks, the #0 only sells for about $75.

The underside of a cast iron skillet with one of the marks used by Griswold.

Another example would be the Griswold #2 skillet. The ones marked "2 Erie 703" with the Griswold circle-and-cross mark bring up to $300, but the same skillet with the mark "2 Erie, Pa. U.S.A. 703 Cast Iron Skillet" and the Griswold circle-and-cross mark brings $375, and if the piece has a wooden handle, the price jumps to around $600.

Yes, it *can* become very complicated, and it is not just Griswold skillets that are valuable. A #15 Griswold parlor stove might bring over $4,000, while a #8 teakettle fetches more than $800. Much the same #8 kettle with a raised spider and web on the lid only brings about $600. In addition, a #2800 wheat-and-corn pattern corn-stick pan sells for over $1,200, but it should be noted that other Griswold corn-stick pans start at $75 and escalate from there.

The variety of collectible Griswold items is astounding. A letter box (the kind that hangs on an outside wall) can go as high as $250, a charcoal grill about $500, a bundt pan $1,200, a cake mold shaped like Santa Claus $700, an ashtray $95, a wall coffee-bean grinder $1,400, and so on, *ad infinitum*.

Hand-Hammered Aluminum

Turning from a heavyweight metalware champion to a more light-weight contender, there does seem to be growing collector interest in hand-hammered and spun aluminum ware. It is hard to believe, but there was a time when aluminum was so expensive that it was used to make jewelry, and in the mid-nineteenth century, French emperor Napoleon II commissioned an aluminum flatware set that was only used for his most exalted guests.

Better, more efficient refining methods lowered aluminum's cost dramatically, and today we tend to think of this material as that cheap metal from which soft drink cans are made. In the 1920s, the Alcoa Aluminum Company was looking for ways to expand their product line and so they hired artist-blacksmith Wendell August to come up with some ideas.

August created relief designs onto which aluminum sheets were placed and then hammered so that the metal surface acquired a raised pattern. This product really caught on, and in the late 1920s, '30s, and '40s, all kinds of aluminum objects with this type of dec-oration became popular wedding gifts because they were attractive, fairly inexpensive, sturdy, useful, and tarnish-proof.

Wendell August Forge, which is still in business, was noted for its quality workmanship and naturalistic designs of dogwoods, pinecones, and bittersweet, among others. A 20-inch rectangular tray decorated with larkspur now sells for $85, while a large tray table decorated with a leaping marlin might garner a little less than $600, and a wastebasket with dogwoods might bring $175.

Another leader in this field was Russel Wright, whose spun alu-minum pieces were rather delicate and seldom have survived in good condition. A satellite punch set of his with its wooden handles and covered bowl, complete with ladle and cups, is pushing the $1,500 mark if it is in pristine condition, while a single candelabrum might sell for as much as $300. A smoking stand can bring $1,000, a vase $150, and a gravy boat $200.

In addition to Wendell August and Russel Wright, there are other names that command respect in this category:

Arthur Armour

Armour originally designed patterns for Wendell August, but he broke away in the early 1930s and produced heavy aluminum wares with decorations drawn from old prints and maps. An oval letter basket with a map of the world on it is worth about $200.

Buenilum

This is a trade name used by the Buehner-Wanner Company, which is famous for the sleek modernistic designs that fit in well with the Danish Modern style. Most of the normal trays and baskets made by this company are still fairly inexpensive and can sell for less than $50 each, but an above-average covered bowl might sell for as much as $150.

The Rodney Kent Silver Company

This manufacturer is known for aluminum ware with a very bold tulip design and flamboyant ribbon and flower handles. These pieces are widely sought after by collectors, who will pay $50 for a footed bowl and about the same amount for a bar tray.

Enamelware

Aluminum ware is the sort of thing that is stored in the kitchen and brought out to serve guests in the living room or on the patio. Enamelware, on the other hand, is the sort of item that company seldom sees—such as the turkey roaster that only comes out once or twice a year, teakettles, scoops, ladles, basins, buckets, and bread boxes.

The term "enamelware" refers to metal objects that have a white or colored enamel coating on them. Usually, on American-made examples, a background of a solid color such as gray (by far the most common color), blue, green, brown, or red is accented with flecks or swirled veins of color (usually white or gray)—which suggests the look of granite to some people—thus the name "graniteware" (also called "Agate" or "Agateware").

"Granite" was also a trade name for this product at one time, and it is speculated that the name was supposed to give the impression that these wares were as tough as granite—which they are not. In fact, these pieces are so prone to damage that collectors will even excuse a chip or missing flake of enamel if it is not too unsightly, and the little dings and bangs that come from intense daily use are thought to give a piece character rather than detract terribly from its value.

Earlier pieces of graniteware are usually heavier than their more modern counterparts, and will often display rivets and wooden handles in their construction. Some of these items bring amazing amounts of money. The price depends largely on the color and the form of the particular piece in question.

A good example is a ladyfinger pan. In gray, one of these might be valued about $300 (which really is quite a sum for an old baking pan), but one in some color other than gray—such as cobalt blue or red—with a white interior can fetch in excess of $5,000! Another good case in point is a soup ladle, which in gray or brown sells for only about $75. In cobalt that figure jumps into the $100 to $125 range, but in red it zooms all the way to the neighborhood of $1,500!

Other expensive forms include rolling pins ($1,200), syrup jugs ($1,100), water pitchers (from $600 to $2,000), spooners ($2,000), churns ($2,000), and milk cans ($1,000). Of course, all the prices fluctuate up and down depending on color and condition, and any prices mentioned are only meant to give an idea of the possibilities.

Sifters and Muffin Tins

Alongside the iron skillets and enamelware pieces in the cabinet there are probably sifters and old muffin tins. Patented flour sifters first appeared in the mid-1860s, but the collectible ones that are most likely to be found in American kitchens today are the all-metal variety that were mainly in use during the 1930s and '40s.

In truth, these are not very valuable, but they strike a nostalgic chord with collectors and they do make interesting kitchen decorations. Common tin ones with advertising on the sides sell for about $10, but nicer ones with lithographed decorations and wooden squeeze handles might sell for as much as $35.

Muffin tins have been made in a wide array of materials—not just tin. Cast iron examples are some of the earliest, and they can be priced into the hundreds of dollars each. Pans made from soapstone as well as enamelware and earthenware also exist. However, the muffin trays found in most of today's kitchens are made from unadorned tin, and the value for those that were made between the two World Wars (and perhaps slightly thereafter) is generally in the vicinity of $5 to $25 each.

There are so many little things around the kitchen that are avidly collected that we could go on and on and on. Helaine insists that we cannot end this chapter without mentioning pot holders, which she collects. The vintage kind from the 1950s or so that are hand-crocheted or have some sort of needlework on them sell from $4 to about $20, depending on how cute and unusual they happen to be.

In addition to pot holders, kitchen collectibles include such items as ice crushers, nutmeg graters, aprons, cookbooks (the best of these start at $20 and go up from there into the low hundreds), butter dishes, refrigerator magnets, spoon rests, and, yes, even dinette tables and chairs. As for this latter item, what pre-1970 kitchen was complete without a Formica-topped, chrome-legged table surrounded by at least four chairs covered with some kind of plastic, vinyl, or oilcloth?

Called the "Hoosier
cupboard," this
came in golden oak,
white enamel, or
French gray. When
it was new about
1925, it was consid-
ered to be a labor-
saving device.

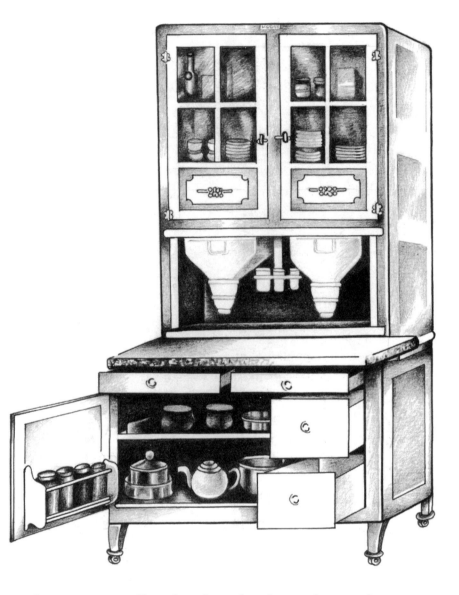

These sets are collected and used today, and examples start in
the $250 range for "plain Jane" sets with little color or interest and
go up into the neighborhood of $750 or so for those sets with color
and style—maybe a red-and-white-banded top on the table and
spiffy, original 1950s coverings on the chairs.

Another type of furniture often found in kitchens is called a
"Hoosier cupboard," or sometimes "baker's cabinet." In the late

nineteenth century, furniture makers began making tables that were specifically designed for rolling dough and slicing bread.

Normally, these had a metal tabletop with a porcelain-enamel work surface and pull-out bins for sugar and flour underneath. By the turn of the twentieth century, overhead cabinets had been added for the storage of spices, condiments, and utensils, and these cupboards were being transformed into kitchen work centers.

Makers such as Hoosier Manufacturing of New Castle, Indiana, Mutschler Brothers of Nappanee, Indiana, and Sellers and Sons of Elwood, Indiana, started advertising these cabinets as work- or step-saving devices. The popular name for these was derived not only from the "Hoosier Manufacturing Company" but also from the fact that many of the cabinets' principal manufacturers were in Indiana—thus the name "Hoosier" came to be attached to a product that was strongly associated with that state.

Up until a few years ago, Hoosier cupboards were fairly inexpensive. Most were under $1,000 (and, as Helaine says, "It was a lot of cupboard for very little money"), but prices are rising rapidly and many have reached the $1,500 level. Some are inching toward $2,000. The best and most expensive have original paint and glass and lots of accessories, such as canister sets, spice jars, and built-in equipment such as flour and sugar sifters, ironing boards, spice racks, recipe boxes, and metal bread drawers. The more original equipment, the better.

One last word before we move on to the pantry. Many of the items we have been talking about are so popular that they are being reproduced, while the pieces that have been in your home for forty or fifty years are probably as they should be. If you go out and purchase something on the current market, be very careful indeed. Be especially wary of juice reamers, anything labeled "Depression Glass," and Griswold cast iron.

CHAPTER FOUR

The Pantry

Walk into the pantry, turn on the light, and what do you see? Hopefully not scurrying little critters, but shelves filled with food containers. Most of these containers will be boringly familiar, and it might be hard to imagine that anyone would be interested in preserving, much less collecting, something like this. But don't be too hasty.

Most of the packages that food comes in are thrown away after the contents have been used, and that means that the vast majority of yesterday's and today's food boxes and tins have vanished into dumps and landfills. Some of the packages that have managed to survive are very rare indeed, and we have seen collectors literally break into rhapsodies over a cardboard milk carton, or have a virtual spasm over a paper egg tray.

It is hard for many people to understand, but old tin coffee cans, cereal boxes, and even spice containers can sometimes bring significant dollars. We are amazed at how eager people are to find these old tins and boxes, and we are equally amazed at how many modern pantries still have vintage examples.

Spice Tins

The value of spice tins depends very much on how interesting and colorful the graphic content of the design is, how uncommon the maker happens to be, and what spice that particular container was designed to hold. After all, most kitchens had dry mustard and pepper, but fewer had such things as turmeric and ginger.

Tin containers for spices originated in the mid-nineteenth century, and early manufacturers such as McCormick, Durkee, J. R. Watkins, and Colburn had a relatively wide distribution. Today, a turn-of-the-century Watkins allspice tin in very good condition might sell for as much as $25 because it is an attractive package, but a Durkee cream of tartar should sell somewhere in the $10 range because it is a common item in an ordinary container from a mass-market maker.

Products from uncommon brands can bring significantly higher prices. A Conquest mustard seed container, for example, might sell for close to $100, while a Dining Car cloves tin with its wonderful image of a railroad dining car should sell for about $175 if its condition is good. Vintage spice containers that were too large for home use can also be very valuable.

A prime example of this is a Moshier Brothers Gilt Edge spice container that measures 11 inches tall by 7½ inches square. It is a glorious container with depictions of nineteenth-century buildings set in a sort of golden sunburst. This whopper is worth an astonishing $800 if it is in good condition. If ever there was a "poster child" for the concept of "Do not throw anything away," it would certainly be these spice tins.

Other tin containers that can bring surprisingly high prices are coffee cans. A 5-pound Blue Bird Coffee pail, for instance, brings $450, while the same size Bagdad Coffee container brings about $175. These items are tremendously popular with collectors, and while prices start at about $25, pieces like the Strong Heart Coffee can with its portrait of a Native American often push the $1,000 mark.

One of our favorite collectible coffee cans is the Clipper Brand can put out by the Merchants Coffee Company of New Orleans, Louisiana. It has a wire handle and a brilliant yellow background with an image of a clipper ship with all its sails fully rigged. Find one of these in pristine condition and it will be one of your favorite things, too, because it is valued at $2,500!

Peanut Butter Tins

Not long ago, Helaine and I were evaluating the estate of a gentle-man who had been a collector of almost everything (or so it appeared). The kitchen, the dining room, and the pantry were stacked to the ceilings with old tins and, frankly, most of them were ordinary in the extreme.

After viewing the entire house from cellar to garret, Helaine was walking through the pantry area off the kitchen on her way to the back door when she happened to notice a small tin on top of a tall stack of practically worthless lard cans. She called for me to bring it down for her, and what we found was a small ($3\frac{1}{2}$ by $3\frac{1}{2}$ inches), round pail with "Wigwam Brand Peanut Butter" printed on the can above a picture of two children playing in the sand at the seashore.

It was in great condition and cute as could be. That one, small peanut butter pail was worth about $650, and it was the most excit-ing thing we found all day. In fact, finding old, small-sized peanut butter or candy tins in a pantry can make anybody's day, because they can be valuable, between $75 and $1,000 each, and wonderful to look at.

Additional tin containers to look for are those that once con-tained popcorn, baking powder, talcum powder, and, although it is seldom found in the kitchen, tobacco. Actually, the tobacco pocket tin is the king of all tin containers; and if one of these such as Uncle Sam's Smoking Tobacco or Essex Mixture should turn up anywhere in the house, be sure to remember that it is not terribly uncommon for a tin like this to top the $1,000 mark, and some, like the Essex Mixture, can sell in the vicinity of $6,000 to $8,000.

Cereal Boxes

Cereal boxes are now popping up on the collectibility radar, but there is a great deal of uncertainty in the marketplace about just how desirable and expensive these items are or may be in the future. Right now, sports collectors seem to be interested in those boxes that are sports-related; character collectors appear to be looking for examples that feature the characters in which they happen to be interested (Disney and such); and premium-nostalgia collectors are attracted to boxes that contain premiums such as records, or a Tony the Tiger spoon.

People who just collect the boxes for their own sake are a bit of a rare breed, but no matter how or why they are collected, cereal boxes do have a following. The first packaged, ready-to-eat cereal appeared on the market around 1900, and most boxes from this era fall into the $100 range. Examples from the 1950s, '60s, '70s, and '80s start at about $5 and go up into the $150 range, depending on their graphic interest and on how resonant of pop culture the packaging happens to be.

Glass Fruit Jars

Also on those pantry shelves might be some glass fruit jars. Over the years, all sorts of odd closing devices have been invented for canning jars, but it was the zinc screw-on lid with a rubber ring seal invented by John Mason in 1858 that made glass canning jars popular and practical.

Most glass canning or fruit jars made over the next hundred years were made in either clear or aqua glass. Examples in cobalt blue, black, and amber are rare, and prices for examples in these colors start in the low hundreds and go into the low thousands.

To illustrate the difference color makes, consider a machine-made Atlas jar marked "Atlas Special." It came in three sizes and had a zinc lid. Examples of this jar in aqua bring only about $5, but specimens in green bring at least $20, and in blue, $30. An even more striking example might be a jar marked "Ball Standard." In aqua this piece is worth only about $5, but in light green the price rises to $25. In dark green, however, it zooms over the $600 level, and in amber, its price clears the $1,200 mark.

We are all familiar with Ball jars, Mason jars, and Atlas jars, but jars with less familiar names can also be quite valuable. A quart-size in aqua marked "Collins and Chapman Wheeling, West Virginia" is worth about $1,000; and a green, handmade quart jar with metal lid and thumbscrew closing marked "Dalbey's Fruit Jar Pat Nov 16 1858" is worth approximately $2,800.

Now, before you trample the cat making a mad dash across the house to check on your old fruit jars, please understand that there are probably a million fruit jars out there worth $5 or less for every fruit jar worth $100 or more. The point we want to make is that if you have a canning jar that is an unusual color, by an unusual maker, or in an unusual size (¼ pints are usually very nice), be aware that it *may* be valuable.

Stoneware and Pottery Canning and Storage Jars

Glass canning jars are popular because the contents are visible, but before these were available stoneware and pottery containers were used to preserve perishable food. Long after glass jars were available, however, pottery vessels were still in use, and late-nineteenth- and early-twentieth-century examples are fairly common.

It might be best here to talk about what is *not* particularly valuable, and this includes the plain brown undecorated jars, crocks, and jugs that are unsigned by the maker fit into this category. The old song about the "little brown jug" romanticized these items, but they are common, and as a general rule have very little monetary value.

Other jars, crocks, and jugs that are white on the bottom and brown on the top are also of little value, as are the plain, gray, generic stoneware jars that are devoid of either maker's name or adornment. The presence of a potter's name on one of these gray crocks or jars can raise the value considerably, especially in the area or region in which it was made.

Anonymous crocks and jars are the rule, and items that are

attributable to a specific manufacturer are the exception. The products of certain identifiable companies such as Monmouth and Red Wing can be very collectible and fairly expensive when compared to their "no-name" cousins.

The Monmouth Pottery was founded in Monmouth, Illinois, in 1892 and became part of the Western Stoneware Company in 1906. Pre-1906 marks are usually "Monmouth Pottery Co.," while post-1906 marks feature a maple leaf and the name "Western Stoneware Company." Small, white, glazed (called "Bristol" glazed) crocks in the 2- to 20-gallon size usually sell in the $100 to $150 range, but add a bit of cobalt blue decoration and that price triples. A pre-1906 Monmouth preserves jar with wax seal is worth $350 or a bit more, and a 60-gallon crock brings about $750.

The Red Wing Pottery Company was founded in Red Wing, Minnesota, in 1878 and stayed in business until 1967. Their products were more varied than Monmouth's, and they made everything from commercial art wares and dinnerware to crocks and canning jars.

The Red Wing crocks that are most desirable to collectors are the ones with cobalt decorations. In the larger sizes, these can command $3,000. Special attention should be paid to the 30-gallon size with stenciled images of lilies or a butterfly. Other, smaller-sized Red Wing crocks with cobalt blue stenciled decoration run in the $150 range for a 5-gallon size with "elephant ear" leaves, to about $850 for a 5-gallon size with a butterfly.

Red Wing jars start at $75 for a 1-quart brown-glazed example (this brown glaze is more properly called "Albany slip"), to about $600 for a 1-gallon size also with Albany slip. The prices seem to be reversed for white Red Wing jars. In these, the quart size fetches $100 to $125, while the gallon only brings $65 to $75. Of course, variations do occur in these prices due to special features, markings, and decorations.

Cobalt blue decoration always adds to the value of old stoneware, but collectors are most interested in the early to mid-nineteenth-century pieces with hand-painted cobalt designs on gray stoneware. These are considered to be folk art, and prices at auction for examples with elaborate decorations have pushed above the $15,000 level. Look for signed pieces coupled with unusual images, such as sailing ships, stags in a forest, horses, people, lions, roosters, and chickens.

Joe remembers helping two elderly women sell part of their possessions. Out in the pantry there was a stoneware crock that had been painted green. One of the two ladies said that they had become tired of the piece and had decided to spruce it up by applying a bright, fresh coating of a color that reminded them of springtime.

Joe asked if he might remove the paint, and the women replied that they were just about ready to throw the piece out anyway, so he should go ahead. Underneath, there was a beautiful gray stoneware crock decorated with hand-painted cobalt renderings of birds. It was subsequently sold for $1,000 and would have brought more if it had been signed by the maker. The ladies were somewhat surprised to learn that the object in which they had been casually storing paper bags for so many years was actually worth money.

Stoneware canning jars with simple cobalt decorations of swirls and daubs start at about $200 if they are in good condition. From there, prices escalate to the neighborhood of $3,500 to $4,000 for items with rare designs such as a man's face seen in conjunction with a star, or perhaps a deer set among grasses.

Large, extensively embellished crocks, churns, and jugs usually surpass the value of jars because they have a much more significant graphic impact on the eye of the viewer. As was said earlier, values here can approach the $15,000 level at auction and surpass it at retail. If, for example, you own a crock depicting a horse at a hitching post, it might be worth in excess of $10,000 at retail, and a piece with a detailed landscape should command a price in the same neighborhood.

Another prized type of stoneware that might be found in a pantry is generally referred to as "blue and white stoneware." Items that fall into this category have no painted decoration at all. Instead, they have molded designs and a surface that appears to be covered with a blue wash over off-white. Gradations and shadings are characteristic of the blue coloration, and there are said to be more than 150 patterns in this ware.

The article that is most associated with blue and white stoneware is the pitcher, which is sometimes called a "buttermilk pitcher" because, as older Americans from rural parts of our country can recall, buttermilk was once kept in these vessels and stored in the icehouse. When dinner was served, the pitcher—and the milk it held—came to the table frosty cold.

Today, these "buttermilk pitchers," which served such an unglamorous purpose, can be quite valuable. One with an image of a peacock on it is worth over $1,000; and another with an eagle, shield, and arrows is worth just a bit less. More common ones start about $150. It should be noted that one pitcher that people often believe to be quite valuable is actually one of the least expensive. It is the one that features a Native American good-luck symbol shaped like a swastika, and its value is around $200.

Other items found in blue and white stoneware include butter crocks, salt containers, rolling pins, lavatory sets, batter bowls, cuspidors, mugs, grease jars, canisters, and bean pots. Among the most expensive items are coffeepots and large, barrel-shaped water coolers, with prices for the best of these soaring above the $3,000 level for coffeepots and above the $4,000 level for water coolers.

It should also be mentioned that these wares came in other colors besides blue and white, most commonly, green and white.

CHAPTER FIVE

The Dining Room

In most modern American homes, the dining room is only used for special occasions, and it is here that many cherished items are displayed and stored. If the family silver is not in a bank vault (as it often is these days), it can usually be found here, along with the fine china, crystal stemware, and crisp linens that many people consider to be necessities for setting an elegant table.

Limoges China

Often when we go into homes, we are proudly taken to the dining room and shown the family's Limoges china that has been passed down from generation to generation. (Limoges, incidentally, is a city and region in France famous for its production of fine-quality pottery and porcelain.)

Usually we are shown these delicate heirlooms because there is some expectation on the part of the owner that we are going to gasp in awe and tell them right there, on the spot, that they have a treasure of great monetary worth. Unfortunately, we generally have to disappoint our host because, for the most part, this type of china has a very modest value and only rarely can it be converted into an amount of cash that is anywhere near the amount that a new set of high-quality fine china would cost.

To be sure, the Limoges tureens, covered vegetable dishes, and sauce and gravy boats bring fairly decent prices on today's antiques market, but plates and the other parts of individual place settings can go begging. This is because modern homeowners, as a general rule, do not want to care for this fancy, fragile, "dishwasher-unsafe" dinnerware that is often just a little too fussy for contemporary tastes.

Also, it should be noted that Limoges dinnerware (and this includes Haviland) is far from rare. In its day, almost every household in the United States with any claim whatsoever to affluence had a set of this china, and on more occasions than we care to think about, we have been in homes that have as many as six sets, or partial sets, which have trickled down from various branches of the family.

The two of us do not believe it to be an exaggeration when we say that if we gathered all the Limoges dinnerware within a 25-mile radius of our respective homes, each of our individual accumulations would easily fill an aircraft hangar. Therefore, unless a set is very extensive, relatively undamaged, complete with many serving pieces, and in an extremely pleasing pattern, it is very hard to sell—and even then, the price can be remarkably low.

Going to an estate auction and watching old sets of dinnerware sell can be a very instructive experience. An above-average Limoges service for twelve (such as we have been talking about) often sells in the $1,000 to $1,200 range, and, unless it is very special, a vintage Lenox service for ten or twelve can go for even less.

We have seen large, fine sets of twentieth-century Meissen (arguably some of the best china made in the world) with wonderful serving pieces go for less than $4,000. If you were trying to buy a new set, that amount of money would probably buy you little more than a tureen, a meat platter, and perhaps a few plates. Indeed, buying new fine china can be an exercise in extravagance, and this dinnerware tends to hold its value only as long as the manufacturer produces it and it remains in open stock.

Once a pattern is not in open stock, the value a private individual can realize tends to drop like a rock. Certain modern patterns, however, have held their value, and can be quite collectible. Noritake's Azalea pattern comes to mind as a prime example.

Typically, obsolete patterns become the bailiwick of the replacement services, which assemble huge stocks of no-longer-manufactured wares in order to sell them to those unlucky individuals who break a cup or destroy a plate. This is an extremely valuable service for those who need a piece to complete an extensive set, but many people who have found themselves in need of this assistance are astounded by how much the replacement piece can cost.

But the real shock comes when the hapless china owner decides to sell his or her wedding or heirloom china to one of these services, only to be offered some tiny fraction of the price being charged to customers for these same pieces. Although it outrages many of those who want to sell, this is the way a free-market economy works, and sometimes the facts of life are hard to understand.

Noritake "Azalea"

We are not going to dwell on this china issue much longer, but since we have mentioned Noritake's Azalea pattern, it might be a good idea to go into it in a little more depth. This design originated about 1916 and was made exclusively for the Larkin (Soap) Company, which gave pieces away as premiums.

This china continued in production until the 1930s, and pieces should have the pattern name, "Azalea," printed on the back. As is the common rule, the plates in this series are fairly inexpensive, with the 4- and 6½-inch-diameter sizes selling for about $10 each and the dinner plates bringing about $30.

Unusual plates such as the three-compartment grill plate fetch about $175, and the 12- and 14-inch platters bring about $60 to $70 respectively, but the 16-inch size is worth closer to $500. In this pattern, the #182 coffeepot sells for close to $600, the #450 relish for $475, and the #452 vase is valued at $1,200. But, beware, the #182 fan-shaped vase is much less, at $200.

As a last thought on this subject, we want to mention that sets of china made in the eighteenth and early to mid-nineteenth centuries by such important companies as Derby, Worcester, and Meissen can be exquisitely expensive. For example, a one-hundred-piece, circa 1820 Derby set with a soup tureen, two dessert sauce tureens, and four graduated platters in the classic Ivy pattern is worth approximately $20,000, and prices for rarer sets can go much higher than that.

Sterling Silver Flatware

The situation with sterling silver flatware is much the same as the one with fine china: As long as a particular pattern is being manufactured, prices stay high. Once a design is discontinued, its price tends to fall. The products of certain upper-end manufacturers such as Unger Brothers, Tiffany, Georg Jensen, and Buccellati buck this trend, and typically retain more of their value; but, for the most part, when a pattern is no longer made, pieces that initially retailed at $80 to $120 each drop to the $15 to $45 level on the secondary market.

Certain flatware designs, however, are more sought after than others, and while we cannot list them all, here are a few that generally bring premium prices:

Kirk-Steiff's Chrysanthemum, Smithsonian, Dancing Surf, Paramount, and Williamsburg Shell

International's Cloeta, Cleone, Mille Fleurs, Northern Lights, Silver Iris, Vision, and DuBarry

Reed & Barton's Les Cinq Fleurs, La Parisienne, Intaglio, Love Disarmed, Florentine Lace, French Renaissance, Cameo, and Tapestry

Whiting's Lily and Imperial Queen

Dominick & Haff's Labor of Cupid

Alvin's Morning Glory, Orange Blossom, Raphael, and Majestic

Wallace's Romance of the Sea, Sir Christopher, and Grand Baroque

Gorham's Fountainbleau, Paris, Medici, Poppy, St. Cloud, Bird's Nest, Medallion, Mythologique, Saxon Stag, Gilpen, Decor, Hunt Club, Classic Bouquet, and Lansdowne

Towle's King Richard, Margaux, and Georgian

Any sterling silver flatware pattern made by Tiffany and Company is prized on today's market, but a few of their patterns are more desired than others. The list is really fairly long, and we are going to name only a few, but special attention should be paid to American Garden, Bamboo, Padova, Hamilton, Century, Flemish, English King, Audubon, Wave Edge, San Lorenzo, Windham, Richelieu, and Provence.

Some of these patterns have been made for a very long time, and it is good to know that modern pieces are usually lighter in weight than older specimens in the same pattern. This means that collectors tend to want the earlier pieces, unless they are trying to fill out a specific set and want everything to match in both age and weight.

One circumstance that devalues old flatware very quickly is the presence of a monogram. The appearance of a family's initials can reduce the value of sterling silver flatware by as much as half, and make the items very difficult to sell on the secondary market. Monograms are great for security and family pride, but bad for monetary value.

Crystal Stemware

No dining-room table with beautiful china and glowing sterling silver is complete without elegant crystal stemware. Any number of companies made crystal glassware in the early to mid-twentieth century, but for our purposes we are going to look at the products of just five: Heisey, Tiffin, Morgantown, Cambridge, and Fostoria.

Heisey is one of the big names in American glass. They were in business in Newark, Ohio, from 1896 until 1957, and one of their patterns that collectors are most eager to find is Orchid.

As the name suggests, this design is festooned with etched images of large orchids, and it is really quite a striking pattern. A 7-inch-diameter salad plate in this pattern is worth about $20, while a 73-ounce pitcher runs about $500, a 1-pint cocktail shaker approximately $300, and a 14-inch-tall vase should be valued in the vicinity of $700.

Stemware in this pattern can be relatively expensive, with a 2-ounce sherry glass costing about $125, a $4\frac{1}{2}$-ounce cordial almost $150, the more common water glass about $45, and the sherbet $30. Over the years, Heisey produced some colored stemware that is highly prized today, but their Orchid pattern pieces are always in clear, colorless glass.

This is the case for most of the stemware that has been made for the past two hundred years. But there are exceptions, and some of the most beautiful are the pieces made by the Tiffin Glass Company in a color called "Twilight." Twilight is a rather odd color because it changes hues depending upon whether or not it is seen in natural or fluorescent light.

Under normal incandescent light or sunlight, Twilight is a pleasant shade of lavender, but when exposed to fluorescent lighting, it turns to blue. This shade was introduced in 1951 and was made right up until 1980.

Lately, we have been seeing Tiffin decorative objects in Twilight priced in antiques malls as high as $600 per piece, but we believe that these prices are a little bit enthusiastic because few pieces of Twilight are actually selling above the $500 level.

These items are a little hard to price because values are going up rapidly, and demand for Tiffin products in general is high, to say the very least. A water goblet, which is one of the most common objects, should sell for about $50, and more unusual pieces such as cocktail glasses (saucer champagnes, etc.), cordial glasses, and sherry glasses should go for double or even triple that amount, depending upon the pattern.

Tiffin stemware in Twilight is extremely hard to find, as is colored stemware by the aforementioned Heisey company—particularly in their Tangerine (a bold red orange), cobalt blue, and Alexandrite (a bi-color ware similar to Twilight made only between 1930 and 1935, which shades from a soft pink/lavender/red to a powder blue). The point of mentioning any of these at all is to make it clear that fine crystal stemware in a shade other than clear, colorless is very uncommon and potentially rather valuable.

If you have an older set of stemware in yellow, green, red, blue, or pink, its value is worth checking, because it could be considerable. To be sure, there are lesser versions of these colored stemwares, and currently these only have a modest value, but if the pieces you own were made by Tiffin, Heisey, Cambridge, or Morgantown, you may not want to undervalue them.

A real "comer" in this field is the Morgantown Glass Works of Morgantown, West Virginia, which began in 1903 as the Economy Tumbler Company. They were in business until 1971, and we are stunned at the value of some of their products.

Morgantown specialized in mold-blown stemware with etched designs, which often had colored glass bowls and clear, colorless stems, or vice versa. Most of their more ordinary wares have prices that range in the neighborhood of $15 to $30 a stem, but goblets with extraordinary etchings such as the Superba (very Art Deco in feeling with semi-nude women and palm trees) on a clear bowl with a black stem and foot can bring prices in excess of $225 per stem.

Some Morgantown pieces were extraordinary because of the design of the piece itself. One of the most striking is called "Summer Cornucopia." It features a simple, non-etched, clear, colorless glass vessel supported by a stem that is shaped like a cornucopia with the pointed end supporting the drinking portion and the end that overflows with fruit resting on the foot.

These start at about $125 each and go up to around $275 for a 1-ounce cordial glass. Other fascinating shapes include Top Hat, which has a stem in the shape of a monocled gentleman wearing a top hat and was primarily made for New York's Knickerbocker Hotel, and Chanticleer, which sports a stem shaped like a rooster.

Of these two, the Top Hat pieces are the most valuable, with prices that range from about $75 to $150 per stem, depending on the particular color combination. Examples of Chanticleer bring about half that amount.

Morgantown also used some special types of decoration on their stemware that produced very striking and elegant effects. One of these was a silkscreening process that placed a colored picture—usually of pheasants or a woman known as "Queen Louise"—in the center of a fancy etched reserve or cartouche. Stems with this sort of decoration start about $125 and go up to $250 each.

Another special decorative technique Morgantown used involved depositing silver onto the surface of a piece of glass to produce a design in very low relief. The pattern that was most often employed on these silver-deposit pieces is a hunt scene, and stemware examples are very hard to find. When they are found, they start at $175 each.

A similar technique featured etched designs into which a gold, silver, or platinum paste was rubbed and fired on in a furnace. This generally appeared as a broad band, and two of the most popular patterns were LeMons with its stylish triangles and diamonds, and Sparta with its classically inspired Greek women arranged around an altar. Prices for these start at $75 and go up to $175 plus.

In 1965, the Morgantown Glass Works was purchased by the Fostoria Glass Company of Moundsville, West Virginia, a firm that is famous for its moderately priced stemware. Earlier, we mentioned their more everyday American pattern, but among their more formal etched lines, their Navarre and Chintz patterns have wide followings.

Navarre was made from 1937 to 1980, and up until the '70s—when pink, blue, and green examples began to appear—all the pieces were colorless crystal. Collectors are not yet sure how they feel about these colored items, so at the moment prices are usually expressed in terms of the colorless crystal pieces only.

Navarre is really a very simple pattern with vine tendrils sparsely festooned with tiny star-shaped flowers. One of the most expensive pieces in the line is the #500 48-ounce footed pitcher, which sells for about $325. Stems start at $25 and go up to $50 for a 1-ounce cordial glass.

Chintz, with its variety of flowers and tendrils, is busier than Navarre, and some people say that it is a bit more in demand. The aforementioned pitcher in Navarre that brings $325 sells for about $25 more in Chintz, but the stems sell in the same price range.

One of the most widely collected of all the stemware patterns was made by the Cambridge Glass Company of Cambridge, Ohio. Called "Rose Point," it was made between 1936 and 1953 and featured an etched design of rose sprays arranged in panels between elongated scroll medallions. This pattern is always found in clear, colorless crystal, but occasionally the design has been accented with gilt enrichment. The design was placed on pieces of almost every conceivable shape, from candelabra and hurricane lamps to cocktail shakers and ice buckets.

In stemware, there is a staggering variety of pieces, including cordials, oyster cocktails, wines, parfaits, sherbets, brandies, and clarets. Most of these are valued from about $20 for a #3500 low-footed sherbet to about $275 for a #3104 3½-ounce cocktail glass.

Table Linens

All the items we have talked about so far are very nice and lovely in and of themselves, but they really do not look their best until they are sitting on a table covered with a fine linen or lace table-cloth. Today, in our fast-paced world, few of us have the time to take care of these very delicate fabrics, and we all know that one misguided glass of red wine can spell doom for these delicate textiles.

Monitoring the goings-on at estate sales, it is not uncommon for us to see customers exclaiming over the beauty of a lace or damask cloth, only to have them unfold the piece, discover a huge stain or a small hole, and just walk away. Buyers are not interested at any price. Therefore, for those of you who have vintage linens made from the 1930s through the 1950s, make sure they stay in excellent condition.

Over-laundering can cause linen fibers to break down, and do not overstarch your linens either, because this can cause unsightly permanent creasing. A little light spray-starching during ironing should do nicely. In addition, do not store your fine linens folded; instead, roll them on cardboard tubes covered with acid-free tissue paper, which will also help prevent permanent creasing.

If you find that you have a problem with heirloom linen, do not attack it as a do-it-yourself project until you have consulted with a cleaning specialist—and then make sure the remedy is appropriate for the specific problem and overall condition of the fabric.

When judging the rarity of a table linen, keep in mind that rectangular and square tablecloths are far more common than the round or oval variety. Quality and workmanship are key ingredients, and the phrase "Irish linen" still strikes a positive chord in the minds of collectors.

Damask tablecloths, with their fine, woven, tone-on-tone weaves, seem to be experiencing quite an upsurge in interest. Currently, a high-quality 108- by 72-inch rectangle in a chrysanthemum pattern is selling in the $200 to $250 range, and if there is a matching set of twelve napkins, these can add $100 to $150 to the price of the tablecloth if they are all sold as a set.

Lace tablecloths are also highly desired, but it is very hard to quantify their value because their quality varies so widely. Nice examples from the 1950s by a quality maker such as the Quaker Lace Company start at about $150 and go up from there depending on size, condition, and just how fancy and well-made they happen to be.

Joe has seen fights at estate sales over fine lace tablecloths, and whenever "linens" are advertised at one of these events, a crowd is sure to turn up just itching to find something wonderful and elegant. Fine linens in general are in demand, and any piece that exhibits handwork—be it embroidery, tatting, drawnwork, or whatever—should be carefully cared for and prized both for its beauty and its monetary worth.

Silver Plate

Earlier we talked about sterling silver flatware, but there is another type of silver in American dining rooms, and that is the silver-plated serving dishes that come out from the sideboard or buffet two or three times a year for parties and holidays. Unfortunately, the vast majority of these items have little value on the secondary marketplace.

The general rule is that the fanciest and most elaborate pieces are the ones in most demand. Large tea trays, for example, are sought after if they are extensively engraved and very decorative. Footed examples and pieces with galleries (raised rims around the edge) are the most desirable, and prices for high-quality, mid-twentieth century trays start at $350 and go up from there.

Other in-demand items include tilt-cradle hot water kettles, chafing dishes, anything that is unusual and attractive, and, among older pieces, tilt-cradle water pitchers with supports that hold one or two cups or goblets. These latter devices are usually mid- to late Victorian, and they retail in the $1,500 and above category.

The silver-plated products of two English companies are especially prized and often bring premiums on today's market because of their quality. The first one is Elkington & Company of Birmingham, which invented the silver electroplating process about 1840. Their marks usually include an "E & Co." inside a shield-shaped device.

The second company—and the one whose name you are most likely to find—is Ellis-Barker, also of Birmingham, England. Their finely crafted pieces are often marked with a representation of a pineapple, a cockleshell, a menorah, an open doorway, or an M superimposed over an S inside a shield.

Works by either maker are highly regarded by collectors but

often overlooked by homeowners, since the marks mean nothing to them. Be aware that one reason Ellis-Barker ware is so highly regarded is that the handles and raised trim are often made of sterling silver, not plated base metal.

Cut Glass

In addition to all of the above, there are generally two other types of collections that are likely to be found in most dining rooms: One is American Brilliant Period cut glass, and the other likely collection is decorative pottery or porcelain plates. The former makes the center of a table or the inside of a cabinet sparkle, and the latter looks festive and appropriate hanging on the walls or sitting behind the plate rail in a cabinet.

American Brilliant Period cut glass is said to have originated with the centennial celebration of the Declaration of Independence, which was held in Philadelphia, Pennsylvania, in 1876. This type of glass was made by cutting a series of deep V-shaped grooves, or "miters," into a thick, lead-crystal body.

The hobstar motif is one of the most commonly encountered decorations on American Brilliant Period cut glass.

These deep incisions form designs such as fans, stars, and hobnails, and were designed to catch the light and cause the glass to glitter—thus the name Brilliant Period. This type of glass was in vogue until the 1910 to 1915 era, and it stopped being made because it was just too labor-intensive to manufacture and its price had become prohibitively expensive.

American Brilliant Period cut glass was made in such large quantities that examples are found in many of today's homes. In fact, it is not uncommon to find Grandma's or Great-Grandma's cut glass bowl or creamer and sugar proudly displayed in homes that do not have a single other antique in them.

The reason this kind of cut glass is so plenti-

ful is that during the thirty or so years that it was being made, it became the gift of choice for brides and wives. In the modern world, if someone is stuck for a gift to give a bride, a crockpot or a piece of china or silver might be a standard choice, but in the late nineteenth and early twentieth centuries, the standard fallback gift of choice was a piece of cut glass. And if a husband needed a birthday, anniversary, or Christmas gift for his wife, if it was not roses, a box of candy, or (heaven forbid) lingerie, it was often cut glass.

The value of any piece of cut glass depends on a number of factors:

Shape

Items such as nappies (small bowls with one or two handles), berry bowls (both master and individual), creamers and sugars, carafes, tumblers, relish dishes, water pitchers, and compotes are fairly common. Baskets, cologne and perfume bottles, tea- and coffeepots, lamps, cake stands, large-diameter plates, humidors, whiskey jugs, cookie jars, and trays are fairly uncommon and command premium prices.

Pattern

Most Brilliant Period cut glass is cut in a rather generic manner with hobstars, fans, and such, but certain special patterns such as Russian, Louis XIV, Brazilian, Macbeth, Coronet, Nautilus, and Dunkirk are desired for their beauty, rarity, and/or intricacy of cutting.

Signatures

Traditionally, cut class signed by the maker is from 20 to 40 percent more expensive than unsigned examples. The tricky part here is that many times the signatures are so hard to see that the owners never know they are there. Signatures are usually found on the inside bottom of bowls, under the handle on pitchers, and near the base on vases. They are hard to see because they were applied using a rubber stamp dipped in acid, which leaves a faint, gray-colored impression that needs to be hit by the light in just the right way before it is visible. Such companies as Hawkes, Dorflinger, Libbey, Clark, Hoare, Straus, Sinclaire, and Bergen used this technique, but, as we have said before, buyers need to be aware that these marks are easy to fake and have been misused with great regularity by unscrupulous individuals.

Color

The vast majority of cut glass is what is known as clear, colorless, but perhaps one in every thousand pieces was made using a solid color glass blank, or by putting one or more colors over a clear, colorless base and then cutting through the color(s) to make a bi- or tri-colored piece. Prices for these pieces are double or, in some cases, triple those of their clear, colorless counterparts.

Type of cutting

The sort of cutting we have been discussing so far is used to make geometric patterns, but there is another type of cutting that was also done during this period that is highly prized as well. It is called "intaglio," and it involves cutting images deep into the glass surface. The items depicted are usually flowers or fruits, but more exotic motifs can also be found. In this country, Hawkes and Tuthill were most famous for using this technique, and intaglio pieces with signatures by either of these two companies can be two to three times as expensive as their regular cut glass products.

Cut glass is very fragile and easily damaged. Abrupt temperature change can make it crack, so do not store cut glass in a bright, sunny window; do not put it in the dishwasher; do not put it in the refrigerator; and do not wash it in hot water. Remember, a cracked piece of cut glass is an all-but-worthless piece of cut glass— except for the family memories it might engender.

In recent years, new cut glass has flooded the marketplace. It is cheaply made, using lasers. It is usually very easy to identify because it is so sharp. The raised points are often uncomfortable to touch, and it should also be mentioned that in many cases the surfaces are not properly polished. This produces gray areas that do not occur on old pieces.

The best way to recognize old pieces of cut glass is to find a reputable dealer with old pieces and examine his or her stock. Once you have picked up several old pieces and examined them closely, the new items should not fool you, because their look, their weight, and their overall "feel" are different.

Decorative Plates

The variety of pottery and porcelain plates that are out there to collect is almost endless, and some of them can be quite valuable. Limited-edition collector's plates litter homes in great numbers, and while a very few of these have become exceedingly valuable, most of them have shown only a modest increase, if any at all, since they were first made.

The first real collector plate was issued by the Bing & Grondahl Company in 1895, and was a Christmas plate called "Beyond the Window." When it was new, this piece cost less than $1, but today it is valued about $7,500!

Other winners in the collector's plate sweepstakes include the 1971 Goebel Hummel plate entitled "Heavenly Angel," which originally sold for $25 and is now bringing more than $600, and the 1969 Wedgwood "Windsor Castle," which originally sold for $25 and is now bringing about $200.

As a general rule, we do not advocate purchasing modern collector's plates for *investment* purposes. Buy them if you like them, or buy them for decorative purposes, but do not buy them expecting to make money from a later resale. Too many times, we have been faced with average collector's plates—still in their original boxes and with all their pertinent paperwork—and almost every time we have found that selling them is an extremely difficult task, bordering on the impossible.

There are, however, other plates that merit special attention, and these include:

English blue and white

Plates with this simple color scheme are always desirable, and they are relatively plentiful. Nineteenth-century examples with images of flowers or generic landscapes are fairly inexpensive and seldom rise above the $100 level, but pieces decorated with historic American scenes can be quite valuable. The most expensive of these are the ones where the blue is a very dark, almost inky, blue; these were primarily made in the 1820s. One plate featuring the sea battle between the ships *Constitution* and *Guerrière* is worth about $1,800, while a view of the Hudson River is about $800. More common images, such as the Boston State House, Commodore MacDonnough's Victory, and the New York City Battery, bring prices that are in the $150 to $400 range. Plates decorated with lighter blue bring less.

English and American flow blue

Originally made from the late 1820s until about 1860, flow blue was reintroduced in the 1880s and remained popular until about 1910. It is characterized by blue pigment that seems to run, or "flow," into the white areas. The earlier, generally more eagerly sought-after examples are distinguished by a darker blue color, and by decorations that strongly suggest the Orient with pagodas, arched foot bridges, and willow and palm trees. The prices for large, hard-to-find pieces such as platters and tureens decorated with flow blue can easily rise into the low thousands of dollars each, while plates are often some of the lowest-priced items. Still, a 10½-inch Formosa pattern plate by Mayer is worth around $175, and a 10½-inch Madras pattern plate by Doulton brings about $115. Other 10-inch flow blue plates start at $75.

Pickard and other china decorating companies

At the turn of the twentieth century, a number of American companies purchased white china "blanks" from European sources and then had them decorated in their workshops by artists. The Pickard China Company, founded in Chicago in 1895, is widely known for their rich depictions of flowers, fruit, animals, and scenic views, which were often greatly enhanced by lavish applications of gold. The simplest Pickard 8½-inch plate decorated with florals starts about $45, but prices really zoom up from there. Collectors are particularly interested in plates with scenic designs, and a Dutch windmill might bring $400, while a Nile scene brings closer to $500. Artist's signatures on these pieces are a plus ("Challinor" is a big favorite), and every piece of Pickard should be signed with the company name. Examples made before 1919 are preferred. These can be identified by a circle mark that has "Handpainted China" around the outside and "W A Pickard" on the inside. Avoid pieces with an all-over gold decoration. These are the least desired. Though generally less expensive, other names to look for include Osborne, Stouffer, Donath, and Brauer.

Royal Vienna

These are usually lovely portrait plates with exquisitely hand-painted images of women in the center surrounded by a richly colored border that is sometimes "jeweled" with drops of enamel. These plates should have a beehive-like mark on the back (actually the mark represents a shield, but it looks like a domed beehive to many), and this should be under the glaze. In reproductions, the mark is on top of the glaze, and it can often be felt with your fingertip. This is a key clue to help you spot some of the plentiful reproductions. Another is that the decoration of fakes is transfer-printed, not hand-painted. To detect a transfer, take a magnifying glass and examine the picture. If little black dots appear, it is a print and a fake. This sort of examination is necessary because a genuine Royal Vienna portrait plate starts at about $500, and zooms into the low thousands depending on the quality and the artist. The artist who signed his work "Wagner" is a very popular choice among collectors.

Limoges

We are not talking here about the ubiquitous dinner plates decorated with small flowers, but about plates that were designed to match special fish-and-game sets, and plates that were specifically made to hang on the wall. These latter plates can sometimes be distinguished by the two holes punched in the footrim so that a string or wire could be threaded through them to facilitate hanging. Plates intended to be used just as decoration are characterized by pictures of birds, animals, fish, people, landscapes, and flowers. Birds, animals, and fish appear on plates used to serve fish or game, and these plates often came with a large platter and a sauceboat. Complete ten- to fourteen-piece fish or game sets can go into the low thousands of dollars, and individual plates sell in the low hundreds. Large, well done decorative plates can bring prices well over $1000. Limoges plates should have two marks on them: the first one, underglaze, tells who made the china body; the second one, overglaze, tells who did the decorating. The best circumstance is if both marks are from the same factory. Next best is if the overglaze-decorating mark is from a professional French or American decorating company, and the least desirable is if the name of an individual is written on the back. This generally signifies the work of an amateur, and their pieces are not prized by serious collectors, who almost always want factory-decorated pieces.

Dining Room Furniture

Most of the things discussed so far are of no use whatsoever unless there is a dining-room table for them to be used upon, plus a china cabinet and perhaps a buffet or sideboard on which to display them. A vast variety of furniture can be found in the average dining room, and much of it is the fairly generic product that comes from the local furniture store. Nice, but not particularly special.

A lot of this furniture is moderately priced, mid-twentieth-century reinterpretations of Queen Anne, Sheraton, or Chippendale styles, and it will be a long time before anyone thinks of these lower-end pieces as being anything other than used furniture. There are, however, other early- to mid-twentieth-century furniture reproductions executed in various seventeenth-, eighteenth-, and early-nineteenth-century styles that are of much higher quality and value.

Many of these better sets were made by noted manufacturers, such as Baker, Berkey & Gay. The quality of the workmanship and the materials on these pieces can be very high, with intricate satinwood inlays and bandings, marquetry, decorative moldings, and solid wood such as mahogany and walnut, or hand-matched veneers. Such pieces were expensive when they were new, and they are expensive now.

We see a fairly large number of dining-room suites made in the 1920s and '30s that look rather grand by today's standards. Although each piece was available separately, most of them were intended to be sold and used as ten-piece sets consisting of a table, a china cabinet, a server (that often doubled as silver storage), a buffet, a host's chair (or armchair), and five side chairs.

Reading the catalogs of the companies that made these suites, it is evident that they were trying to recreate old styles—or at least suggest to the purchaser that they were working in the manner of the past. References are freely made to Jacobean, Elizabethan, Chippendale, Hepplewhite, Louis XVI, Duncan Phyfe, Renaissance, and Sheraton.

These dining suites were usually made from gumwood with exotic wood veneers thinly layered on top. Burl walnut or mahogany were favorites (in those days, "burl" woods were often called "crotch" or "butt"). Original prices for these sets started at approximately $300 and went up to as much as $2,000. Today, the value of these sets starts at about $2,500 for the lower-end models and goes up above the $10,000 level for the better, fancier examples.

During the 1930s, '40s, and '50s, there was a great upswing in artist-designed modern furniture that was either produced in an artist's studio or by a furniture manufacturer such as Herman Miller, Widdicomb-Mueller, or Knoll. There are many designer names to look for. We mentioned Charles and Ray Eames in the first chapter, but there are also such luminaries as George Nelson, T. H. Robsjohn-Gibbings, George Nakashima, Eero Saarinen, Gilbert Rohde, and Hans Wegner, to name just a few.

Most of this furniture is labeled in some way, so if you see a designer label and/or the name of a famous, high-quality manufacturer such as any of the ones mentioned, it is appropriate to do a little investigation to see if you have a potential treasure. A classic Hans Wegner Danish Modern drop-leaf dining table, for example, with its oak top and simple X-shaped legs sells for about $2,000—and that is just the table with no chairs.

A chair that might blend with this grouping is the DCW ("dining chair wood"), also known as the "potato chip" chair, by Charles and Ray Eames. These chairs are made from laminated and molded walnut plywood, and they look very much like office furniture. But a set of four should be valued between $1,800 and $2,000.

We are amazed by the value of things such as the Charles and Ray Eames dining table that resembles one of those collapsible card tables that people kept tucked away in their closets for bridge or poker. This designer model is 34 inches square, and has a plywood top and, yes, folding metal legs. It may look like an ordinary card table, but if you have one, it is worth about $1,000!

About 1940, English designer Robsjohn-Gibbings created a dining-room suite that featured a very simple walnut table with saber-curved legs and matching chairs. These were manufactured by Widdicomb, and when they are accompanied by their six matching chairs, the value in original condition with original upholstery is about $3,500.

One of the most highly regarded manufacturers of American dining room furniture during the mid-twentieth century was the Heywood-Wakefield Company, which was renowned for its rattan furniture. In the 1930s the company introduced a line of modern furniture that was fundamentally based on the high-style designer pieces of the mid-1920s.

This sort of modern furniture had not been a hit in the United States because it was too extreme and too expensive, but Heywood-

Wakefield felt that they could make a mass-produced product that would be stylish in a more subtle sort of way, and relatively inexpensive in the bargain. The designer of this more down-to-earth line was Gilbert Rohde, and, in 1931, Rohde Contemporary Furniture premiered.

This furniture introduced Americans to the idea of sectional and modular pieces, an idea that is still much used in today's furniture design. It also featured the use of bentwood and walnut veneers. By 1934, Rohde had moved on to bigger and better things and was designing more upscale pieces for makers such as Herman Miller, but Heywood-Wakefield was determined to persevere.

Over the next few years, refinements and changes were made to Heywood-Wakefield's modern furniture, and in 1937 the Streamline Modern line was introduced, which was largely made from light-colored birch wood. In 1939, the company pioneered a new finish called "Champagne," which was a light pinky beige that was said to resemble a properly concocted champagne cocktail.

By 1940, this was Heywood-Wakefield's most popular finish and Streamline Modern was hot with the American consumer. Today, blond, modern furniture is once again very popular; and among dining-room pieces, an open corner cupboard retails for about $750, a two-drawer server for about $350, an extension dining table for about $450, and six chairs (four side and two arm) for about $850.

That means that an entire dining room sells for about $2,500, which is really a bargain at the present time, but we feel these prices will greatly increase in the twenty-first century.

CHAPTER SIX

The Living Room

Few of us have furniture in our living rooms—or anywhere in our homes, for that matter—made before the 1840s, and this means that the earliest furniture normally encountered in our homes is from the Victorian era. Queen Victoria ruled England from 1837 until her death in 1901, and this means that Victorian furniture was made for a very long time. It was also made in a large number of forms that are usually referred to as "substyles," and some of these furniture substyles are avidly collected, while others are less highly regarded.

In chapter 2 we discussed the characteristics of many of the Victorian furniture styles, and there is no real reason to rehash them here. What is important to discuss is the tendency for pieces in the Rococo Revival, Gothic, and Renaissance Revival substyles to be more valued by collectors than Eastlake, spool furniture, or the painted, so-called cottage furniture.

Rococo Revival

The king of Victorian furniture is probably Rococo Revival (also called "Louis XV"), which was popular from about 1840 to 1870. Like every other category of antiques, there are plenty of examples of Rococo Revival that are merely good, but then there are also the *great* Rococo Revival pieces, which are what serious collectors are actually looking to find.

Ordinary pieces in this style—of which we see vast quantities— have the requisite cabriole legs and crests carved with flowers or fruit, but they lack the flair and exuberance that distinguishes the best Rococo Revival furniture. Most of these more ordinary Victorian Rococo pieces tend to be made of walnut, but the best ones are frequently made of rosewood. Rosewood is a richer, redder wood than walnut, but caution needs to be exercised because other, cheaper woods were occasionally grain-painted to resemble rosewood, and these can be real foolers.

The very best Rococo pieces were made from laminated wood (think early plywood) that was created by gluing together strips of rosewood veneer to create a layered sheet of wood that was easily shaped and curved in a steam press. When this type of construction is discovered on a piece of Victorian furniture, many want to attribute the item to New York City cabinetmaker John Henry Belter, who arguably made the best examples of Rococo Revival furniture.

Unfortunately, such attributions are not necessarily warranted. Many furniture makers copied Belter's work, and it was not uncommon for manufacturers to infringe upon his patents. Objects crafted by Belter and his company are sometimes signed with stencils and paper labels, but most are not, and attribution has to be made according to the pattern of the particular item in question, rather than any other consideration.

It is important to keep in mind that there is nothing subtle about the best Victorian Rococo Revival furniture. It is excessive, "over-the-top," and outstanding specimens often have pierced carvings in which the wood surface is actually penetrated by the carving, leaving holes and openings among the design elements. Often, the best chairs and sofas have high, arched crests on their backs, which remind Joe of the elaborate combs Spanish women wear in their hair on special occasions.

One of the more commonly seen pieces of Rococo Revival furniture is the "turtle-top" center table. These tables were made with either plain wooden tops or with marble tops, and the latter is far more desired by collectors than the former.

Turtle-top tables get their name from the shape of their top. Looking down, the surface is largely oval, and has four protrusions at the 10-, 2-, 4-, and 8-o'clock positions. These rounded bumps look a bit like stumpy legs protruding from a turtle's shell, thus the name.

The best turtle-top tables have stretchers that run between the legs and meet in the middle under the tabletop, just above the floor. In the center, where the stretchers converge, there is often an ornament such an urn; better examples, however, may have a fully carved basket of flowers or the figure of an animal such as a dog or a lamb.

Earlier, we said that turtletops were "center tables," and this is because they were designed to be placed in the center of the best parlor, not up against a wall. These center tables (not always turtle-topped) were the places where families displayed what they wanted important visitors to know about them. If piety was emphasized, the family Bible might be placed there; if family itself was stressed, photo albums might be displayed; or, if travel was important, there might be a stereoviewer and cards from faraway places.

Prices on turtle-top tables start at about $850 for the plainest-of-the-plain with wooden tops, and increase to the $6,000 to $7,500 range for a fine-quality, marble-topped example that is not attributable to a particular maker. An exceptional turtle top that can be traced to a specific maker of Rococo Revival furniture such as John Henry Belter, Charles Baudoine, or Leon Marcote should command triple that price or more.

Always check to make sure that the marble top on a Victorian table is original. Gently lift up the marble; if you find a solid wooden top underneath, the marble is an addition. Tables that were designed to have marble have an open top with a flange running around the outside and a crossbar across the middle to support the weight of the stone.

Gothic

One of the other highly respected Victorian substyles is Gothic, which was most popular from the mid-1830s to 1865. This form, with its pointed arches, trefoil and quatrefoil elements, and legs that sometimes end in animal hooves, was not a very popular style when it was originally made, and has a somewhat limited following today.

In Victorian days, it was a style that architects loved, and as a consequence the best pieces are those that architects designed or had made for particular building projects. This style was somewhat elitist then, and on the current market it is often undervalued because the demand is not very widespread.

Yet the best pieces—made by such people as A. J. Davis, J. and J. W. Meeks, and Richard Byrne—can be very fine and expensive. The more architectural and medieval looking an example happens to be, the better; and pieces made from rosewood and mahogany usually command a premium. Objects in the Gothic style were also made from walnut and oak, with the oak stained dark to resemble ebony or another dark wood.

The pieces that collectors are most likely to encounter are the chairs with high-pointed backs that look like church windows without the stained glass. The more imposing and "throne-like," the more desirable. Abundant "cathedral-type" tracery elements are a plus as well.

Renaissance Revival

Another Victorian substyle that we need to discuss in detail is Renaissance Revival pieces. In the living room there might be a large, square, or rectangular secretary with inset burl walnut panels and carved three-dimensional heads of either animals or people.

Renaissance Revival pieces are primarily constructed of walnut. They should have an architectural feeling and, in addition to the burl walnut panels, they might have elaborate inlays of exotic woods or even mother-of-pearl. Renaissance Revival pieces also have shallow line carvings and design elements placed in decorative medallions.

This style was based on classical antiquity (that is, Greek and Roman styles) and was most popular from 1865 to 1885. Renaissance Revival also includes a style called "Egyptian Revival," which featured sphinx heads, palmettes, zigzag lines, lotus capitals, and legs that ended in cloven hoofs.

One of the more interesting forms of Victorian Renaissance Revival furniture is the Wooton Patent Desk, which was invented by William S. Wooton of Indianapolis, Indiana. These desks were made between 1875 and 1884 and they are quite extraordinary.

Massive in size, a Wooton Patent Desk is really an office contained in a single case. The front of these pieces was divided in half, and when each section was opened, file drawers and cubbyholes were revealed in the right- and left-hand portions. In the center section, there was a desk unit and more storage.

This Superior Grade Wooton Patent Desk is an entire office unto itself.

Wooton desks came in four grades: Ordinary, Standard, Extra, and Superior. Ordinary examples were indeed fairly ordinary with very plain fronts, and Superior Grade pieces were elaborately ornamented and extravagantly fitted. Originally, an Ordinary Grade desk cost a little less than $100, while the price of a Superior Grade specimen was about eight times as much or around $750. Today, Ordinary Grade Wooton desks start at more than $10,000, and Superior Grade examples in excellent condition can exceed the $100,000 mark.

Eastlake

One last Victorian style that needs to be discussed is known as "Eastlake" because it was loosely based on the ideas of Englishman

Charles Locke Eastlake. In all fairness to Eastlake, his ideas were debased and corrupted by other furniture makers, but the objects that rightly or wrongly bear his name were very popular in America in the latter days of the nineteenth century. They were made from walnut or oak (the oak specimens were largely made after about 1890) and tend to be very rectangular, rather austere, and decorated with machine-made ornamentation.

Eastlake pieces were mass-produced and fairly inexpensive when they were new and, for the most part, they are not very pleasing to modern eyes. It is the kind of furniture that authors of books on Victorian furniture either try to ignore because there are so few quality examples, or to emphasize because there is so much of it in American homes. Many pieces of Eastlake furniture are revered because they are "family" pieces or "heirlooms," but their owners should be aware that their value is mostly sentimental, not monetary.

Some large pieces in the Eastlake style (secretaries and the like) push above the $2,000 level at retail, but few should be valued at more than $4,000. Most Eastlake pieces are valued in the hundreds rather than the thousands of dollars. Simple Eastlake side chairs bring $125 or even a bit less, and that is really very little for a piece of furniture that has been around for more than one hundred years.

Arts and Crafts or "Mission" Furniture

At the end of the Victorian era, a new style arose, one that was opposed to the aesthetic sensibilities of the Victorian furniture makers. This style was called the "Arts and Crafts Movement" and it got its start in England during the third quarter of the nineteenth century. It was an attempt to return to the craftsmanship of earlier (namely, medieval) times and to set new standards of beauty.

The leader of this movement, William Morris, believed that there were two types of furniture: "workaday," and "state." Workaday furniture was meant to be used every day—and encompasses items such as dining tables and chairs. Morris felt that these needed to be simple and functional, with spare ornamentation that allowed their handmade nature to be evident.

State furniture, on the other hand, was for show, and these pieces could be elaborately—but tastefully—carved, inlaid, and hand-painted. Sideboards are good examples of pieces that Morris would have considered to be of the state variety.

Starting in the 1870s, Morris and a group known as Morris and Company designed furniture, jewelry, carpets, wallpaper, metalwork, tapestry, and stained glass. Morris' name itself is attached to a chair that is commonly seen in American living rooms.

A "Morris chair" is a reclining "easy chair" with open arms that are often padded. They usually have loose padded seats and backs, and there are sometimes vertical slats under the arms, and the backs have slats in a "ladder-back" configuration. Morris chairs are usually made from oak, and one unattributed to a maker is worth $750 to $1,000 on the current market. An L. & J. G. Stickley example (#830) should be valued in the $1,400 to $1,600 range, and a box-arm Morris chair by Gustav Stickley (#336) is worth between $7,500 and $8,500.

Both Gustav Stickley and Elbert Hubbard were greatly influenced by Morris and the English Arts and Crafts Movement. Both men traveled to England, and when they returned Stickley founded his "Craftsman Workshops" and Hubbard his "Roycroft" community. Both concerns produced a variety of products, including metalware (mainly copper) and furniture. The Craftsman Workshops also turned out linens and the Roycrofters specialized in bookbinding.

Actually, there were five Stickley brothers involved in furniture making: Gustav (the oldest), Leopold, Charles, Albert, and John George. Besides Gustav's

Gustav Stickley's #369 Morris chair. If it is in good condition with its original finish and leather cushions, it is worth more than $7,000.

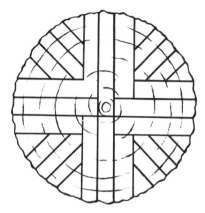

Diagram of a quartersawn log.

Gustav Stickley #820 bookcase. Despite its simple appearance, it is worth almost $3,500.

Craftsman Workshops, they operated L. & J. G. Stickley in Fayetteville, New York, and Stickley Brothers in Grand Rapids, Michigan (not to mention an original Stickley Brothers, for which they all worked, in Binghampton, New York). The items produced by Gustav are by far the most highly regarded and the most valuable. Look for his mark, which may feature a joiner's compass and the phrase "Als ik Kan" (literally, "The Best I Can"), and may be in the form of a brand or on a paper label.

The furniture made by the Stickleys, the Roycrofters, and others was generally made from quartersawn oak, was square in design, and had for its ornament only the handmade hardware or the mortise-and-tenon joints which were left visible. From the last days of the 1890s through about 1920 (Stickley's Craftsman Workshops actually went out of business in 1915, but the Roycrofters continued until the 1930s), this furniture was popular in the United States, where it was often called "Mission" furniture.

There are actually two theories as to the origins of this name. Some say it is derived from the simple furniture found in the Spanish missions of California, but others claim it is derived from the fact that the makers felt they had a "mission" to reform the taste of the people in the United States.

American Arts and Crafts furniture can be extremely expensive, yet much of it can still be found hiding in attics and other storage spaces where it was banished when it initially went out of fashion. Marked pieces by the Stickleys, Limbert, Greene and Greene, Roycroft, and others are preferable to unsigned pieces. A signed Gustav Stickley #208 settle (or sofa) is worth around $10,000, while a similar unsigned and unattributed settle is valued about $2,800.

A signed settle by L. & J. G. Stickley in their style #222 or #223 is worth about as much as the Gustav Stickley #208, but a Limbert settle #653 with spade-shaped cutouts in the side and back splats is worth only about $4,000. Some Gustav Stickley settles (such as the #206) can sell well above $20,000, but for all this furniture to retail at anything near the values mentioned above, it is critically important that they be unrefinished and still have their original leather cushion covers.

After reading the above, you may have the impression that all American Arts and Crafts furniture is expensive. This is not the case. An L. & J. G. Stickley #816 armchair, for example, might sell for less than $500, while a Limbert #59 magazine rack should bring less than $850, and a Limbert plant stand less than $700. Even some Gustav Stickley pieces can bring prices only in the $1,000 range or slightly below.

Modern " '50s" Furniture

Walk into any American living room and the first thing you will see is upholstered furniture. There are sofas, armchairs, wing chairs, love seats, club chairs, and so on—but unless they are very unusual, these pieces are probably just used furniture worth very little on the collectors' market.

Exceptions to this include items such as George Nelson's Marshmallow sofa, which looks like numerous round vinyl cushions mounted in four rows on a tubular steel frame. This sofa was made

George Nelson's Marshmallow sofa.

about 1956 by the Herman Miller Furniture Company, and if one of these happens to grace your living room—*and* it is in perfect shape—you can value it at close to $17,000!

If you are not lucky enough to have one of these, maybe you have a "swan" sofa designed by Arne Jacobson and made by Denmark's Hansen. This sofa from the late 1950s has a fiberglass body, a trestle-shaped aluminum base, flip-up sections at the end of the seat, and a back that wraps around slightly. This is not quite as expensive as a Marshmallow sofa, but at about $4,000, it is still a nice piece to have around.

American and Danish furniture from this time period had all sorts of weird names: there was the Pretzel chair (George Nelson for Herman Miller, $3,000), the Coconut chair (George Nelson for Herman Miller, $3,500), the Diamond chair (Harry Bertoia for Knoll, $500), and the Grasshopper chair (Eero Saarinen for Knoll, $1,800). There are also Kangaroo chairs, Papa Bear chairs, Eiffel Tower chairs, and, of course, the famous "670" chair and "671" ottoman by Charles and Ray Eames.

The 670 and 671 are perhaps the most famous of all the designer furniture pieces from the mid-twentieth century. This set was introduced in 1956, and was made from laminated rosewood and down-filled black leather on a five-branch cast aluminum base (the ottoman is four-branch). At last report, this grouping is still being made, but the original ones sell for a little less than $3,000 if they are in excellent shape.

Many of you may be thinking that this expensive furniture does not turn up very often, but Joe

The famous 670 chair and 671 ottoman created by Charles and Ray Eames.

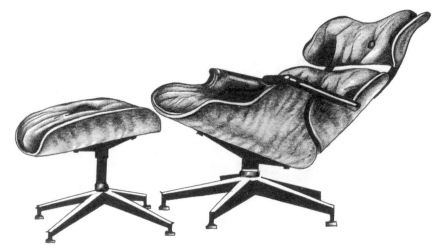

remembers going into a mobile home located behind a junkyard in an industrial park to see about doing an estate sale. It was a dismal place with debris strewn everywhere, but what Joe noticed when he walked in through the trailer door was an Eames 670 chair and 671 ottoman in fair condition. These were truly jewels among junk.

We wish we could give you more details about this type of potentially very valuable seating, but whole books have been written on the subject. What we are trying to get across in this brief space is that if you have 1940s or '50s furniture with wire, tubular metal, fiberglass, or bentwood construction; and if it was made by Herman Miller, Knoll Associates, or a Scandinavian concern; and if it has a designer name on it—or even if it *looks* like it might be a designer piece—it should not be discarded without a little investigation.

It does not matter if the piece looks like it came out of your grade-school principal's office, or out of a doctor's waiting room. It does not matter if it looks a bit weird (it should), and it does not matter one whit if it looks out of place at the turn of the twenty-first century. What does matter is that its owners think and do a little research before they throw this piece away just because it is out of style or because they cannot imagine that this relic might be valuable, rather than just "in the way."

Coffee Tables

One other piece of living room furniture we need to discuss is the coffee table. Many people do not realize that this form of furniture is always twentieth century! George and Martha Washington would not have known what to do with one, nor would Abraham and Mrs. Lincoln. Low Victorian-looking tables that appear to be coffee tables are either reproductions or nineteenth-century tables that have been cut down. When this butchery occurs, it greatly diminishes the value of the original table.

Since coffee tables are not yet technically "antique," collectors

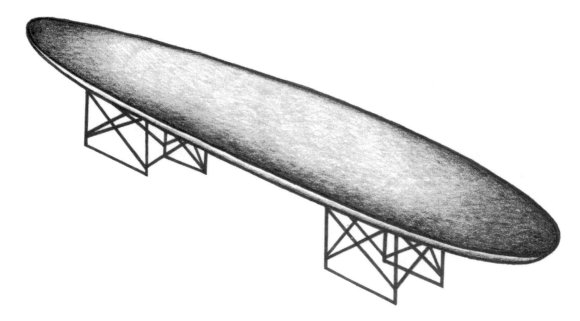

An Eames
Surfboard table.

are only interested in the ones that have great style and quality. Marble- and leather-topped examples often do well, and pieces with elaborate carvings from the 1920s and '30s also have a following.

But the mid-twentieth-century coffee tables that are most sought after are the "amoeba" or "biomorphic" items designed by such names as Isamu Noguchi (for Herman Miller) and Edward Wormley (for Dunbar). These pieces usually have free-form glass or, in some cases, wood and glass, tops that are shaped like a single-cell organism or a triangle with curved sides.

Other oddly shaped pieces fall roughly into this group: one, by Robsjohn-Gibbings, has a three-tiered, raised top that looks like a relief map of an amoeba's back, and another, by Charles and Ray Eames, is a long, slender oval supported on twin wire bases that is called the "Surfboard" table. Both of these coffee tables are very expensive and run in the $2,000 to $2,500-plus range, but other designer tables start around $750.

Knockoffs of these tables abound, and the imitations are much less expensive. These are actually very simple to make, and Joe was once in a house with wonderful '40s and '50s furniture that included a number of these amoeba-shaped tables. He was somewhat surprised when he discovered that the gentleman of the house had carefully examined pictures in design magazines and gone to his workshop and recreated what he saw.

This points out rather vividly how tricky this business can be, and these look-alikes and wannabe items can be real foolers. Their value, however, is very limited, and examples not actually made to a designer's specifications by a company such as Knoll, Herman Miller, Johnson Furniture, Dunbar, or Widdicomb are worth very little. In other words, in most types of mid-twentieth-century furniture, it is pedigree that counts, not just appearances.

Lighting

Every living room has to have light, and the torchère floor lamps that date from the 1930s, '40s and '50s interest some collectors. These fixtures, with their typically heavy bases, long poles, and upturned, flaring shades of glass or metal, are becoming moderately valuable. Prices generally fall into the hundreds unless the glass shade is made by a famous company such as Durand or Steuben, and then values can push well beyond the $1,000 mark.

Examples with marble or lighted bases and fancy decorations at the top and bottom of the poles are pluses, but all too often these lamps were rather plain, and the metal parts were merely brass-plated. These latter items can suffer from peeling metal, discoloration, and general unsightliness, and they go begging now and will continue to do so in the foreseeable future unless they are carefully refurbished by a professional.

Table lamps are much more complicated to assess because they come in such a huge variety. A good general rule might be that any lamp that was high-quality and expensive when it was new is probably still high-quality and expensive.

Currently, anything that has a Neoclassical look is desired, as are figural pieces (both human and animal), and examples made by famous companies such as Lenox or Wedgwood. There are all sorts of fabulously expensive glass lamps out there that were made by Tiffany Studios, but for all intents and purposes, these *must* be signed—and they should be signed both on the base *and* on the shade.

It needs to be understood that during the first and second quarter of the twentieth century, many companies made leaded-glass shades. None of them came up to the Tiffany quality then, and none of them come near the Tiffany prices now. Please, do not call a lamp a "Tiffany" unless it was made by that company and bears its trademark. You also need to be aware that "darn good" fakes do exist, and have existed for some time. Just because a lamp is signed "Tiffany" does not make it the real thing.

The type of lamp that we see erroneously labeled "Tiffany" most often is the slag-glass panel lamp that is sometimes decorated with metal cutouts to give it a semi-leaded glass look. These were very common in the 1910s, '20s, and '30s, and they are fairly inexpensive today.

Slag-glass panel lamps such as this one are often called "Tiffany" lamps. They are not.

More times than we would like to remember, someone has brought in one of these lamps swathed in layer after layer of wrapping, and told us they want us to evaluate the family "Tiffany" lamp. When the heirloom lighting fixture finally comes out of its wraps, all too often it is one of these panel lamps, and it is difficult for us to tell the owner that it is worth less—sometimes much less—than $1,200 at retail.

Another grouping of twentieth-century table lamps that are desired by modern collectors are the ones with "reverse-painted" shades. These usually consist of a metal base that supports a more-or-less dome-shaped shade decorated on the inside with hand-painted scenes or images of animals or flowers.

Again, these were produced by any number of

manufacturers, but the two that make some collectors break out in hot sweats of desire are those made by the Handel Company of Meriden, Connecticut, and the Pairpoint Manufacturing Company of New Bedford, Massachusetts.

Handel made a variety of products, including some Tiffany-style leaded-glass shades, but the company is best known for its reverse-painted products. On these pieces, a design is painted on the inside—or reverse—of the glass lamp shade, and it really does not show to its full advantage until the lamp is lit. (A word to the wise: Use very low-wattage bulbs in these lamps because higher-wattage bulbs produce too much heat and may crack the shade, which will greatly devalue it.)

As an adjunct to the reverse painting, Handel often employed an interesting and very distinctive decorative technique on the outside of the shade, called "chipped ice." To create this look, the outside of the glass shade is sandblasted and then coated with fish glue and baked in an 800-degree Fahrenheit kiln until the glue contracts and pulls off tiny pieces of the glass.

Magnificent Handel Birds of Paradise reverse-painted lamp.

The shades of Handel lamps should always be signed but, on occasion, the company marked its bases with a cloth or felt strip that was easily removed or lost. As a general rule, the larger the shade's diameter, the more valuable the lamp, but decorative subject matter is also very important. Examples that feature images of birds (parrots, birds of paradise) are much more valuable than pieces with simple floral borders.

A lamp with an 18-inch-diameter, reverse-painted shade decked out with a design of birds of paradise might sell for close to $12,000, while a fixture with a 16-inch parrot-and-rose decorated shade might push the $15,000 mark. On the other hand, a lamp with an 18-inch shade and reverse-painted cherry blossoms will probably fetch less than $4,000.

Keep in mind that lamps with smaller shades and common decorations can bring prices less than $1,000. Also, it should be understood that the prices quoted are for lamps and bases that started out life together. Shades on non-Handel bases or shades on Handel bases that are not original to the piece bring much less money.

Another really important maker of lamps with reverse-painted shades, as we have already mentioned, was the Pairpoint Manufacturing Company, which bought out the famous Mt. Washington Glass Works in 1894. The conventional reverse-painted shades and metal lamp bases that Pairpoint created seldom run above $10,000, and most fall in the $3,000 to $5,000 range.

The real jewels of the Pairpoint lamps are the "puffys," with "blown-out," or three-dimensional, images that are enhanced on the reverse side with painting. These are truly spectacular because the shades were usually made to look like bouquets of roses, poppies, azaleas, hollyhocks, or some other flower. Butterflies can also be found, and there is one shade that features lotus plants and dragonflies. The colors painted on the inside make these shades breathtakingly beautiful; and if you own a 14-inch-diameter puffy shade in a

Albert Steffin's design for a Pairpoint puffy lamp shade.

sort of bonnet shape with poppies on it, you should value it at more than $20,000 if it is in perfect condition. A similar lamp with a dome shape instead of a bonnet sells for about $12,500.

Pairpoint lamps should always be signed on both the base and the shade. On the base, the signature is often a *P* inside a diamond, and the shade should have "Pairpoint Corporation" and/or some sort of patent information, such as "Patented July 9, 1907."

Tiffany, Handel, and Pairpoint lamps are very serious works, but in the mid-twentieth century, some interesting lamps were made that are not so serious. We are particularly taken with the Easy Edges lamps designed by architect Frank Gehry in the early 1970s. These lamps were made from round sections of cardboard in such a way that the internal corrugations show and form the decoration around the circumference of the base and shade. Today, a pair of these is worth about $1,200. Matching cardboard side chairs with hairpin-curved bases and rectangular backs were made as well, and these sell for more than $1,500 each.

Hummel Figures

You could almost say that a living room serves as a house's museum, and its collections could consist of anything from Hummel and Precious Moments figures to Pilgrim and Charles Lotton art glass. Hummel figures are one of the things that seem to turn up in houses all the time—and while some of them are quite valuable, others are not.

In general, the monetary value depends on when the figure was made, the mark it carries, how large it is, and how intricate it happens to be. Large multi-figured groups often demand a premium, and a Hummel piece that is marked with a crown intertwined with a "WG" can bring a significant premium.

Hummel figures were first made about 1935 by the W. Goebel Porzellanfabrik of Rodenthal, Germany. They were modeled after the drawings of Sister Maria Innocentia (née Berta Hummel), a Franciscan nun born in 1909. Each authentic piece should be signed "M. I. Hummel," and should bear the Goebel factory mark in use at the time it was made.

The first mark used was the aforementioned crown over a "WG," which was employed from 1934 to 1950. From 1940 to 1959, the company also used various marks that employed a large flying bee inside the letter V. Starting in 1960, the bees became stylized. In 1979, both the V and the bee disappeared altogether and were

Goebel's Full Bee mark (upper) and Crown mark (lower) used on Hummel figures.

replaced with several marks that prominently used the company's name, "Goebel."

Collectors tend to pay a premium for the Hummel examples made between 1934 and 1950 that carry the crown mark. To illustrate this, let's examine the 4¾-inch-tall figure known as "Joyous News" (#27), which shows an angel sitting down, blowing a horn. Pieces with the original crown mark sell for as much as $2,000; but examples with the V bee mark, which was used from 1940 to 1959, bring only about $1,000. The same piece with marks signifying it was made after 1979 is valued at only about $200.

Size is also important. A good example of this are the Ba-Bee Rings wall plaques (#30A and 30B) that feature a baby's head inside a ring. Perched on the ring is a bee, which has captivated the baby. The plaques came in pairs, and in two sizes—a 5-inch and a 6-inch diameter.

A 5-inch-diameter pair with a crown marking is worth only about $450, but a crown-marked, 6-inch diameter brings more than six times that figure at approximately $3,000. If the ring happens to be red instead of tan, the price can jump to as high as $9,000!

Color can be a very significant variation in Hummel figures, and odd little rarities can make prices jump like jackrabbits. One of the more frequent variations that makes a difference is when a figure is decorated all in white instead of in color. Usually if in white, this raises the value, but on other occasions it can actually lower it. Let us give you a few examples.

One of the figures that we often see in estates is the Flower Madonna (#10), which came both in white and in color. The 9½-inch-tall white version with the crown mark is worth about $450, while the same size and mark in color is about $1,000. Usually, the all-white Hummel pieces are considered to be quite rare, and a good case in point is Friends (#136), which shows a little girl petting a fawn.

The colored and crown-marked, 5-inch version of Friends sells for about $500, but in all-white the price soars to more than $4,000! On very rare occasions, Hummel figures are found in all terra-cotta—

a kind of red earthenware—and when one is, it can be very costly indeed. As a case in point, the same crown-marked Friends figure we have just been talking about should be valued at more than $10,000 in terra-cotta!

Details are so important in Hummel figures, and we will give you one last case in point. There is a baby plaque that is similar to Ba-Bee Rings, but this one shows a child in bed with the covers pulled up and a small ladybug on the outside ring. Appropriately enough, it is called "Child in Bed," and its impressed mold number is 137B. (All the numbers mentioned so far can be found incised on the bases of Hummel figures; they are the easy way to identify what a particular figure is called.)

The 137B with a crown mark is worth about $450, but there is a rare mirror-image version incised "137A." If you find one of these, value it at $8,000, and remember how just a little thing like a letter B or letter A can make a huge difference when a price is being determined.

Precious Moments

Now, let's take a quick look at what have been called "American Hummels": the Precious Moments figures created by Samuel J. Butcher and made by Enesco Corporation. They originally came on the market in 1978, and twenty years later they could boast about having a collector's club that was more than a quarter of a million souls strong.

While a few of these retailed in the $200 to $600 range when they were new, most Precious Moments figures were fairly inexpensive when they were issued. Interestingly, at this time most of the more costly upper-level pieces have shown only a modest gain since they first appeared on the market, but some of the more modestly priced versions have shown significant gain.

A good example of this is the 1977 He Leadeth Me (E1377A), which sold for $9 when it was new and is now pushing $300 on the secondary market. Yet the 1972 limited edition Ye Have Touched So Many Hearts initially retailed for $500, and now sells for only about $100 higher at $600.

Without going into a lot of detail, the most important thing to remember about Precious Moments figures is that, almost without exception, when a piece is retired or undergoes a change in the mold, prices on the secondary market go up. The future for these figures looks bright, and this is mainly because there are so many people out there collecting them (which makes for a healthy secondary market).

Lladro figures, made in Iavernes Blanques, Spain, are also very popular with collectors, and retired items and limited editions have a following on the secondary market. They can be bought for as little as $40 on the resale market, but rarer examples can sell in the $1,500-plus range.

Like Hummels, which were widely copied in Japan, there are look-alike Lladro pieces, and in our opinion these have very little interest now nor will they in the foreseeable future. It is the real thing or nothing at all.

Czechoslovakian Glass

Another type of decorative collectible that we find in many living rooms is beautiful art glass made in the former nation of Czechoslovakia. Glass has been made in this region for centuries, but currently there is a focus on pieces made after 1918 that are signed with the name of the country of origin.

This last factor, "signed with the country of origin," is very important, because collectors truly prefer to collect signed pieces. If, for example, you have two pieces that are exactly alike in every particular except one is signed and the other is not, the signed one will sell first, and will sell for more money—sometimes as much as 50 percent more.

Czech glass is usually brightly colored, with striking color contrasts, such as red and yellow, red and black, brown and orange, and so forth. There are also frosted-glass pieces done in the manner of Lalique, and the most desirable of these have an "Art Deco" flavor.

At the present moment, prices for Czechoslovakian glass are not astronomically high, and ordinary pieces can be had for as little as $50. The best pieces, however, go above the $1,000 mark, and these are usually the very fancy items with oil-spot, luster, cameo, and/or metal-mounted decoration.

Czechoslovakian Pottery

Czechoslovakian pottery is also sought-after, and names such as Amphora and Royal Dux can command significant dollars. Geography complicates things here, because Amphora and Royal Dux were made in the part of Bohemia that was a part of the Austro-Hungarian Empire—that is, until 1918, when the region became a part of Czechoslovakia (currently called the Czech Republic). This means that some of their work is marked "Austria" and some is marked "Czechoslovakia."

Prices for these pieces start about $100 and go up into the low thousands (usually $3,000 or less), depending upon size, style of design, and intricacy of workmanship. The most favored designs tend to be Art Nouveau, which is characterized by sensuously curving lines, portraits of women with masses of curly hair, and naturalistic, rather than stylized, flowers. Most of these will be signed "Austria" or "Bohemia," rather than "Czechoslovakia."

Pieces marked "Czechoslovakia" will often be in the Art Deco or other, more modern style. Art Deco is characterized by more brash colors, and angularity rather than curves, and the women who are depicted have straighter hair and seem to be having more fun. Art Deco pieces made by Amphora and Royal Dux generally do not reach the price levels of their earlier, Art Nouveau wares.

Identifying these pieces is not difficult. The name "Amphora" can generally be found somewhere in the mark, which might also include the place-name "Turn." Identifying Royal Dux is a little more difficult because you have to know that the old wares are marked with a raised pink triangle with the letter *E* inside and the word "Bohemia." On post–World War I items, "Bohemia" is dropped in favor of "Made in Czechoslovakia." On modern wares, the *E* is also eliminated.

Wares marked "Erphila" are a sometimes-Czechoslovakian pottery that is also widely collected. By "sometimes" we mean that Erphila is an acronym for Eberling and Ruess, Philadelphia, a Pennsylvania importing company, and while many of the products they brought into this country were made in Czechoslovakia, others were made in Italy, Germany, and elsewhere.

Hand-painted Czechoslovakian products garner the most interest, and collectors are particularly interested in the more colorful and highly decorated wares. Prices here can start as low as $25 for small, relatively uninteresting items and go to the mid-hundreds or low thousands for better pieces with style, hand-painting, and vibrant hues.

Italian Pottery

Italian pottery of the mid-twentieth century is also being collected. Look for the country of origin mark, "Italy," coupled with either an artist's name or the name of a quality importer such as Raymor. Pieces that are only marked "Italy" are much less desired; artist-made pieces can command prices well into the mid- to high hundreds of dollars, and occasionally more.

Venetian Glass

Of even greater interest to collectors is the Italian glass made on the island of Murano, near Venice. It is not uncommon to find examples priced above the $1,000 mark, and occasionally above the $10,000 level. Pricing is very much a name game, and many of the best pieces will have the name of the maker written—actually, scratched or acid-stamped—on the bottom.

Unfortunately, many of the companies used paper labels, and these were either taken off after purchase or washed off during cleaning. This leaves these pieces in a distressingly anonymous state, and they often remain that way until they are spotted by a knowledgeable individual who sometimes buys them for next-to-nothing from an unsuspecting homeowner.

There is no way we can tell you what to look for every time you examine a piece that may be Venetian glass, but we can tell you that most of the free-formed ashtrays and bowls so often seen on coffee tables are worth less than $50 and seldom rise above the $250 level. Venetian glass objects can be recognized by their heavy form (often starfish- or amoeba-shaped), with pink, green, blue, gold, or red glass that is sometimes encased in a layer of clear, colorless crystal. In many instances, these pieces are embellished with streaks of gold flecks and maybe a series of carefully controlled bubbles.

The better pieces are usually very artistic, and they tend to be rather elegant in a '50s sort of way. Color is often a big component of their design. They might, for example, look something like a patchwork quilt, or even like a lava lamp with all the colors writhing and flowing together in layers and spots. Other items might resemble glass mosaics, and some highly regarded pieces have designs in them that look like pleated Austrian puff draperies.

There are also Venetian glass objects that look as if they were assembled from shards of different kinds of glass, and still others that look as if they were assembled from a network of lace. In addition, spectacular sculptural figures of musicians, courtiers, blackamoors, fish, birds, and animals were made, but these seldom rise above the $1,000 level unless they are truly exceptional.

Before we give you a short list of some of the names to look for, it is important for us to make clear that there are fakes out there. It is easy to scratch a name on the bottom of a piece of glass. You can do it, we can do it, and certainly a dishonest opportunist can do it. Just keep in mind that if a piece has been in your home for thirty to fifty years, it is probably all right, but if it has been bought on the secondary market within the last ten years, it needs to be examined by a professional.

And one last word of caution: Several of the companies that are going to be mentioned below are still in business, and they do—to some extent—still make glass in the styles of the 1940s and '50s. These new products are expensive on the primary retail market, but at present collectors are cool toward them, and the secondary market shuns them. So be careful.

Here are some of the names to look for:

Venini & Company

Paolo Venini was a lawyer who founded Vetri Soffiati Muranesi Venini in 1921, now widely considered to be the best twentieth-century Venetian glass maker. The better products of this company are highly prized. Pieces are often signed with the name "Venini" scratched or acid-stamped onto the bottom, plus "Italy" or "Italia," and "Murano." Venini also used a paper label, which is often missing, leaving the piece essentially unsigned. The Venini label is a circle with a vase in the center and "Venini S. A. Murano" around the edge.

Seguso

Archimede Seguso started his glass company, Seguso Vetri d'Arte, in 1946; and, while he used paper labels extensively, scratched signatures do occur. The paper labels are shaped like shields and read "Seguso Vetri D'Arte Murano Made in Italy."

A Venini Pezzato cylinder vase. This 11-inch-tall patchwork quilt of red, blue, and green glass should be valued about $14,000.

Barovier and Toso

This firm as such came into being in 1942, but it can trace its actual origins back to the 1300s. It is one of the most highly regarded of the Murano art glass makers. They commonly marked their pieces with an an easily removed red-and-white rectangular paper label that included the company's name, "Murano," and "Made in Italy."

Salviati & Company

This firm originated in the 1850s and played a role in the revival of Venetian glass in the mid-nineteenth century. They often scratched in their name or used a seal-like paper label with their name and "Venice" plus "Made in Italy."

Cenedese

Gino Cenedese opened his glass works in 1946, and he often marked his wares by scratching in his last name. A rectangular, black-and-white paper label was also used.

A couple of other names of importance include Alfredo Barbini, and Arte Vetraria Muranesé—or A.V.E.M.—who did not sign their work at all.

Scandinavian Glass

In addition to the Italians, the Scandinavians were heavily involved in making art glass in the postwar period, and most of their products were signed with scratched-in signatures. The wares of companies such as Kosta, Flygsfors, Holmegaard, and Nuutajarvi-Notsjo are very collectible and often quite valuable, but the work of the Swedish company Orrefors is the most prized.

Collectors are particularly interested in the Orrefors wares that have pictorial or geometric decorations encased inside colorless crystal. Items with this kind of embellishment carry the line names Ariel, Graal, Ravenna, and Kraka; and they have various types of intricate, modernistic designs, some of which are embellished with simple lines and stripes, while others feature images of people, birds, animals, and plants.

These images seem to float, encapsulated, in the clear glass, and it is much too difficult in this short space to describe all the technical differences and methods used to make them. All we really need to say is that any piece of Orrefors glass with this kind of decoration is potentially valuable, with prices that start at $500 for small, fairly simple pieces and rise above the $4,000 level for larger, more artistically made examples.

This type of art glass started being made around 1916, and we have seen fine examples that were manufactured quite recently. Age is not the issue here, artistry is. What also impacts the value of any Orrefors piece is who the designer was, and this information is often included as part of the mark.

Most Orrefors signatures include a letter that refers to either the type of glass it is or to the designer. Some of the letters for the more important designers are *D* for Ingeborg Lundin, *G* for Simon Gate, *H* for Edward Hald, *L* for Vicke Lindstrand, *P* for Sven Palmqvist, and *V* for Eva Englund. Most of the Orrefors glass found in American homes is plain, heavy, colorless crystal; and while this is of very high quality, its value on the secondary or collector's market does not begin to approach that of the items discussed above. Also found in great numbers are the clear, colorless glass vases decorated with engraved pictorial designs. Some of the more finely done of these items can sell into the low hundreds of dollars each, but they simply do not command the same respect and admiration enjoyed by items with more colorful embellishments.

Charles Lotton, Dominick Labino, and Pilgrim Glass

There are other modern makers of glass whose products promise to be very valuable in the future. These artists-craftsmen are consciously making art objects that command significant dollars on the retail market, and if they manage to acquire a reputation and a following, their products should continue to be expensive in years to come.

One of the most important names that comes to mind is that of Charles Lotton—and therein lies an interesting story. Lotton started his professional life as a hairdresser, but since he was fascinated with glass, he began to experiment by melting down Coca-Cola bottles and using the material to learn how to create hand-blown glass.

He must have learned his lessons well, because today his art glass products are considered by many to be the best since Louis Comfort Tiffany and Frederick Carder (of Steuben fame), and he now has a worldwide reputation for artistic excellence. In many instances, Lotton successfully sought to master the technical problems that daunted both Tiffany and Carder, and his achievements have been something of a triumph.

His greatest achievement is probably the Multi-Flora glass, which is similar to some of Tiffany's ultra-rare reactive glass items but more intricate and highly developed. These pieces usually consist of a colored glass base in which flowers "bloom" and seem to float like blossoms in a shimmering pond. Multi-Flora pieces are elegant and beautiful, and they are often sold at antiques shows or at prestigious auctions that feature art glass of the nineteenth and twentieth centuries.

His most sought-after Multi-Flora objects are usually lamps, and these can sell on both the primary and secondary market for many thousands of dollars each. In fact, something as simple as a 10-inch-diameter Lotton Multi-Flora bowl made as late as 1995 can sell for around $2,000 on the resale market.

Another name to look for on the bottom of a piece of glass is Dominick Labino, who made art glass in Ohio until about 1985. One of the interesting things about Mr. Labino is that he was a ceramics engineer by trade and helped develop the tiles that keep the space shuttle from burning up on reentry.

Labino was famous for his colors and his color combinations, and he made everything from paperweights to figures of ducks and owls. Currently, a 7-inch-tall pitcher that shades from red to brown might bring about $600, while one of the aforementioned figures might bring between $450 and $800.

These prices sound fairly modest, and they are for Labino's less ambitious works, but for pieces in his Emergence series and for examples that are major works, values can rise to the $5,000 mark and even beyond.

A third name to keep in mind is that of Kelsey Murphy, which is usually seen signed "Kelsey Pilgrim," Pilgrim being the name of the glass company for whom Ms. Murphy works. We feel that the product here that will become increasingly valuable is the cameo glass that is, in our opinion, some of the finest glass made since the French products of the late nineteenth and early twentieth centuries.

Murphy and her co-workers at the Pilgrim facility just outside Huntington, West Virginia, are creating multicolored cameo pieces decorated with images as diverse as Santa Claus, fruit, flowers, swimmers, runners, horses, the Statue of Liberty, and square dancers. This cameo glass is created in much the same way as cameo jewelry, with varying layers of colored material being cut away by carving, acid, or sandblasting to create a picture.

Pilgrim cameo can be found with only two layers of glass, but the best pieces have five or six layers of variously colored glass that have been laboriously sandblasted away to create lavish scenes. These can cost thousands of dollars when they are new. For the most part, these pieces have not yet reached the secondary market, and this makes it hard to judge their potential, but this is a quality product with all the earmarks of being a real winner in years to come.

We mention Lotton, Labino, and Murphy because we want to make it clear that quality products did not stop being made years ago. Not everything being made today is plastic debris belched out of factories in a tidal wave of cheap construction, bad taste, and planned obsolescence. No, wonderful things are still being made. They are collectible now, and they will be even more collectible in years to come.

Fenton Glass

One last glassmaking company needs to be mentioned, and that is the Fenton Art Glass Company of Williamstown, West Virginia. The company has been in business at this location since 1907, and their products are so pervasive that it is impossible to go into an American home and not find at least one object made by this firm.

Some of the early Fenton glass can be quite rare and hard to find—so rare, in fact, that many collectors do not even recognize it when it comes up for sale. Karnak Red is really very distinctive, with an almost tomato-red body decorated with dark, heart-shaped leaves and vines. Often—but not always—it has a black base and/or black handles.

Joe remembers seeing a piece of Fenton's Karnak Red at a very prestigious art glass auction company. The piece was so uncommon that the auction house's specialist had incorrectly labeled it "Loetz," which was a producer of Austrian art glass. Luckily, it was correctly identified before the sale, but because it was a fairly unknown entity, it sold for only about $450.

Another piece showed up for auction in North Carolina early in the year 2000, and this time the vase brought $2,300 (plus a 10 percent buyer's premium), which was double what was actually expected. When recognized and appreciated, this early Fenton glass can be quite expensive. Collectors also look for pieces similar to Karnak Red but with a base glass of blue, green, or ivory instead of red. There is also a great deal of interest in an early Fenton glass called "Mosaic," which has a black base and inlaid splotches of red, yellow, and/or gold glass.

Over the years, Fenton has made a variety of other types of glass. Most of these products have been fairly unpretentious, although the company has made a few stabs at creating more upscale art glass. Collectors seem to like products by Fenton because they are pretty, non-threatening, and with a few notable exceptions, easy to find. Fenton glass is characterized by decorations that tend to contain such things as hobnails, coin dots, opalescent stripes, swirls, dancing nudes, and fancy ruffled edges.

They are also famous for reproducing earlier types of glass such as Burmese, which is a heat-shaded glass that gradually changes color from pink to yellow. There is an almost infinite variety of Fenton glass, and they are the pieces that everyone's grandmother and mother had—the candy dish on the coffee table, the dresser jar, and the lemonade pitcher and glasses that only came out when company called.

Prices for modern Fenton glass are all over the board. They start at about $10 for a small, commonly found piece, and go up to about $400 for a cranberry-colored, ice-lipped water pitcher with a coin dot pattern. Pieces made after 1970 are signed with the word "Fenton" inside an oval.

Carnival Glass

Fenton's reputation was founded on the making of what is known as "Carnival glass," and they were responsible for some of the most interesting patterns made in this medium. To name just a few, there are pieces with dragons, birds and cherries, butterflies, coral, elks' heads, orange trees, and panthers stalking through undergrowth.

Carnival glass, with its iridescent luster finish over a colored glass base, was first made about 1905, and although its initial popularity faded in the late 1920s, it was revived in the 1970s and continues to be made to this day. Carnival glass was an inexpensive product then and, contrary to popular belief, much of it continues to be relatively inexpensive today.

In Fenton, for example, a Beaded Star pattern bowl in marigold can be bought for $50, while a Cut Arcs compote in blue is worth less than $60. Pattern is very important to value, but so is the shape of the object itself, and the color of the glass from which it was made. Consider a bonbon dish in Fenton's Cherry Circles pattern. In marigold, this little dish is only worth about $45, but if you happen to have the same piece in red glass, that value jumps well above the $2,000 mark!

Shape is important, too, and this is aptly demonstrated by Fenton's Lattice and Grape pattern in which a tumbler in marigold is worth a mere $40, while a spittoon in the same color and pattern brings closer to $2,500. Certain Carnival glass shapes tend to be relatively rare: spittoons are one, plates are another, hatpin holders are still another, and banana boats are a fourth.

Many other companies made Carnival glass beside Fenton. Perhaps the best known is the Northwood Company, which often signed their products with an *N* inside a circle. The Northwood name is magic to some people, but, like Fenton, the value of their Carnival glass pieces runs the gamut from very inexpensive to very dear—once again, it all depends on the color, pattern, and shape.

There are some who would say that the best Carnival glass was made by the Millersburg Glass Company of Millersburg, Ohio. Surprisingly, this company was founded when John Fenton split off from his brother Frank, who stayed with the original business in Williamstown. John went off to open his own glass factory, but it was very short-lived and was in operation only between 1909 and 1913.

The products of this company are highly sought after, and one way to distinguish them is by their distinctive Radium finish, which was first used in 1910. This process left a luster finish only on the front or top surface of the pieces, and it was more reflective than the normal finish seen on Carnival. This wavery, mirrored look was very popular, and it was eventually copied by the Imperial Glass Company, which also made Carnival.

American Art Pottery

We have already discussed Czechoslovakian and Italian pottery in brief, but the most important—and potentially the most valuable—of all the pottery items found in the typical American home is American art pottery. The art pottery maker Roseville in particular has practically become a household name, and this company did indeed make some wares that are now valued in the thousand of dollars each for important and rare specimens.

When collectors speak of "American art pottery," they are primarily talking about pieces made by specific companies between about 1880 and 1950. There were dozens of manufacturers engaged in making this sort of ware, and since there is no way that we can describe all of them and what they made, we will give you a short list of some of the most significant firms, and indicate the ways you can identify their wares.

Rookwood

This Cincinnati, Ohio, concern virtually invented the American Art Pottery movement, and their products are some of the most highly regarded. Most of their pieces are marked with a back-to-back R and P with flames around the top and sides. Any piece whose mark includes the initials or signature of an artist is worth checking out.

Roseville

Most of the later wares made by this company are signed with its name, but early items might have "Rozane," a foil sticker with the company name, or nothing at all on the bottom. Hand-painted and hand-carved pieces are the most valuable, but among later molded pieces, look for items decorated with pinecones and blackberries.

Weller

Although, like Roseville, this pottery company did not sign some of its earlier wares, most of its later products do carry the company name. Some of the most desired wares have an iridescent glaze in shades of blue, green, and purple; usually the name "Sicard" is written on the side. The molded pieces are not as desirable as Roseville's are, but the prices of their hand-painted wares are comparable in many cases.

Newcomb College

This pottery was made at Sophie Newcomb College, a women's college in New Orleans, Louisiana (now part of Tulane University), and it is hard to find a piece of it for less than $1,000. It is usually marked with an N inside a C—but beware: Some Japanese porcelain has much the same mark. Items with a high-gloss glaze are usually more valuable than the ones with a matte glaze.

Grueby

This firm primarily made tiles and vases. The tiles are not cheap, and the vases can go for many thousands of dollars. Signatures found are "Grueby Pottery Boston U.S.A.," "Grueby," and "Grueby Faience Co. Boston U.S.A."

Fulper

Signed both "Fulper" and "Prang" in a long rectangle, the pieces to look for from this company include lamps and pieces with crystalline glazes that look like snowflakes on the surface.

Marblehead

Pieces from this company with plain, single-color glazes are far less expensive than those with any sort of decoration. Decorated pieces can command prices above $1,000. Look for "Marblehead Pottery" in an oval, or a sailing ship with the letter M on one side and P on the other.

Saturday Evening Girls

Look for "S.E.G." plus a date on the base. Examples with an artist's initials on them are highly prized. These charming pieces were decorated by immigrants—the "Saturday Evening Girls"—and they usually feature images of such things as flowers, chickens, and ducks or geometrics. Prices start in the low hundreds for pieces with little or no decoration and rise into the low thousands for rarer depictions.

Teco Gates

Large pieces with unusual handles and flamboyant forms have brought prices well above the $10,000 level. Look for the name "Teco" with the "eco" running down the upright of the T.

Dedham Pottery and Chelsea Keramic Art Works

Any pottery piece marked "CKAW," "Chelsea Keramic Art Works," "CPUS" inside a four-leaf clover, or "Dedham Pottery" is potentially valuable. These are the products of the Robertson family, and they

are famous for their plates with rims decorated with rabbits, elephants, dolphins, and wolves seen in profile. Watch out for reproductions of Dedham ware.

This list just skims the top of American art pottery, but it does
include most of the important companies whose work we see in
homes on a regular basis. Pottery of every description is one of the
hottest collectibles categories going, and pre-1960 examples found in
your home should not be taken for granted.

CHAPTER SEVEN

The Bathroom

The bathroom is not a fertile field for finding hidden treasure in the typical American home, but there are a few things that should not be discarded. Helaine, for instance, is an avid collector of "rubber duckies" and figural hot-water bottles shaped like penguins, Little Red Riding Hood, or Donald Duck.

Helaine has paid as much as $225 for a single rare rubber bed warmer, although it is hard for many to imagine that these things can be worth that much money. Non-figural hot-water bottles with embossed scenes on them sell in the $25 to $75 range, and the common, plain-red-rubber variety are practically worthless.

Figural Bubble-Bath Containers

Hot-water bottles are not the only bathroom items to come in figural shapes—there are also the bubble-bath containers that were meant to be used by children. Designed to make bath time a little more fun for water-shy kids, they came in a wide variety of snazzy character shapes. Colgate-Palmolive, Purex, and Fuller Brush all produced these products in plastic forms, which range from Bullwinkle Moose all the way to Godzilla.

The problem is that these containers cracked easily, and their decoration was easily destroyed. They were not meant to last, and most did not. The most desired ones were made in the 1960s, and examples from the '80s and '90s are less highly regarded. Among the most expensive of these are the ones in perfect condition found in the form of Batman's Robin ($100), Frankenstein ($100), Paul McCartney or Ringo Starr ($125), and Huckleberry Hound (Knickerbocker, $75; Selcol, $145).

Condom Tins

All this goes to illustrate that for every object in the American home—no matter how bizarre—there is probably someone out there who is collecting it. At the risk of being indelicate, some of the most unusual bathroom items that are being sought are old condom or prophylactic tins.

We are not going to belabor this subject, since some of you may find it objectionable, but, like it or not, condom tins are desirable to some. In general, these lithographed tins were made in the 1910 to 1950 era, and while some were rather generic in design, others had colorful pictures of birds, leaping animals, knights on horseback, and desert nomads.

Paper and cardboard condom containers are also collectible, but the tin ones are the champs. Prices for those in good condition with no rust and only minor scratching start at about $20 and can exceed $1,000 for rarer examples. In excellent condition, a condom tin entitled "Sovereigns" with a crown and "For those who discriminate" is valued at about $900, and one marked "Sphinx" with the image of three pyramids and a bemused-looking sphinx is worth about $1,200!

These tin boxes are usually a little larger than the more familiar, square aspirin containers, and it needs to be stressed that almost any old tin box found in the bathroom that once contained medicine or beauty products and has interesting graphics or advertising on it is potentially worth at least a few dollars.

Aspirin Tins

Old tin aspirin containers are one of the things that we see collectors trying to find. Right now, prices start at just a couple of dollars each for forty-year-old Bayer containers, but they can rise to about $35 for something like "Cofer's Headache Tablets." All sorts of medicine boxes are collected, including boxes that once held laxatives, cold remedies, salves, and corn plasters, and prices can push above the $100 mark for the rarer and more interesting examples.

Most of the time, however, prices for medicinal items are modest, but on occasion when we have emptied old medicine cabinets and bathroom closets and offered the contents for sale, these items have been snapped up both by collectors and by individuals who are interested in using the vintage items for decoration.

Medicine Bottles

Medicine bottles often find eager buyers, and any cobalt blue example with a label or interesting embossing that was made before the beginning of World War II is salable. Some older medicine bottles can be very valuable, but others are very cheap. Small, clear-glass examples with simple embossing on them can bring less than $5, but rarer, more interesting specimens can carry price tags that approach the $2,000 mark.

A bottle such as the amber "J L Giofray & Co. Hair Restorer" is an example of one of the more expensive bottles, and another amber bottle, "Smith's Green Mountain Renovator," brings close to $1,500. Unfortunately, there is no intuitive way to tell if a given bottle is a $2,000 winner or a $10 loser. There are no reliable rules for judging a particular medicine bottle's worth; to find its value, each one has to be researched.

Razors

Bathrooms are the place to find men's shaving razors, and the straight-razor variety is becoming a really sharp item. Most of these have plain black handles and undecorated blades, and they currently command a price in the $10 to $25 range, depending on their condition and the company that made them.

For a straight razor to be more valuable than this, it needs to have a handle made from a higher-grade material, as well as a blade that has been etched with some fancy design. Carved handles contribute greatly to the value, as does the reputation of the maker. Some of the best and most-desired manufacturers include Case, Rattle Razor, Wade and Butcher, Queen City, KaBar, Boker, Winchester, Holley Manufacturing Company, and Robeson Cut Company.

Handles made from ivory, tortoiseshell, mother-of-pearl, sterling silver, and stag horn raise the value by three or four times. Bone and celluloid are slightly less desired, but many celluloid straight razors were made with figural grips shaped like women, eagles, boats, or deer, and these are very desirable. In addition, intricately etched scenes that run along the entire length of the blade enhance the value of a straight razor greatly. When you put handle material, a desirable maker, and artistic decoration together, a top-quality straight razor might be worth $250 to $300 or more.

Safety razors began replacing the treacherous straight razors about 1900, but at the present moment there is not quite as much interest in these as in their earlier cousins. Fancy safety razors with ivory handles and their original cases can bring more than $150, while others with fancy openwork or engraving on the surface that covers the razor blade are gaining favor. Some of these can be valued in the $100 range if they are complete with their cases.

Safety razors often came in lithographed tin boxes, and these can be very valuable even without the razor inside. Prices start about $50, but a large, square box for "The Fox Safety Razor and Stop" by F. Lothar Schultz is worth $2,000 in tip-top shape. A round box for a "Star Safety Razor" starts around $300 and goes up to $450 for a blue one with the picture of a man shaving. Rectangular boxes issued by Star are somewhat less valuable, and bring prices somewhere in the the $75 to $100 range.

CHAPTER EIGHT
The Children's Bedroom

A child's bedroom is a hotbed of popular-culture items, and the potential for finding really valuable items is very high. The problem, however, is that everything found here—toys, books, games, etc.—has been extensively played with and used. The records are scratched; the posters are Scotch-taped and thumbtacked; the action figures have been mutilated; the games have pieces missing; and the books have crayon marks scribbled throughout.

Sometimes it seems like collectors have very unrealistic expectations for things that have been through a childhood. They want the toys to be unplayed-with and in their original boxes, and the comics unread.

Helaine, who is always the consummate collector, had a "brilliant" idea when her children were little. She says—and Joe is surprised that she admits it—that every time someone gave one of her boys a toy, she went out and bought a duplicate, which she stored in the attic for posterity.

Helaine felt that all these "MIB"s—or "mint-in-box"—would be very valuable someday. Unfortunately, she reports that although her attic looks like the after-Christmas sale at Toys "R" Us, 90 percent of the items do not command much interest on the current collectors' market.

Part of the problem is that it really is too soon; the toys are only twenty-five to thirty years old, and while the value of some things of that vintage has shot up into the stratosphere, most have not. That will take many more years, and the people reaping any sort of benefit at all will probably be Helaine's yet-to-be-even-thought-of great-grandchildren.

This is a good lesson. After reading this chapter, many of you are going to be convinced that any toy found in a child's room is a potential treasure, and this is simply not true. If every toy were going to be valuable in a short time span, all a collector would have to do would be to go out, buy an attic full of toys, wait twenty years, sell them, and retire. Helaine can testify that, as much as she would have liked this dream to come true, this approach does not work.

Dolls

It is amazing how valuable late-nineteenth- and early-twentieth-century dolls can be, as was aptly demonstrated at a *Treasures in Your Attic* appraisal clinic.

A doll came in wrapped in an old towel and its owner explained that it was part of a collection that had been left to her by a deceased friend. The figure inside the towel was fairly small, only about 14 inches tall, and the woman thought it might be a Jumeau, which is a very desirable maker of French dolls.

However, when Joe raised the doll's hair looking for a mark, he discovered the so-called circle dot mark used by Bru Jne, & Cie, another famous French doll maker. Glancing up from his reference, Joe informed the woman that this was a very rare doll, and that in its particular size and condition, it should be insured for about $15,000. To say that she was flabbergasted would be something of an understatement.

As a follow-up to this story, this lucky lady called Joe about six months later and asked him to take a look at the rest of the dolls that she had been given. Joe discovered about fifteen other dolls, not one of which was worth less than $1,000, and two together were actually worth about $75,000!

Barbie

Dolls of almost every description and age can be quite expensive. We all know about Mattel's Barbie, and so much has been written about her that there is probably not even a hermit mumbling arcane incantations in a cave in the wilds of Outer Mongolia who is not painfully aware that Barbies and Barbie outfits and accessories are potentially valuable.

The hottest of these items is the elusive #1 Barbie, which first appeared in 1959. She was made from vinyl, had a light complexion, white irises, a ponytail, arched eyebrows (as opposed to the later rounded ones), a black-and-white bathing suit, and, most importantly, holes in the balls of her feet so that she could fit on a stand. She came with either blond or brunette hair. The brunette is harder to find and commands more money.

We hesitate to quote prices for First Barbies because, like the stock market, they tend to change each morning; but unlike the stock market, their value has only gone up. This upward rise cannot go on forever, and there is a hint that at the current moment Barbie prices may be softening just a bit. In any event, for right now, a First Barbie brings big bucks if she is in mint condition and in her original box. A minimum value seems to be about $10,000, and we have heard $14,000 bandied about.

Not long ago, Joe received a telephone call from a woman who had a First Barbie and wanted to sell it. She said that it was very valuable and she knew that one MIB (mint-in-the-box) brought about $8,000 at that time. She then expressed a willingness to be realistic and said she only wanted $7,000 for hers. "Oh, by the way," she continued, "I don't have the box; the color is worn off Barbie's lips, and I cut her hair when I was a little girl."

The lady was outraged, indignant, and offended when Joe diplomatically suggested that her doll was worth a "tad" less than what she wanted, and she hung up with a bang and a huff. Despite this kind of reaction, the market says that once the box is gone, the potential value of a First Barbie drops in half, and after the doll has been even gently and lovingly played with, the value drops another 25 percent.

Other Barbies that bring more than $3,000 if they are still MIB include Second Barbie (just like the first, only without holes in the feet); Bendable Leg Barbie (circa 1965) with a side part in her hair; Evening Splendor Barbie (#861, circa 1960); and Busy Gal Barbie (#881, circa 1960). Interestingly, Second Barbie is now bringing close to $9,000 if she is MIB and has blond hair, but MIB-and-brunette brings just a bit less than $8,500 (just opposite of First Barbie).

If they are still in the package, there are certain Barbie outfits that are valued at $1,000 or more. These include Roman Holiday (#968), Easter Parade (#971), Pan Am Stewardess (#1678), Here Comes the Bride (#1665), and Commuter Set (#916). Remove any Barbie outfit from the package and the value drops 50 percent; lose a part or do any kind of damage, and the value drops even more precipitously.

Most Barbie vehicles run in the $100 to $300 range, but two bring somewhat more. One is the Barbie Sport Plane, which is valued in excess of $3,000; the other is a red-and-white Austin Healy that brings about $4,000 if it is still MIB. But, beware—a similar orange Austin Healy retails for just 10 percent of the red-and-white version.

Barbie's buddies—Ken, Midge, Skipper, Francie, and the rest—do not sell nearly as well as the "grande dame" herself. Just about the only ones that break the $750 barrier (if they are MIB) are black Francie (1966), Twist 'N Turn Francie (1966), black Twist 'N Turn Francie (1967), and no-bangs Francie (1970). This latter doll is just what the name suggests—a Francie with a swept-back hairdo and no bangs. Once again, little details can make a big difference.

Madame Alexander Dolls

Madame Alexander dolls also have a following among a large number of collectors, and there is a great variety in this category. The Alexander Doll Company went into business in New York City in 1923, and their cloth dolls of the 1930s are somewhat difficult to find. Usually unmarked except for a clothes tag, the most expensive of these is probably the 24-inch-tall Dionne Quintuplet, which, in excellent condition, sells for $1,500. Other Madame Alexander cloth dolls such as Alice, Susie Q, Bunny Belle, and Oliver Twist sell in the $200 to $1,000 range.

Besides these cloth creations, Madame Alexander also made composition dolls in the 1930s, and, again, a Dionne Quintuplet is among the most desired. A set of five in the 7- to 8-inch size, complete with their original wicker carrying case and extra clothes, sells for about $2,400, and the 14-inch-tall Doctor Dafoe, who delivered the quints, is $1,800.

The 1937 composition Scarlett O'Hara is very desirable as well, and the 11-inch version in tip-top condition sells for $750, while the 21-inch size brings about $1,000 more. Hard-plastic Madame Alexanders started being made in 1948, and some of these can bring very high prices.

Reportedly, the 21-inch-tall dolls known as Ballerina Debra and Bride Debra, which were made between 1949 and 1951, are pushing the $5,000 mark. Other hard-plastic dolls such as Aunt Pitty-Pat (1957), Cousin Grace (1957), Little Minister (1957), Me and My Shadow (1954), Queen Elizabeth (1953), and Princess Margaret (1953) all bring more than $1,000 if they are either still boxed or in immaculate condition. Many of the more modern all-vinyl Madame Alexander dolls bring somewhat less money.

Madame Alexander's Ballerina Debra.

Paper Dolls

Plastic dolls, porcelain dolls, wooden dolls, metal dolls, wax dolls, and cloth dolls are all worth keeping. Some of these are more fragile than others, but the most easily destroyed dolls are paper dolls, which should be preserved with great care. Like everything else, collectors want their paper dolls to be in pristine condition.

This means that for the dolls that came in books, or the dolls that came on single sheets of paper, collectors want them uncut. Prices plummet for examples that have been cut and, heaven forbid, played with.

To illustrate the role that cut versus uncut plays in paper dolls, if you have a set of *Brady Bunch* paper dolls featuring Greg and Marcia in cut but otherwise excellent condition, the value is about $40. If the set is uncut, that price would more than double to approximately $100.

The value of uncut books of paper dolls seldom rises above the $500 level, and the most valuable items tend to feature celebrities and movie stars of the 1930s and '40s. Comic strip characters also are sought after, as are the 1939 and 1940 examples based on the movie *Gone with the Wind.*

Raggedy Ann and Andy

Another doll that often turns up in a child's bedroom is Raggedy Ann or Andy. These cute little moppets, the creation of illustrator Johnny B. Gruelle, have been around since 1915, and the Volland Company started making Raggedy Ann rag dolls shortly thereafter. Today, one of these yarn-haired, button-eyed dolls in good condition and in its original clothes is worth upward of $1,800.

Raggedy Andy did not join his Ann until 1920, but a Volland representation of him is worth about the same as his aproned sweetie. Even more expensive than Raggedy Ann or Andy is Beloved Belinda, the kerchiefed African-American character in the Raggedy Ann series. A Volland 15-inch Beloved Belinda should be valued at approximately $2,500.

After Volland stopped making Raggedy Anns in 1934, Mollye Goodman started making them. The Volland examples are marked "Patented Sept. 7, 1915" and the Goodman pieces are signed on the chest with "Raggedy Ann and Raggedy Andy Dolls Manufactured by Mollye's Doll Outfitters." In perfect condition, these dolls should be valued between $1,000 and $1,200 depending on size.

Georgene Novelties started making Raggedy Anns and Andys about 1938, and while these are generally less valuable than the Vollands or the Mollye's, they still bring prices in the $150 to $400 range—unless you find one with an isosceles triangle nose outlined in black.

The one with that nose in the 19-inch size is worth about $800 and in the 32-inch size $1,500. The normal Georgene Raggedy Ann and Andy dolls had noses that were more in the shape of equilateral triangles, and they were more neatly outlined. However, the real Georgene treasure is once again Beloved Belinda, and this rarity is currently selling for $1,750 in excellent condition.

The Knickerbocker Toy Company made Raggedys from 1963 to 1982, and even these late editions have a value that is not altogether inconsiderable. They range in price from about $50 for the smallest to about $225 for the largest (36 inches), and their version of Beloved Belinda goes for as much as $900.

Bisque-Headed Dolls

Some of the most prized dolls are the bisque-headed examples that were primarily made in France and Germany during the late nineteenth and early twentieth centuries. Some of these have values that reach into the tens of thousands of dollars, but others can be surprisingly inexpensive.

If we find a bisque doll in a home, there is a good possibility that it will be a product of Armand Marseille of Koppelsdorf, Germany, a firm which went into business in 1885. This company supplied such mass merchants as Sears and Montgomery Ward with a fairly large quantity and variety of dolls, which means that the majority of these dolls are not all that hard to find today.

Most of these dolls are marked "Armand Marseille," or "A. M." They also tend to be marked with a number and perhaps a name, such as "Rosebud," "Alma," "Baby Phyllis," or "Queen Louise." One of the most commonly found Armand Marseille dolls is the #390

Floradora doll, which must have been made in vast quantities. In pristine condition, this doll in the 10-inch size retails for just a bit more than $250. The Floradora doll comes in a large variety of sizes and the value goes up with the size, but it does not surpass $1,000 until the doll's size exceeds 32 inches—and that is an unusually big doll.

Most Armand Marseille dolls are fairly inexpensive, but there are some notable exceptions. Some of the maker's "character dolls" are quite hard to find and valuable. A "character doll" is defined as one that has a head with a lifelike expression such as pouting, laughing, crying, or serenity. Marseille made a model #230 and #231 Fanny doll (one had molded hair, while the other had a wig) that are now valued in the $5,000 to $6,000 range if the condition is optimum.

Other commonly seen manufacturers of bisque-headed dolls include:

Kämmer and Reinhardt

This company was founded in Waltershausen, Germany, in 1896 and their products can often be identified by their mark, which was their initials on either side of a six-pointed star. Like Armand Marseille dolls, most Kämmer and Reinhardt products can be quite reasonably priced, and also like Armand Marseille, the happy exception is some of their character children. A 22-inch-tall character child with mold number 102 should be valued around $175,000; a number 103 or 104 in the same size $80,000; and a number 108 has sold for a little more than $275,000.

Simon & Halbig

This company began in 1869, and they often made heads for other doll makers. Their full name can be found written out, or their initials may be coupled with numbers. Simon & Halbig dolls are eagerly collected, and prices for their large character dolls (such as the #153, #1388, and #1448) can bring more than $25,000. Simon & Halbig's Lady dolls are also in demand. These dolls have adult faces and bodies. In this category, the 20-inch #1303 is valued at $18,000; the 25-inch #152 at $25,000; and the Mary Pickford model at $35,000.

Kestner

This famous company was founded in Waltershausen, Germany, in the early part of the nineteenth century. This maker is said to have been one of the first firms to produce dressed dolls, and once again its character child dolls are some of the most valuable. Kestner's #206 and #208 fetch over $10,000 in optimum condition, and a pair called "Max and Moritz" have reportedly sold for more than $35,000.

These are a few of the most common makers of bisque-headed dolls found in modern homes, but others include Jumeau, Gebruder Heubach, and S.F.B.J. (for Société Française de Fabrication de Bébes et Jouets). This is a huge field, but there is perhaps one more specific doll that we should mention because it holds such a warm place in the hearts of many doll collectors and enthusiasts.

Bye-Lo Baby

The famous "Bye-Lo" baby was created by Grace Story Putnam in 1923. This doll, which is supposed to represent a newborn baby, was made in a wide variety of configurations—there are examples with bisque heads, wax heads, composition heads, celluloid heads, and wooden heads; there are also all-bisque Bye-Los, cloth-bodied Bye-Los, and composition-bodied Bye-Los.

Legend says that Putnam went to the hospital to sketch newborn babies, trying to find just the right look. She failed to find what she was looking for until she saw a baby that had just died, and it was that baby that became the model for the Bye-Lo. There is also a rare variation of the Bye-Lo called the "Fly-Lo"; this is merely the Bye-Lo baby with green, gold, or pink satin wings sewn to the body.

Fly-Lo babies are worth as much as $5,000, but the wingless By-Los with bisque porcelain heads generally sell in the $500 to $1,800 range, with the larger examples bringing the most money. A wax-headed version should be valued at $2,200 and a wooden-headed model by Schoenhut is worth a little less than $2,000.

Action Figures and Toy Soldiers

Both boys and girls play with dolls, but boys tend to call them "action figures" or "toy soldiers." Dolls of every variety are hot, and the ones that your children played with should not be discarded unless they look like they were the test dummies used for the development of TNT. Speaking of high explosives, the whiff of gunpowder brings to mind many a child's favorite doll—oh, excuse us, "action figure"—G.I. Joe.

The Hasbro Company originated G.I. Joe in 1964, and the first-year pieces are distinguished by hard plastic heads that have a scar on the right cheek. By 1966, this facial scar had disappeared. In great condition, these early figures—the Action Soldier, Sailor, Marine, and Pilot—bring about $300 each, with the exception of the Black Action Soldier (#7500), which commands a price of nearly $1,000.

Some of the foreign fighters from the 1966 editions also bring good money, and the top four are probably the British or Canadian Commando, the Japanese Imperial Soldier, the German Soldier, and the Russian Soldier. The British or Canadian Commando is the top lot of this grouping, fetching prices of approximately $900, while the other three have values that generally fall in the $600 range.

Interestingly, one of the most expensive of all the G.I. Joe collectibles is the figure of a woman—namely the G.I. Nurse, which appeared in 1967. This dispenser of mercy has ash blond hair, and in her "starched" white uniform can bring $1,200 if she is MIB.

G.I. Joe disappeared from the marketplace in 1976, but he was reissued in 1991, and the figures from this commemorative series currently do not rise much above the $100 level for the most desirable examples, which seem to be the four G.I. Joe Commemorative Gift Sets.

G.I. Joe was not the only action figure that captivated the attention of little children. There were also Ideal's Captain Action, Marx's Johnny West Adventure Series, Kenner's The Six Million Dollar Man, Mattel's Big Jim, and Gilbert Toys' The Man from U.N.C.L.E., to name just a few. All of these are interesting and collectible, but few if any of them reach the price level of G.I. Joe at the present moment.

Spiritually related to G.I. Joe are the small lead, iron, or rubber military figures bought by the millions from the now vanished 5 and 10 cent stores such as Woolworth's. Many of these were made by Barclay, Manoil, Grey Iron, Auburn, Dinky, and others.

Smaller, more detailed examples were made by Britains of England, and these were seldom if ever sold in the dime store. They are high-quality, and a rare set of ten Royal Navy Bluejackets still in the original, like-new box should sell for about $2,000. Other, more easily found sets in similar condition are somewhat less expensive, and prices can start as low as $25.

Figures of medieval knights on horseback or in other stances by Courtenay are also highly prized. They can be very elaborate, with helmeted knights carrying elaborately painted shields and weapons. Values on these start at $150 and go up to ten times that amount or more. A simple, 2-inch-tall standing figure of Sir Miles Stapleton should be valued about $175, while a larger mounted image of Sir John Havering on a charger decked out with an elaborate saddle blanket is worth $1,400 if there is no more than a little paint loss.

Prices for dime-store variety military figures can be all over the board. Single Barclay figures with most of their paint intact start at $7 and go up to about $170 for an uncommon item such as a soldier in a bayoneting position but without a bayonet on the end of his rifle. Barclay's representations of vehicles such as airplanes, aircraft carriers, and car carriers can motor into the $100 range.

Stuffed Animals

The leading name in stuffed animals is Steiff. Margaret Steiff, a victim of polio who lost the use of her left arm and hand, somehow became a dressmaker, and in 1879, started making little elephants stuffed with lamb's wool to give away as gifts.

By 1883, she was displaying her elephants in Stuttgart, where she got so many orders that she expanded her line with other animals and opened a factory. The company made stuffed bears as early as 1892, and Richard Steiff, Margaret's nephew, designed a jointed bear that was first shown in 1903.

This bear met with little success until Hermann Berg, a buyer for New York's George Borgfeldt Company, saw it and ordered three thousand. It was shown at the St. Louis World's Fair in 1904, where it became associated with Theodore Roosevelt's well-publicized sparing of a bear cub's life while on a hunting trip in Mississippi in 1902. The Steiff jointed bear became "Teddy's bear," or teddy bear, and turned out to be one of the most beloved toys of all time.

It should be mentioned that the Ideal Novelty and Toy Company also claims to be the originator of the teddy bear. It is said that Ideal created the "Teddy" bear for the 1904 presidential election as a campaign gimmick for Teddy Roosevelt.

Usually, teddy bears made by any of the early manufacturers can be identified by their long, curved arms; long snouts with stitched or *gutta percha* noses; wooden shoe button or clear glass eyes with painted backs; large feet with felt pads and stitched-on claws; and distinctive humps on their backs. In addition, early bears were stuffed with excelsior, which is nothing more than wood shavings in long, thin strips.

Few teddy bears survive childhood because they are literally loved to death. Fur flies, buttons pop, and poor Teddy goes to toy heaven. Those that do survive in good order can be very valuable, and some of the first Steiff examples in rare colors, unusual styles, and superb condition can sell well above the $100,000 mark. Many pre–World War II examples top the $1,000 level, and even bears from the 1950s can be worth somewhere in the $150 to $600 range, depending upon their makers and how well they have stood the tests of childhood.

Board Games

What child's room would be complete without board games? Most kids had Monopoly, Candy Land, Clue, The Game of Life, and so forth, but most of these only have a very modest value. A 1950s Clue, for example, is worth only about $35, while a 1962 Candy Land sells for about $20, and a 1970s Game of Life brings about $15.

Circa 1895 board game by McLoughlin Brothers called "Game of Mail, Express Accommodation." Its cover art has a wonderful Currier & Ives feel.

All the prices mentioned above are for board games that are complete with all their pieces and instructions, and in a box that has not been abused. In general, values depend on rarity, condition, the quality of the graphics on the box lid, and, for more modern games, nostalgia.

A game such as McLoughlin Brothers' 1895 Game of Mail, Express Accommodation is sought after not only because few survived intact, but because the picture on the lid—which shows a locomotive being shoveled out of the snow by a group of men—has a great deal of graphic punch. It is reminiscent of a Currier & Ives print and, in excellent condition, its value exceeds $1,200.

A more recent board game with a lot of appeal is Ideal's 1965 Addams Family, which retails for $275. Other television- and movie-related games are also very desirable, and some of the most expensive include Star Trek (1967), Three Stooges (1959), Outer Limits (1964), Wanted: Dead or Alive (1960), Godzilla (1963), King Kong (1963), and Twilight Zone (1964). The appeal is mainly nostalgic, and almost any mass media–related board game that pushes those "Remember when?" buttons has potential.

We cannot leave a discussion about this topic without mentioning the quintessential board game, Monopoly. It was invented about 1933, and some of the early, handmade versions are very valuable. Parker Brothers began making it in 1935, but a game in great condition from that date is worth only about $35. A thirty-year-old example is worth about $20, unless it is the deluxe edition, which is worth almost triple that figure.

Battery-Powered Toys

There is nothing more charming or delightful than a battery-powered toy that can walk, talk, smoke, play a musical instrument, swing at a baseball, tend bar, barber hair, or do one or more of a zillion and one other things. Most of these toys were made in Japan from the 1940s through the 1960s, and they are popular with collectors because many of these toys were engineering marvels. As a general rule, the more actions a battery-powered toy performs, the more interesting it is to enthusiasts.

It is important that these playthings be in working condition (so always remove the batteries after use), and an original box adds about 50 percent to the value if the box is in reasonably good shape. To illustrate how expensive these can be when they are in fine condition and still in their box, a Smoking Popeye is worth $1,400, a boy with a camera called "Shutter-Bug" brings $675, a vehicle called "Million Bus" is worth $2,000, and a Mr. Magoo Car sells for a more modest $350.

Representations of characters and pop-culture figures can add greatly to the value of any given battery-powered toy. Good examples of this are a Ford automobile featuring vinyl figures of the Beatles inside, which is worth more than $4,000 if it is in mint condition, and a Superman turning over an army tank, which is valued at a little more than $1,500.

Transportation Toys

What child's room is complete without trains, planes, and automobiles—not to mention trucks, buses, and helicopters? Matchbox, Hot Wheels, Corgi, Buddy L, Tekno, Structo, Lionel, Marx, American Flyer, Tonka, and Tootsietoy are just a few of the companies that made transportation-related vehicles that can really grab a collector's interest.

Buddy L was founded in 1921, and some of their cars can command prices above $4,000, and even their more common pieces generally bring more than $250. Their products can be divided into categories such as firefighting equipment, construction equipment, cars and buses, and trains and trucks.

Firefighting equipment has great interest for some collectors and a Buddy L #205D Hydraulic Water Tower Truck should be valued around $3,000 in excellent condition, and a Hook and Ladder Fire Truck #205 in the same condition is worth more than $3,500. Of course, some other Buddy L firefighting equipment toys are less expensive, and examples with missing parts, chips, scratches, and rust have prices that range in the low hundreds rather than the low thousands.

Corgi cars are another hot item. They originated in 1956, and prices range from about $2 for a Corgi Junior car in good condition to about $3,000 for a rare item such as the #1110 Shell Tanker. Corgi cars that are related to a character (such as Batman, James Bond, or Captain Marvel) are some of the most desired, but values depend very much on the particular model.

Captain Marvel's Porsche #262 is only about $75, James Bond's Moon Buggy #811 is $600, and James Bond's *Diamonds Are Forever* Ford Thunderbird #391 is approximately $300. The Monkeymobile

#277 is $350, and the #267 Batmobile ranges from $175 to $600 depending on the type of wheels it has (the ones with red "whizz-wheels" are the most valuable).

The variety of Corgi vehicles is absolutely mind-boggling, and if you are interested in vintage movies, television, or cartoons, you can find Kojak's Buick (#290, $85), Chitty Chitty Bang Bang (#266, $400 for the original, $125 for the remake), The Saint's Volvo (#201, $175), or Popeye's Paddle Wagon (#802, $650). You can even find a Charlie's Angels Van (#434) for $75.

Japanese-made tin automobiles of the 1950s and '60s can be very valuable, with prices that can run over $4,000, although most are somewhat less. They were either friction- or battery-powered, and were accurate representations of actual automobiles. In size, they range from 6½ to 28 inches long. Some of the top items are: the 1956 Ford Sedan by Marusan, the 1962 Chrysler Imperial by Asahi Toy Company, the 1954 Cadillac Convertible by Alps, the 1956 Lincoln Continental Mark II by Line Mar, and the 1955 Chevrolet by Marusan. Although prices generally do not go as high as the automobiles, Japanese tin airplanes of this same era are desired as well.

The Tonka Corporation (now part of Hasbro) has been making metal trucks, construction equipment, and tractors in Mound, Minnesota, since 1947. The value of Tonka toys tends to run in the $50 to $700 range for examples in great condition, but, unfortunately, Tonka toys tend to be found in poor condition. They were "built to be tough," and children often responded by hauling rocks in the dump trucks and digging sand with the construction shovels.

They were left out in the rain, and this means that rust and paint loss are big problems. Just remember, a red Tonka gasoline truck in near mint condition may sell for $600, but the same gasoline truck with rust, dents, and little or no paint (or, heaven forbid, repainted) is worth only a small fraction of that figure—probably less than $100.

Since 1968, many children have enjoyed playing with Hot Wheels miniature cars. It has been estimated that since the late '60s more than two billion of these have been sold, and because of these huge numbers, most Hot Wheels models can be bought for less than $25, with many selling in the $5 to $10 range. The rarest examples of Hot Wheels cars can sell above the $750 level.

Some of the most desired models are those that are called "red lines." These are cars made before 1971 that have red-wall, rather than black-wall, tires. It must be understood that for Hot Wheels, "mint" condition means that the item must be in its original package (which could mean it is mounted on a card). An example in perfect condition without its original package is worth at least 50 percent less than the same item still in the box—and any defect at all to a boxless item drops the value another 25 percent.

As an example, a blue Mongoose Rear Engine Dragster with red-line tires is worth about $500 on its original card if the card itself is in near perfect condition. The same car without the card and in unplayed-with condition is worth only about $200 to $250, and if there is any sign of wear, the price drops to $125 to $150.

Collectors can be very passionate about model trains, and this may be because many adults have fond childhood memories of their "choo-choo train" whizzing around a track. It was also a toy that a parent and child could enjoy together—although sometimes Mom and Dad did try to take over.

Perhaps the most famous maker of electric trains was the Lionel Company, which was founded by Joshua Lionel Cowen. The company can trace its origins back to 1901 when Cowen produced the Electric Express, a battery-powered train car with people inside it that was designed to be a display in a store window. Windup trains were popular toys, but a battery-powered one was a novelty, and the shop's customers were enthralled and clamored to buy an Electric Express.

In 1902, an electric trolley car was added, and if you happen to find one of these in the back of a closet or in the bottom of an old toy chest, it may be worth fairly big bucks. In excellent condition (no rust, no dents, and only a few scratches), an example with a cream-colored body and a blue roof is worth approximately $3,000, while the same trolley with an orange roof is worth closer to $4,500.

Lionel almost went under during the Great Depression, and the company's salvation is often attributed to a very special pair of mice—namely Mickey and Minnie Mouse. The #1100 Mickey Mouse windup handcar sold like hotcakes, and if you have one today in tip-top condition with an orange body, it is worth a little over $1,000. (With a green base, the value drops to $700; and with a red base, $575.)

The next year, a Peter Rabbit and a Santa Claus handcar were introduced; the Santa Claus model is much more valuable than either the Mickey Mouse, the Peter Rabbit, or the still-to-come Donald Duck. In superb condition the Santa Claus handcar with a green base is worth almost $2,000, and with a red one about $1,700.

The golden age for Lionel trains was the late 1940s into the mid-1950s. Sets and individual pieces made during this time frame can be very desirable, and a beautiful, circa 1950 #2343 Diesel Locomotive (Santa Fe Railroad) is worth about $600 and a circa 1952 #2345 Diesel Locomotive (Western Pacific Railroad) is worth about $1,800 if in prime condition. Other cars and locomotives from this time period generally run in the $50 to $5,000 range.

One of Lionel's chief competitors was American Flyer, which in 1938 was acquired by A. C. Gilbert, of Erector Set fame. As a general rule, American Flyer trains are a little less expensive than Lionel, but a #449 locomotive might sell for $1,700, or a #436 for $1,200. Other American Flyer components sell for as little as $30 even in excellent condition, but prices top out around $12,000 for a mint-in-box set made for the J.C. Penney Company. This set has a #3113 locomotive with "Nationwide Lines" on it.

Erector Sets and Building Blocks

Since we have mentioned A. C. Gilbert, perhaps we should make a brief mention of Erector Set. This toy first appeared around 1913 and, despite popular opinion to the contrary, most vintage Erector Sets are not very valuable.

Even complete and in the original box, a set seldom rises above the $200 level, and most are $100 or less. One big exception to this is the giant Deluxe Set #10. With this big box of pieces and parts, an enterprising child could make a dirigible, a locomotive, or a truck. A complete #10 set in great condition should bring close to $2,500. The #8 complete and in its wooden box is also rather desirable and brings close to $1,000.

Somewhat related to Erector Sets are the various and sundry types of building blocks. We see lots of Lincoln Log sets, but these are usually in bad condition, and average examples from the 1950s in near-mint shape normally bring prices of less than $100. Among building block sets, the Richter Anchor Stone sets can be extremely valuable.

These originated in the 1880s, and while they are far from common in the modern home, they do turn up from time to time. Prices for these start as low as $50, but the bigger, rarer specimens such as Great Castle can command prices that push the $10,000 mark if they are complete, in the box, and in great condition.

Character Toys

It does not matter if it is a cartoon character, a Disney character, a character from a movie such as *Planet of the Apes*, a character from a television series such as *The Munsters*, or a real-life "character" from pop culture such as Elvis Presley—all items that relate to the character are collectible and potentially valuable. Save anything having to do with Snoopy, the Beatles, *Howdy Doody*, Miss Piggy, Mickey Mouse, *Indiana Jones*, *The Six Million Dollar Man*, *E.T.*, Betty Boop, *The Flintstones*, *Masters of the Universe* . . . and the list goes on and on.

Recent reports are that prices of Snoopy and other "Peanuts"-related items have escalated dramatically since the death of Charles Schultz in 2000. Frankly, Joe cringes every time we do an appraisal clinic and someone comes in wagging a Snoopy-related item, hoping that it has become fabulously valuable practically overnight. Joe usually states that he does not know the value of the item in question because the market is much too volatile at the moment, and he goes on to explain that once the hoopla, hype, and frenzy has settled down, prices should stabilize. Then and only then can realistic values be assigned.

Some of the most valuable character collectibles are those that feature Walt Disney's creations. The most valuable tend to be from movies made in the 1930s and '40s, but newer characters, such as *The Nightmare before Christmas* dolls, also attract attention. The Sally doll from this 1993 animated motion picture is currently valued at almost $400, and Jack brings a little less, about $250. Even a *Nightmare before Christmas* keychain is worth $5.

Who Framed Roger Rabbit items are also doing fairly well with collectors, and a 24-inch stuffed doll is valued at $100, and a 6-inch-tall bendable figure of Jessica is worth about $35. For those who were captivated by the original *Toy Story*, the 3-inch-tall figures of Woody and Buzz Lightyear are worth about $8 each and heading for $10.

Of course, the quintessential Disney character is Mickey Mouse. A 1930s stuffed-cloth Mickey doll by Charlotte Clark is worth about $2,400. Mickey dolls by the famous German company Steiff (of teddy-bear fame) start at about $750 and go up to around $2,800 for the rare open-mouth version. Mickey Mouse dolls from the 1950s, '60s, '70s, and later seldom rise above the $100 level.

There are so many different Mickey Mouse items that it is hard to even grasp how diverse this field is and how varied the prices. A Mickey Mouse gas mask (1936), for example, is worth more than $3,000; a gum ball machine (1968) is worth only about $65. There are also Mickey dominoes (1935, $200), a Mickey Mouse toy chest (1935, $500), moccasins (1930s, $1,200), soap (1939, $150), swim masks (1970s, $50), and a Mickey Mouse Hoop-La game (1930s, $350).

The list of collectible Disney character items could go on forever, and it would include such animated icons as Donald Duck, Cinderella, Snow White, Bambi, Dumbo, Goofy, Pluto, Pinocchio, and Sleeping Beauty. Memorabilia associated with lesser-known characters is also collectible; a Ferdinand the Bull doll by Knickerbocker is worth about $600, and a Panchito doll (one of the *Three Caballeros*), $300.

Futuristic Toys

This category includes space toys of every description, plus robots. Space toys span the years from *Buck Rogers* to *Star Wars,* and currently a Buck Rogers Sonic Ray Gun in mint condition and in its original box is worth about $500, and a Tootsietoy Buck Rogers Flash Blast Space Ship in its box brings about $400.

The range of *Star Wars* collectibles is huge, and encompasses characters, vehicles, and accessories from four very popular movies. It is much too early to know how valuable the items from *Episode I* are going to be in the short term, but it is thought by some that items from the first three films will be the most desired.

Some of the more valuable items are the vehicles, such as Micro Collection's Millennium Falcon ($650 MIB) and a Jawa Sandcrawler ($450 MIB). As for the *Star Wars* figures, the 12-inch versions are usually much more valuable than the 3³/₄-inch size. Look for the 12-inch Boba Fett ($300 in box), Ben (Obi-Wan) Kenobi ($400 MIB), and Han Solo ($450 in box).

Please keep in mind that almost any played-with toy in the *Star Wars* category is worth only 10 to 25 percent of the value of the same toy still in its original packaging. A good example of this is a *Star Wars* Darth Vader figure. In the box, it is worth about $200, but its value drops to only about $40 in very good, played-with condition.

Robots can be very expensive, and some models go into the $10,000 range, but others are much more affordable. For every Showa Mechanized Robot (MIB $2,750), Robby the Robot (painted tin, played with but in the box, $1,500), or Musical Drumming Robot (mint $9,000), there are hundreds of Ideal's Zeroid Robot (mint-in-package $500), Bandi's Pete the Spaceman (MIB $200), and Masadaya's vinyl Robby the Robot ($75).

Marbles

No, we have *not* lost ours! Handmade marbles are so popular that they are usually immediately snapped up when they are offered for sale, and the best ones go for thousands of dollars each. The marbles that are the most interesting to collectors tend to be large, with elaborate internal decorations, and they tend to have small indentions at their poles where they were gripped by marble "scissors" during their making.

Some of the most desired are called "sulphides." These have small, clay people, animals, numbers, or objects suspended in their interiors. When one of these marbles is large in size, in good condition, and in a color other than clear, colorless, or if the suspended figure has any color other than white or silver, then the value can run as high as $4,000 or beyond!

Later, machine-made marbles are not usually very desirable, but a major exception is the comic marbles made in the 1920s and '30s. These feature such characters as Betty Boop ($200), Kayo ($300), Skeezix ($150), and Moon Mullins ($300). But be careful: There are recent versions that may fool you. The thing to keep in mind here is that any old, handmade marble is potentially valuable, so do not overlook them.

Fisher-Price Toys

Toys made by this company have become very popular, and a paper-covered wooden pull toy in great condition, still in its original box, can be a prize indeed. The #175 Gold Star Stagecoach from the mid-1950s, for instance, brings about $750 if it has its box and has been played with gently.

Almost any Fisher-Price toy featuring a Disney character is good, and this is aptly demonstrated by the Donald Duck Choo Choo from the 1940s, which should be valued at $300, or by the

Mickey Mouse Xylophone (either first or second edition from 1939 or 1942), which fetches around $500.

Even more modern Fisher-Price toys have something of a following. The late 1970s Sesame Street Clubhouse, complete with characters and accessories, is worth $85, and the first McDonald's Restaurant that appeared in 1990 is valued about the same price or just a bit more.

Fast-Food Toys

Speaking of McDonald's, this brings to mind the toys that fast-food restaurants have become famous for selling or giving away, either in or with their children's meals. A good example might be those California Raisins characters that were available at Hardee's during the 1980s and early 1990s. Well, we "heard it through the grapevine" that some of these now have some value.

There is, for instance, a raisin marked "CALRAB-Applause" in the shape of Mom Raisin with yellow hair and a pink apron that is worth in excess of $150. Also, look for Lenny Lima Bean and Cecil Tyme (a carrot), and a key chain in the shape of graduates (raisins in mortarboard caps). Prices for California Raisins figures begin at $5 and rise to close to $200 for the very rare few.

Among others, Arby's, McDonald's, Burger King, Dairy Queen, Jack in the Box, Pizza Hut, and Wendy's all gave away toys to kids, and all the toys are collectible. Many came in sets that need to be complete to have their highest value, and it also helps if the toys are in their original package.

Most of these should be valued in the $2 to $10 range, but something like the Beanie Baby Pinky the Flamingo from McDonald's sells for $30, and all seven cars of the Sonic Food Train are worth $25. Dairy Queen's *Baby's Day Out* books are valued at $15 each, and the price of all four together should be around $75.

Toy Guns

Children have played cowboys or cowgirls and Indians, and cops and robbers for a very long time, and traditionally, this pastime has required toy guns. Before World War I, most toy guns were cast iron, but since that time they have evolved through nickel-plating to die-casting. A cast iron example from the late nineteenth century might bring $500; while a circa 1940, nickel-plated Cowboy Cap Pistol by Hubley in very good condition should bring $200.

Die-cast cap guns became popular in the era when the television cowboy reigned supreme, and examples carrying the names of such small- and big-screen legends as Gene Autry, Hopalong Cassidy, Roy Rogers, and The Lone Ranger were all the rage. Slightly earlier guns featuring heroes such as Buck Rogers and Tom Mix are very collectible as well.

Despite their age, Tom Mix guns are not terribly expensive, and a whole outfit—gun and holster—might bring somewhere between $100 and $150, depending on the type and model. Buck Rogers guns tend to bring a little more, but here, too, prices start at $100 for a 1952 Sonic Ray Flashlight Ray Gun. They go up, however, to about $850 for a MIB 1948 U-238 Atomic Pistol gun-and-holster set by Daisy.

Some rare cap pistols can command prices in the range of $2,000 if they are perfect and still in their original boxes, but guns that command these prices are very rare indeed. Coming close are items such as the Roy Rogers Forty-Niner Pistol and Spurs set, which should retail at around $1,200 MIB, and a Gene Autry Flying A Ranch Holster Set with white-plastic grips decorated with horses, which retails for a bit less—$1,000 if it is MIB.

Paper Items

While treasure-hunting in a child's bedroom, be sure not to over-look the items made from paper. We all know about comic books and baseball and other sports cards. Horror stories abound about parents who tidied up their child's former room and disposed of the cards and comics, only to find out in later years that the collection could have been sold for tens, if not hundreds of thousands of dollars.

We are not going to dwell on this well-trodden ground, but we do want to reiterate that comic books that have torn pages or loose backs, or that generally look as if they were stored under a rock out in a swamp, have very little value unless they are the rarest of the rare. Even then, the greatly diminished value (90 percent or more) could make you burst into tears when you think about what might have been.

Items related to comic books are Whitman's Big Little Books, which were introduced in 1933. Popular until the 1950s, Big Little Books were blasted into obscurity by comic books. These books were all about adventure, and they had exciting illustrations on the right-hand page and text on the left. It was here that kids learned about the derring-do of Dick Tracy, Flash Gordon, Tarzan, and Buck Rogers, as well as any number of cowboy heroes such as Gene Autry. They also got to enjoy the antics of Felix the Cat, Mickey Mouse, Donald Duck, and Little Orphan Annie.

Few of these books rise above the $100 level. Most sell in the $20 to $45 range, and then only those in good condition. Such titles as *Tarzan Twins* (1934), *Flash Gordon and the Monsters of Mongo* (1935), and *Donald Duck Says Such Luck* (1941) bring between $100 and $300 each if they are near-mint.

Other companies produced similar books, and examples by Dell, Golden Press, Saalfield, Lynn and Engel-Van Wiseman are sought after as well. Little Golden Books published by Western Publishing Company are currently attracting a lot of collector interest. When they first came out in 1942, they had blue paper spines; later the blue paper was replaced by gold paper, and even later, gold foil.

Early Little Golden Books in good condition (no crayon scribbles, no torn pages) are eagerly sought after, and collectors particularly like those with dust jackets and those that include paper dolls.

Also, look on either the title page or the last page for a designation "1/A." This is the sign of a first edition and, like any other first edition, it is more valuable. Right now, prices start at $4 and go up to about $40, but a first edition of *The Poky Little Puppy* with its dust jacket in like-new condition is worth a little over $100.

All kinds of children's books are valuable. Pop-up books with pages that raise up to form a three-D picture can be very expensive. Mickey Mouse pop-ups are particularly valuable, and a 1934 *Mickey Mouse Waddle Book* sells for almost $4,000 in mint condition. *Mickey Mouse in King Arthur's Court* can sell for a little less than half that amount.

Early editions of L. Frank Baum's *Wizard of Oz* books can be very valuable: If you happen to have the first edition (and first issue) of *The Wonderful Wizard of Oz* (1900) with its dust jacket and in excellent condition, its value may exceed $40,000! Few of these have survived, and the condition of most *Wizard of Oz* books tends to be marginal because they were loved to death.

First-edition Oz books with their dust jackets tend to sell for more than $1,000, and some can go into the $7,500 to $15,000 range, but most of the Oz books either do not have their all-important jackets or are not first editions. These less-valuable books typically sell in the $25 to $500 range, with only a few non-dust-jacketed first editions going a tad higher.

It should be noted that other authors penned Oz books, and these include Ruth Plumly Thompson and Jack Snow. Like the Baum versions, these Oz tales have value, but as a general rule prices do not rise above $1,000. The first edition of Thompson's *The Cowardly Lion of Oz* (1923) is worth about $500 in excellent condition, and the first edition of Jack Snow's *The Magical Mimics of Oz* (1946) with its dust jacket can fetch as much as $650.

Moving on from books, another large category of paper items commonly found in children's rooms that should be preserved are the posters of music stars, outer space, television shows, movies, movie stars, and other kinds of posters that hung on their walls. Most of these were and are destroyed by tape, tacks, staples, and cruel and unceremonious removals that created rips and tears.

The appeal of posters from the halcyon days of a child's youth can be almost visceral, and can generate an overwhelming urge to re-own a piece of the past. This is one way that things become collectible, and one way that they become valuable. This is also a good example of what we mean when we say "nostalgia."

Concert posters from the 1960s with psychedelic designs are now considered to be quite uncommon and desirable and, in fact, anything psychedelic is becoming hot, hot, hot. Many of these posters were put up on telephone poles and in other public places, and summarily disposed of after the event—so they are now quite rare.

Rock 'n' Roll Memorabilia

Along with concert posters, your child's room might yield other pieces of rock 'n' roll memorabilia, such as concert programs, tickets, photographs, and even luggage. An Elvis Presley overnight case, for instance, is worth $1,000 (depending on condition), and an Elvis zippered school binder from 1956 entitled "Love Me Tender" is valued at $1,200. A simple Elvis pennant from the 1970s, however, is worth only about $50.

A KISS backpack with its original thermos is valued at $100 or a bit more, and a Marie Osmond makeup kit is worth about $35. Rolling Stones concert programs from the 1960s bring up to $200, while the ones from the '70s bring closer to $50. A throwaway item such as a Supremes concert flier can be worth in excess of $100, and one for Jimi Hendrix can bring more than $300.

An unused 1980s vintage Led Zeppelin concert ticket could bring as much as $200, and a Doors ticket from the '60s (also unused) should fetch about $350. The possibilities here are endless, but keep in mind that some old rock 'n' rollers are a little too lackluster for their memorabilia to bring big money. A good case in point might be a Shaun Cassidy notebook with a picture of this teenybopper heartthrob on the cover—it is worth less than $10. Items from New Kids on the Block are not doing well at the moment either.

Records

We think that there was not a child's room in the United States that did not have records in it right up until very recently. These vinyl discs were obligatory childhood equipment until CDs made them obsolete. There is a great deal of buzz going on right now about how valuable records either are, or are not, going to be, but let us tell you right now that most of the records that we find in estates only sell for a few dollars each.

The reason? Well, most of them are damaged, and most of them are by an artist that nobody really wants. It is hard for many people to believe, but a record that has been played even once is a record that has been diminished in value. It is similar to driving a new car off the showroom floor: As soon as it hits the pavement, depreciation sets in big time.

Collectors prefer their records to have the factory-fresh plastic covering over them, and to be unopened and unplayed. A small scratch, a tear on the label, almost anything at all, can turn a $1,000 Elvis Presley rarity into a $300 (or less) Elvis Presley could-have-been. This means that any record found in a child's lair is not likely to be at anywhere near optimum value.

Records tend to be collected in categories. Popular choices are classifications such as early Rock 'n' Roll, Rockabilly, Jazz, Blues, Rhythm-and-Blues, Country and Western, and Big Band. Certain big names are also desirable, and these include Elvis Presley, The Beach Boys, the Beatles, Buddy Holly, and Bill Haley and the Comets.

Transistor and Figural Radios

What child of the 1950s, '60s, or '70s did not cherish his or her transistor radio? Compact and portable, they took rock 'n' roll and sports broadcasts to the beach and (clandestinely) to the classroom. Every adolescent had to have at least one, and today the radios are collectible, and some of them are quite expensive.

At first glance it may be a little hard to tell just from looking at a given transistor radio which one is worth $5 and which one is worth $400. Unusual shapes are something of a clue, and a Sharp model BH-352, which is configured something like a jet engine, is worth about $200.

Unfortunately, most of the transistor radios of this era are unapologetically rectangular. Some of them, however, do manage to have a real "cool" look to them despite the fact that they are basically—well—"square." Joe is particularly fond of the Arvin #9577, which to him looks like a man's electric shaver. It is valued at $175.

Helaine, on the other hand, is partial to Dewald model K-701, which dates from about 1955. This model has a colorful two-tone plastic case and a round dial in the lower middle. It screams " '50s!" and is worth about $300. Another two-tone plastic radio that screams " '50s!" is the Automatic TT 600 Tom Thumb, which retails for $200.

One of the most valuable of these rectangular plastic radios is the Mantola M4D, which is so nondescript that if you found one you would probably just ignore it. This model has a single-color case and nothing to recommend it except an atomic symbol (orbiting electrons) in the center of the dial. Still, this example is valued at close to $400 in pristine condition because of its rarity.

Some of the most valuable radios that one might find in a child's room are the novelty pieces shaped like everything from Cadillac convertibles to toilet-paper rolls or ones with character figures on them. Some of the most valuable of these were made in the 1930s. A good example from this period is the Charlie McCarthy radio made by Majestic, with a three-dimensional metal figure of the famous ventriloquist's dummy sitting on a Bakelite case. If you find one of these, value it at $2,000 if it is in pristine working condition! But, beware—we have seen damaged ones priced at less than $200.

The king of the 1930s novelty radios, however, may be the one that features Snow White and the Seven Dwarfs, which is worth in excess of $3,000! A radio from a little later that is well worth preserving is the one that features Mickey Mantle and Roger Maris. Currently an example in good condition should be valued at a bit over $1,000.

Other, more modern radios that are shaped like some object or character are very collectible, but most of them have a value of less than $150. Bozo the Clown, for instance, is worth about $100, but a Bullwinkle Moose fetches almost $300. There are all kinds of radios in the shape of Coca-Cola bottles, cans, and vending machines, and these start at $25 and go up into the $400 range for a MIB, small-sized upright vending machine from the 1960s (the large example of this machine brings about half this amount).

Coca-Cola novelty radios made from the 1930s to the 1950s can be much more expensive, as evidenced by the 1933 24-inch-tall, bottle-shaped radio that is worth almost $5,000 if it is all original and in excellent working condition. Also, there is a wonderful Coca-Cola cooler-shaped radio from the 1950s that has a value of around $800.

Other fun novelty radios to save are the Gumby radios from the 1970s, valued at $175, the Hershey's Syrup can radios, worth $100, and the radio in the shape of the Michelin Man, which brings about $500 or a bit more. A Snoopy on top of his doghouse radio brought about $45 a year before we wrote this book. As we write now, the value has risen to closer to $85, and by the time this book appears in print, the value will probably have passed the $125 mark.

Banks

Other interesting things may be scattered around a child's room that would attract collectors' attention. Banks are one of them, and a Franciscan china pig is worth about $325, while a Miss Piggy of Muppet fame might fetch as much as $60. Old tin and cast iron "still" banks—meaning they have no moving parts—are a fascinating area of collecting and it has been estimated that there are more than three thousand varieties of these.

Some of these vintage still banks can be fairly pricey. A 4½-inch-tall elephant on wheels is worth $400, while a 2⅛-inch-tall John

Brown's Fort is worth $1,250. A 7¾-inch-long Yellow Cab by Arcade is $3,500, and a 6¾-inch-tall rocking chair by C. J. Manning is just a little less at around $3,200.

Old "mechanical" banks—banks with moving parts—can be even more expensive than their still cousins. Great caution needs to be exercised here because there are far more reproductions than originals, and both of us have seen seasoned collectors fooled by well-done fakes.

Values on some mechanical banks can go above the $20,000 level, but most are priced well below $10,000. One of the cuter mechanical banks shows a boy milking a cow; when the money is deposited, the cow kicks over both the boy and the stool. This bank is worth around $11,000, depending on the condition of the paint and the bank's working order.

Some really interesting banks with lesser prices include one that features a mule entering a barn ($2,000), a frog on a bicycle entitled "Professor Pug Frog's Great Bicycle Feat" ($1,500), and a horse race ($3,500). More common mechanical banks start at $150 and go up to $1,000.

Clocks and Watches

Clocks and watches are items that are commonly found lurking in a child's room, and a circa 1935 Buck Rogers pocket watch in its original package should be valued at $700, while a Beatles' "Yellow Submarine" alarm clock might sell for as much as $2,000 if it is in good shape and working. Wristwatches are often prized, and a Lone Ranger from 1951 with a round face and MIB is worth $700, and a MIB Howdy Doody by Ideal Watch Company about $600.

Mickey Mouse wristwatches are kind of a cliché, and prices for these are all over the board. The 1933 Ingersol Mickey wristwatch is currently pushing the $1,000 level if it is MIB, and the Ingersol pocket watch of the same vintage with its original fob is approaching $2,000. Mickey Mouse wristwatches from the '50s and '60s tend to bring less than $250 each.

Lunch Boxes

Lunch boxes are still another denizen of a child's life. The world of lunch boxes is so huge that it boggles the imagination. There are metal lunch boxes, vinyl lunch boxes, and plastic lunch boxes, and all are sought after by collectors—who call themselves "boxers." The lunch boxes need to be in good condition with no rust, and it is a big plus if they still have their original thermos bottles.

Some of the most desired are the barn-shaped boxes called "domes," and a *Star Trek* version in pristine shape might sell for as much as $800, a *Hogan's Heroes* for $350, and a Home Town Airport for $1,000. Old metal lunch boxes without pictorial decorations start at $20 and go up to about $50 for a white dome.

Prices for rectangular metal lunch boxes are all over the board. A Care Bear from 1984 might be worth less than $10, while a Toppie, which features a plaid elephant and balloons, will command as much as $2,400. In between, there is everything from the *Partridge Family* (1971, $75), the NHL (National Hockey League, from 1970, $550), and *Howdy Doody* (1954, $500) to Blondie (1969, $145), the Beatles (1966, $500), and 240 Robert (1978, $2,000).

In vinyl and plastic, such items as Linus the Lionhearted (1975, $575), Dr. Seuss (1970, $600), Dream Boat (1960, $850), Dudley Do-Right (year unknown, $1,600), and Barbie Lunch Box Ponytail (1961, $800) are among the top lots. More common examples include *101 Dalmatians* (1990, $20), *Back to the Future* (1989, $35), and *Sesame Street* (1979, $100; 1981, $65).

Sporting Goods

Children's rooms, sporting goods, and sporting memorabilia seem to go together like Mark McGwire and home runs. The scope of collectible objects in this category is huge and encompasses everything from old baseballs, baseball bats, and baseball mitts to World Series programs, tickets to past sporting events, sports character figures, and Olympic items.

The best rule is that if an object is sports-related—no matter how trivial it may seem—do not throw it away. We should also mention that if you live in a town or even a state where there is a collegiate sports team that is a "big deal" and has a doggedly devoted fan base, any vintage item relating to that team will be collected with great enthusiasm.

To give any kind of idea concerning the breadth and depth of this market is difficult, but as an illustration of how much money can be involved here, a 1903 World Series program in pristine condition is worth approximately $30,000, while a fielder's glove used by Hank Aaron in the 1970s is valued at $8,000.

Children do not often have these kinds of things in their rooms because they are generally big boys' toys. Items that may turn up somewhere in a house, however, are such things as a Mickey Mantle player-model glove in mint condition, which is worth $500, and a Louisville Slugger bat with Joe DiMaggio's facsimile signature on it, which is worth about $250.

Plastic figures of baseball players are not uncommon, but they are collectible. The ones made by Hartland Plastics were sold at baseball-park concession stands in the 1960s, and today some of these can be fairly expensive. The rarest of these is of the Pittsburgh Pirates' Dick Groat, because only five thousand of these were produced in the original run.

If you happen to have one of these with still-white plastic, and if it has its original hang tag and box, it should be valued in the $1,750 range. Other figures in this series are much less valuable, and in pristine condition a Hank Aaron goes for $300, a Roger Maris for $650, an Eddie Matthews for $200, and a Yogi Berra for $300. Reissues of these were made in 1988 and should have a label on the back of the belt.

Several other companies made baseball and sports figures, but the only other ones we are going to discuss are the "nodders," which derive their names from their spring-mounted heads, which seem to nod when they are moved. Starting in 1960, these were imported from Japan in vast quantities, but the early ones that have squared, brightly colored bases are now fairly valuable.

The rarest of these is probably the one representing the Washington Senators, which in excellent condition brings about $450. Other hard-to-find teams include the Baltimore Orioles ($250), the Boston Red Sox ($325), and the Cincinnati Reds ($325).

Playing House

In Victorian times, little girls were given toys that would help them learn how to be better "homemakers" and hostesses when the time came. Today, Easy-Bake ovens, tea sets, and all this mini-domestic equipment can be very collectible.

Toy ranges

Modern parents are a little queasy about giving their children cooking toys that use a light bulb for a heat source, but in days gone by things were different. Both stove and toy companies made cast iron or porcelain-finished ranges that were miniature versions of the big kitchen units used by Mother. Often these diminutive cooking apparatuses are found with burned sticks and charcoal in them, because little Mary or Janie actually built a fire and did some very real cooking. Some of these toy stoves were rather large and came with a variety of accessories such as pots, pans, kettles, and skillets. The most desired of these are the ones made by the stove manufacturers who made real kitchen appliances. Some of the rarer of these can go as high as $6,000 (or a bit more), but most sell in the $150 to $1,500 range. Stove companies making these include Buck, Charter Oak, and Karr, and the more expensive models often are large and elaborate or have an enamel finish with nickel or chrome trim. Toy companies such as Arcade and Bing made toy stoves and these normally sell in the neighborhood of $100 to $1,500.

Tea sets and toy dishes

Many companies made these, but one of the most famous was the Akro Agate Company of Clarksburg, West Virginia, which was in business from 1914 to 1951. Their glass dishes came in a variety of colors and patterns that were sold in boxed sets, and it is amazing how often these sets turn up still in their original box. Large MIB sets (usually with twenty-one pieces) bring prices that generally fall into the $150 to $800 range, depending on the pattern and color of the dishes in question. Smaller sets in the seven- to seventeen-piece size start at a little less than $100 and go up to around $700 for a seventeen-piece set in the Miss America pattern in green. The same set in white is a bit less valuable at $550. Besides Akro Agate sets, we see a lot of German tea sets made by anonymous makers, and sets with common decorations such as flowers and nonspecific children playing should be valued between $75 and $150. German- and Japanese-made sets with Mickey Mouse on them, however, are somewhat more valuable, with prices that generally run between $300 and $1,200. A set with images of Sunbonnet Babies on it is quite valuable as well. Sunbonnet Babies are images created by Bertha Corbett, and they feature little girls going about their daily chores wearing large sunbonnets that completely cover their heads and faces. These are collectible in any form in which they are found, whether it is on postcards, in the original books by Eulalie Osgood Grover, on adult-size items such as creamers and candle-holders, or shown on children's play dishes. A sixteen-piece child's tea set complete with teapot and cake plate is valued between $1,200 and $1,500, and a regular-sized candleholder made by the Royal Bayreuth China Company is worth $700.

Miniature sewing machines

We may think of these small sewing machines as toys, and in many cases they were. But they were commonly used as traveling machines for use in making quick repairs in faraway places, and, even when a child was "playing" with one, the purpose was quite serious. These devices were designed to teach little girls how to perform a necessary household task skillfully—namely, sewing for a family. These little machines were made for a very long time—from the late nineteenth century all the way to quite recent times. Most of the ones seen in homes are the black-enameled Singer models with gold trim, some of which came in trunks or in hatbox-shaped containers that may have also contained a doll and patterns for doll clothes. Top price for a Singer model with trunk and doll is around $750, but the machines alone seldom rise above $300 for World War I vintage machines. Modern plastic machines from the 1980s bring $25 to $50.

CHAPTER NINE

The Master Bedroom

The master bedroom is a good place to look inside drawers, to peek into closets, and to examine the tops of dressers, vanities, and tables. Lurking in these dark and dusty places are often treasures that are easily overlooked.

Men's Ties

No one really knows why men get such awful ties on Father's Day and Christmas, but they do and with great regularity. Some of these from the 1930s, '40s, and '50s are actually collectible, and a Salvador Dalí with a surrealistic print and his name on the label brings between $200 and $300.

Other artist-designed ties such as the ones by Peter Max are not quite so highly regarded and currently do not command significant dollars. Ties by the famed Italian designer Emilio Pucci are also not in great demand.

How about the ties with hand-painted naked ladies? Well, they sell for between $100 and $150. In general, the hand-painted ties from the '30s and '40s that sport images of horses, bold geometrics, and scenes of some sort should be valued between $35 and $75 each.

Photo-print ties from the late '40s, and '50s that feature pictures of rodeos, bucking horses, fishing scenes, and lighthouses are entrants in the "Tacky Tie" competition as well, and these usually sell in the neighborhood of $35 to $50. Although we may joke about these today, when they were new they were fashionable; and because they speak eloquently of the tastes of the times in which they were made, they are worthy of being collected and being respected for what they are.

Bowling Outfits

In the back of a closet or the bottom of a drawer, there might be a vintage bowling shirt from the 1930s to the 1950s. There it has languished for decades, forgotten, unworn, and unappreciated. Collectors do not want the ones made from polyester, but examples made from rayon and gabardine are prized if they have strong graphics on the back and maybe some interesting embroidery on the front.

There should be a name stitched on the front, and it does not really matter what that name is. Normally, bowling shirts come in bright—even garish—combinations of colors, and the more striking these are, the better. Helaine reports that she recently saw a 1940s bowling dress bedecked and bedazzled with rhinestones sell for $150. As for bowling shirts, most of them are in the $50 to $75 range right now—but great ones go somewhat higher.

Hawaiian Shirts

So far we have mentioned bowling shirts and ties, but the winner of the kitsch clothing contest might be the Hawaiian shirt, which is the butt of more jokes than we care to contemplate. These originated in the 1920s when Hawaiian tailor Ellery Chun crafted a loose-fitting garment from flowery fabric and called it an "Aloha Shirt."

Renamed the "Hawaiian Shirt," they became popular when such stars as Bing Crosby, Arthur Godfrey, and Elvis Presley began wearing them in the movies and on television. The most sought-after examples are those made in the 1930s, '40s, and '50s; have Hawaiian labels such as Kameameha, King-Smith, and Branfleet (later renamed "Kahala"); are made from silk or rayon; and have buttons made from pieces of coconut shell or bamboo.

In terms of images, the most desirable ones depict hula dancers, are photomontages, or have Hawaiian themes, but design, fabric, and coloration also play important roles in determining a particular shirt's value. Most collectors want the baggy look, so larger sizes are preferred, and these routinely sell between $250 and $600 depending upon condition and graphics. Really outstanding examples, however, have brought as much as $5,000!

Women's Fashions

Women's clothes are a little harder to analyze than men's. Garments made from polyester are not desired at the moment, and the outfits that are considered to be treasures carry a designer label. Chanel, Dior, Courrèges, Givenchy, Gernreich, and Hattie Carnegie, among others, all have cachet, and premium clothes with any of their labels still inside can bring prices well over $1,000 each—just as they did when they were new.

To receive top dollar, the garment must be in absolutely pristine condition, clean, and spot-free. Joe often tells the story of finding a Galanos gown in an estate. The dress had been stored in a cedar-lined attic for years and years, and the white fabric had turned an ugly shade of brown from extreme heat, dust, and other adverse environmental factors. Otherwise, the dress was in excellent condition, but it would not sell at any price because of the discoloration.

To be sure, buyers dithered and speculated, but no one wanted to take the chance of having it cleaned and the stain not coming out. This was a painful lesson, and it brings up the point that individuals should never try to clean a designer original on their own. Always send the garment to a professional who specializes in this kind of delicate job.

Another factor that can limit the value and even the basic salability of a fashion garment is size, and it is the small sizes that dominate the marketplace. It has been said that if a dress is larger than an 8, it is too big!

Handbags and Purses

Beaded bags with floral decorations such as this one are not quite as valuable as those with well-executed scenic designs.

As we said earlier, buying designer outfits can require a well-filled pocketbook. And speaking of pocketbooks—or handbags, if you prefer—these are very collectible, too. Beaded bags, mesh bags, the plastic bags of the 1950s, needlepoint and tapestry bags, hand-tooled leather bags, and designer bags are all hot sellers, and they can bring prices that are quite respectable.

Beaded bags have been around for two hundred years, and the ones that have drawstring closings are called "reticules" (actually, any bag with a drawstring closure is a "reticule," not just the ones that are beaded). Of course, the condition of a bag is very important. The fringe needs to be intact, and the beads need to be attached securely and in good condition. Bags that are falling apart are hard to save, and collectors really frown on fixer-uppers.

A high-quality, late-nineteenth- or early-twentieth-century beaded bag with a scenic design might bring as much as $600, while one with an intricate garland of roses might bring $500. Bags with less fine work seldom bring more than $200. Examples with floral motifs usually fetch less than bags of similar quality decorated with landscapes or with images that include people.

When deciding whether or not a particular beaded bag is valuable, be sure to check the frame to which the cloth bag is attached, because sometimes these are sterling or 800 silver, ivory, or even gold. Any one of these can enhance the dollar value of a given purse, and if the frame is jeweled or ornamented with elaborate figural decorations, that too can be a plus.

Commercially made beaded purses, beaded bags with no pictorial content, and beaded bags of the mid-twentieth century are usually far less expensive and sought-after than their earlier, more elaborate cousins. At that time (mid-twentieth century), quality bags were still being made in France and Belgium, but pieces with a "Made in Czechoslovakia" label are quite common and of lesser quality. These might sell for as little as $35, while the better mid-twentieth-century bags seldom rise above the $175 mark.

Expect to pay as much as $200 for a beaded bag from the 1940s marked "An Original Fre-Mor Creation," or about $100 for a bag marked "K & G Charlet Bag, Paris, New York." Other names to look for include DuBonnet, Jasly, and Fabienne.

In the early nineteenth century, mesh handbags were made from either gold or silver, but by the late 1800s, steel-mesh purses appeared that were affordable enough for the masses. Of course, silver and gold mesh bags were still being made in the twentieth century, but the ones that are most likely to turn up today are steel. These start at $75 for a small, plain-Jane version, but they can increase to as much as $800 for a large example that is nicely decorated with enamel.

Some of the more desired mesh purses carry a label that identifies them as having been made by the Whiting and Davis Company of Plainville, Massachusetts. Mesh bags marked "Mandalian Mfg. Co." are also in great demand, and these tend to have tapered bottoms and rich designs with a Middle Eastern flavor that can be traced to the Turkish background of the company's founder, Shatiel Mandalia. Some of these bags have surpassed $1,000 in value.

Lucite bags of the late 1940s and '50s are nifty, and collector interest in these can be intense. They were made in some rather odd shapes, and are characterized by a variety of decorations that include rhinestones, glitter, seashells, and lace.

The leading manufacturer was arguably Willardy of New York City, but top contenders for collectors' dollars were also made by Gilli Originals, Patricia of Miami, Evans, Rialto, and Llewllyn. Prices start at $35 for a clutch bag and quickly escalate into the hundreds for more avant-garde models.

For those whose taste is a little more traditional, needlepoint and tapestry bags are exciting finds in the master bedroom. High-quality French tapestry bags with eighteenth-century scenes often bring as much as $250, and an outstanding *petit point* purse should be valued between $500 and $600.

Some people find alligator handbags with the legs—and sometimes the heads—still attached to be a little distasteful, but there is interest in these, and they can sell for as much as $250. Any purse that is stylish is worth looking into, and particular attention should be paid to the more fashionable bags of the 1920s, '30s, and '40s.

Some names to search for on post–World War II bags include Schiaparelli, Bienen-Davis (look for the "b-d" logo on the lining), Harry Rosenfield, Koret, Balenciaga, Lucien LeLong, Molyneux, and the name of any upper-end department store such as Saks Fifth Avenue or Bonwit Teller.

Hats

Women's hats are another fashion accessory that need to be evaluated before they are sold for a few dollars or thrown out because they appear to be too unfashionable to be of interest. Figural hats by Bes Ben of Chicago bring prices above $10,000, and the creations of famous designers such as Lilly Daché, Peggy Hoyt, and Balenciaga should not be overlooked.

Simple, uninteresting designs even by these famous makers often command prices of less than $50, and only their most daring, innovative, or inspired efforts bring sums in the high hundreds of dollars each. Style and condition are really the important factors to consider, and a fine hat with good, classic elements but no special maker's name can bring $200 to $300.

Some men's hats are also collectible, and three of the names to look for are Borsolina, Harley-Davidson, and Stetson. Top hats are desirable as well and these have prices that range from $250 to about $600 for a fine-quality piece.

Costume Jewelry

So many times when we go into the master bedroom of an estate, the costume jewelry is pushed to one side and ignored. Too often the heirs think that if a piece of jewelry is not made from gold and does not contain diamonds or other precious gems, it is not worth their time. Nothing could be further from the truth.

One of the primary things that Joe likes to look at when he goes into a house for the first time is the jewelry box, because he knows that he is almost always going to find buried treasure. One time it was a genuine ruby ring worth $600; another time, it was four rhinestone pins signed "Eisenberg Original" that together were worth over $1,000.

In the 1920s, Coco Chanel made costume or "faux" jewelry an acceptable part of high fashion. Ever since that time, there has been an explosion of this kind of "fabulous fake" ornament. Some of it is well-made and well-designed; some of it is poorly conceived and crafted; and some of it is just plain ugly. What this means is that not every piece of old costume jewelry is valuable— ugly, poorly made, and unfashionable fashion jewelry usually goes begging.

An impressive Eisenberg rhinestone pin.

Among collectors, Eisenberg is one of the most sought-after makers of costume jewelry. The company was founded in 1914 as a clothing manufacturer and did not start making costume jewelry until about 1930. Early examples of Eisenberg jewelry are often unsigned, but the "Eisenberg Original" signature was used from 1935 to 1945.

"Sterling" was used in conjunction with this mark from 1941 to 1945. After that, the jewelry was rhodium-plated base metal. Starting in 1941, some pieces were signed "Eisenberg Ice" with block letters. This name was discontinued in 1958, but revived in the 1970s, using script instead of block letters. The simple designation "Eisenberg" was used from 1945 until about 1958.

Both block and script letter *E*'s were also used as signatures in the 1940s and '50s.

All this is important because collectors have been traditionally more interested in pieces with the signatures "Eisenberg Original"; "Eisenberg Original" in conjunction with "Sterling"; and "Eisenberg Ice" in block letters, but less interested in pieces simply marked "Eisenberg."

When confronted with a large assortment of costume jewelry, the first thing that needs to be done is to separate the various objects into piles of damaged pieces and undamaged pieces. Unfortunately, this kind of jewelry is prone to the loss of stones and "pearls," which greatly diminishes the value of the affected item.

Therefore,271 serious collectors of costume jewelry often keep a stockpile of old stones and pearls so that they can make repairs, but this is not a fact they normally advertise when they are buying. Even though they can probably make a repair quite easily, most collectors will pay only a modest amount for damaged jewelry. An individual without these repair-and-replacement capabilities will generally not consider buying a piece with missing stones.

After sorting your jewelry, you should examine each piece for signatures, because these are the pieces that will be the most eagerly sought after. Names such as Bogoff, Weiss, Miriam Haskell, Hobé Art, Trifari, Coro, Eisenberg, and Schiaparelli are encountered with some frequency. Pieces with these names (and others) are the heart of the market and usually the most valuable.

It should be noted, however, that many high-quality items are not signed, and despite the lack of a name, they are eagerly collected by those who know what they are doing. In addition, certain quality makers such as Chanel, Schiaparelli, and Miriam Haskell often did not mark their early pieces, and these will take a professional to identify.

One other category of costume jewelry that needs to be mentioned is Bakelite. Jewelry made from this colorful plastic during the 1920s and '30s can command significant dollars. Very plain pieces of Bakelite jewelry bring only a modest amount of money. Collectors are particularly interested in the items that appear to be carved, or those that have combinations of colors. A red Bakelite bangle bracelet with black dots should be valued at $500, and a vari-colored pin with dangling cherries at about $475.

Adult Wristwatches

In among the costume jewelry in the master bedroom old wristwatches often turn up, and they can be valuable. It is important that they be in working condition, because repairing them can be difficult and very expensive.

Helaine had this point driven home recently when she took her Patek Philippe wristwatch to a local jeweler to be fixed. Helaine was not particularly worried about how much it would cost, but the jeweler insisted that she be given an estimate before the work was done. The last time he sent a watch like hers in, it was gone for nine months and the repair cost $800!

We all know that wristwatches from famous makers such as Rolex and Patek Philippe are expensive, and perhaps we should mention that a few of the Patek watches are worth as much as $300,000! Men's watches are generally preferred to women's, and the rectangular "tank" style, along with unusual and futuristic shapes, are some of the most sought-after.

Upper-end wristwatches are few and far between, but timepieces by such companies as Bulova and Timex are not. There must literally be millions of vintage Bulova Accutron watches out there, and some of them can have a fair price if they are in good working shape.

A circa 1960 Accutron Space View (with the mechanism visible through the face) is worth $850 if the case is 14-karat gold, but only $400 if it is gold-filled, and $300 if it is stainless steel. Other Accutrons start at $75 for common examples and can go above the $2,000 level for Astronaut models with 18-karat-gold cases and bands. Non-Accutron Bulova wristwatches start at $45 and go up to around $1,000 for designs with gold cases accented with diamonds and gold bands.

At this time, Timex watches are not widely collected, but that may change. Other brands of wristwatches to look for include Benrus, Cartier, Elgin, Gruen, Hamilton, Illinois, Jules Jurgensen, Le Coultre, Longines, Movado, Omega, Vacheron, and Wittnauer.

Photographs

While rummaging through the bedroom drawers, we might run across some family photographs. Most of the snapshots made in the last one hundred years or so are never going to be valuable monetarily, but we do find nineteenth-century photographs on metal and glass, which can have a substantial value.

These photographs are often found in leather or *gutta percha* cases, and the daguerreotypes—or photographs on copper plates— are usually the most valuable. They came in a variety of sizes that range from a sixteenth plate (15/8 by 2 1/8 inches) to a full plate (6 1/2 by 8 1/2 inches). The larger sizes are much more rare than the smaller sizes, and any daguerreotype that is something other than a simple portrait is potentially worth a considerable amount of money.

Outdoor scenes are very unusual. Photographs of people either performing their occupation or displaying their occupational tools are, like the outdoor scenes, very desirable. In addition, daguerreotypes of famous people and images of military personnel are highly sought after. Finally, there is one last category that collectors look for, but, be warned, it is a little distasteful.

These are pictures of dead children. Ghoulish? Yes. But in the nineteenth century, parents often had a portrait taken of their deceased child as a remembrance. To us, this is a little bizarre, but photographic enthusiasts find these "interesting."

Large, artistic, or unusual daguerreotypes made by famous photographers can sell at prices that run into the tens of thousands of dollars, but the ones found in most homes are much less costly. Ordinary small portraits sell in the $30 to $65 range, or a bit more if the subjects are children, or if there are toys or animals in view. Military subjects can sell above $1,000 if the image is a good size and if the person shown is in full uniform with weapons and other paraphernalia.

Photographs on iron are called "tintypes," or ferrotypes, and those on glass are called "ambrotypes." For the most part, these are not as highly desired as daguerreotypes, but outdoor scenes, "occupationals," military-related topics, dead children, and famous people still command good prices.

The cases for these metal and glass photographs are also collectible. They were made from leather, papier-mâché, *gutta percha* (which is a "rubbery" material derived from the latex sap of certain kinds of Asian trees), and a substance made from mixing wood fiber and shellac, called "Union" (see chapter 2).

A full-plate-size Union case (approximately 9¹⁄8 by 7 inches) can go above the $2,000 level if it has a rare, intricate design on its cover, such as "The Landing of Columbus." A half-plate size (approximately 4⁷⁄8 by 6 inches) with a design called "The Wedding Procession" is worth $500 in pristine condition. Collectors often call these Union cases "thermoplastic" or "hard" cases, and they should not be confused with *gutta percha*, which is an entirely different material.

Original photographs on paper made in the nineteenth and twentieth centuries are wildly desired if they were done by a famous artist such as Man Ray, Edward S. Curtis, Alexander Gardner, Alfred Stieglitz, or Edward Weston. The list of collectible photographers is actually very long, and values can be surprisingly high. These usually can be recognized by the artist's penciled signature in the bottom right-hand corner on the mat or on the reverse side.

Some of the photographs produced by the individuals listed above can generate prices above the $50,000 level at auction. Be very careful, however, because new photographs made from original negatives by someone other than the original photographer do exist, and these are much, much less valuable.

Joe went to an estate auction many years ago, and there, in a mid-nineteenth-century frame, was a picture he recognized. It was a Carleton Watkins view of Yosemite, and Joe knew it was worth about $5,000. He was excited when he bought it for less than $100, but when he got it home and took it out of its frame, Joe discovered to his absolute dismay that the margins had been cut off to allow the photograph to fit into the frame. The photograph's value had been compromised by more than half, and the lesson here is not to trim the margins on either a print or a photograph to enable them fit into a frame.

Always store your photographs in a cool, dry place away from sunlight. If they are framed, make sure they are in an acid-free environment with no cardboard or wood touching them. Also, do not store your family photographs in those sticky albums (it is bad for them), and always identify the people and places shown.

Sewing Items

Other valuable items sometimes found in the master bedroom are sewing-related, and demand for these mundane objects can be quite amazing. Pincushions, thimbles, needle cases, scissors, sewing birds, tatting shuttles, darners, and many other kinds of sewing accessories are prized by a large group of devoted collectors.

For anyone not familiar with the ins and outs of stitchery, a sewing bird is simply a clamp used when hemming a garment. Sometimes called a "third hand," this device was affixed to a tabletop, and it held the fabric in place while the seamstress worked. The clamp was often made in the shape of a bird—thus the name "sewing bird"—and when the seamstress pressed a lever at the bird's tail, the beak opened to receive or release the material.

Sewing birds often had a pincushion attached to the bird's back, and sometimes an additional one was attached at the base, underneath the bird's beak. These devices originated as simple iron birds with no pincushions in the mid-eighteenth century, but the brass examples that are most often seen today were first patented in 1853 by Charles Waterman, who should not be confused with Lewis Edson Waterman, the inventor of the Waterman fountain pen.

Unusual examples, such as one in which the clamp is in the form of a dog rather than a bird, can sell in the $1,000-plus range, but most of the sewing birds found in Grandma's sewing basket will fall into the $250 to $450 range. Keep in mind that reproductions of antique sewing birds have been available for almost twenty years, and care should be taken when buying.

Pincushions are an interesting collectible because they came in a fascinating variety of shapes and sizes. Most commonly seen are pincushions placed inside miniature shoes that are usually made of metal, although examples crafted from wood and leather do turn up. Generally, these sell for between $35 and $65, with a small sterling-silver example bringing $75 to $125.

Other collectible pincushions are shaped like camels, elephants, birds, pigs, foxes, ducks, swans, bears, pigs, and snails. Most pincushion collectors focus on these figural pieces, and prices start at about $50 and escalate to as high as $175 for a small animal in sterling silver.

Many of the figural pincushions discussed above are late Victorian or early twentieth century, and it is unusual to find any pincushion made before 1800. Turn-of-the-century English specimens can be found, and these are often shaped like silk- or velvet-covered balls with silver bands around the middle. Ball pincushions with tattered coverings bring about $100, but examples in better condition can command prices as high as $350.

There is probably no more widely collected sewing item than the not-so-humble thimble. Thimbles were made from gold, silver, aluminum, steel, porcelain, ivory, horn, and plastic. Some were jeweled, some were enameled, some had fancy engraving, and some displayed advertising. All are collectible.

Prices for nineteenth-century and later thimbles top out at about $250 for a very fancy one made from 14-karat gold, and descend all the way to $1 for a plastic one that advertises Singer products. Surprisingly, utilitarian thimbles made of brass or bronze from the fourteenth through the eighteenth century bring very little. The values for these start around $20 and rarely rise above $50.

One sewing item that is often overlooked because it seems so simple is the tatting shuttle, which looks like an elongated oval with pointed ends. Like thimbles, these came in a variety of materials, but some of the most desirable ones were made from sterling silver with enamel decoration on top, and these can sell in the vicinity of $150. Ivory tatting shuttles bring about $50, and ones with advertising on them are usually priced in the $65 range.

Certainly one of the most amusing sewing collectibles is the figural tape measure. Imagine, for instance, the head of a man smoking a cigar. If you pull on the stogy, out rolls a tape measure. A piece like this is worth about $200.

These tape measures became popular in the late nineteenth century, and they remained in vogue until the 1940s. Most of these were manufactured in Germany, Japan, or England, and were made in a wide variety of materials from celluloid and porcelain to brass and mother-of-pearl.

Some of these, such as one shaped like a German spiked military helmet ($250), are quite expensive, but others are far less pricey. A Japanese celluloid pig may be valued for only $35, or a German celluloid basket of fruit for $75. But a celluloid Indian chief with a tape measure hidden in his neck should be priced at $150, and an ivory acorn about the same.

Few households today have any use for a darner—a device used to mend rips and tears in clothes. Most vintage examples have a ball-, egg-, or mushroom-shaped head attached to a handle. Plain wooden ones are worth less than $10, and the addition of a sterling-silver handle only raises the value into the $65 to $85 range.

Recently, however, Joe was perusing an auction catalog and found some fancy art-glass darners that were quite valuable. One made by Steuben Glass in the early twentieth century was expected to fetch $500 if the glass was iridescent gold, and in the neighborhood of $600 if the glass was iridescent blue. An elaborate multicolored darner by the Durand Glass Works Company of Vineland, New Jersey, was thought to be even more valuable at $700.

Any discussion of sewing items should probably include at least a quick mention of the sewing machine itself. Every year we receive dozens of letters asking about these beautifully detailed machines from the nineteenth and early twentieth centuries. We usually tell the hopeful writer that the machine complete with cabinet and accessories is not very valuable because almost every home in America had one. They are by no means rare.

Most of these are worth less than $300, and they can be very difficult to convert into cash. There are, of course, rare sewing machines that have reportedly brought prices approaching $50,000, but these tend to be very early (1840s, '50s, or '60s), one-of-a-kind specimens that are unlikely to be found in the average home.

One modern machine that does sell well is the Singer Featherweight. In its case, in good working order, and complete with attachments, it brings about $500. It is a mid-twentieth-century product, but seamstresses (rather than collectors) seek it out because it is easily portable and reliable. The wood-and-metal folding table that came with this machine is worth as much as $100 if it is in excellent condition.

No foray into sewing collectibles would be complete without at least a mention of buttons. Yes, buttons. It is hard for many people to believe it, but there are single buttons that are worth in excess of $1,500 apiece! Of course, these are few and far between.

Nevertheless, expensive buttons turn up in jars and sewing boxes all the time, and if you find a button with a cloisonné design on it, its value would start at $450, and go up somewhat for the finer pieces. A shell cameo button—not unlike the cameos that are worn as jewelry—starts at $75, and prices often rise to the $500 level for the best ones.

Realistically, however, you can go through a 10-pound sack of buttons and not find one that is this valuable, but you could find many that are worth a few dollars each—and this can mount up quickly. Pay special attention to the buttons that are made from unusual materials—ivory, bamboo, celluloid, Bakelite, silver, glass—or have intricate designs or figural shapes.

Dresser Boxes and Perfume Bottles

The top of a woman's dressing table provides a fertile field for treasure-hunting. Here there might be mirrors with sterling-silver mountings, brushes with sterling-silver backs, or jars and bowls made of white glass with hand-painted or transfer-printed decoration, some signed "Wave Crest," "Kelva," or "Nakara" on the bottom.

All of these are the products of the C. F. Monroe Company of Meriden, Connecticut, and were made between 1892 and 1916. As a general rule, white glass is hard to sell, but these items are the great exception, and in recent years, prices on C. F. Monroe wares have been rising steadily. Currently, a 2½-inch-square dresser box brings $250, but a larger 7- by 8-inch box might bring as much as $2,500, depending on the decoration.

The Wave Crest, Nakara, and Kelva examples with richly colored backgrounds and elaborate, hand-painted floral decoration, or pieces adorned with representations of human, animal, or mythological subjects demand a premium price. Most of the pieces made by C. F. Monroe were hand-decorated, but some examples were embellished with transfer prints (discernible by the series of black dots that make up the outlines). These are far less interesting to collectors and command less money.

Similar wares were made by several other companies, such as Mt. Washington/Pairpoint and the Handel Company (famous for its previously mentioned reverse-painted lamp shades). Products by both of these companies are highly desired by collectors, and in many cases can be identified by the *P* in a diamond on the Pairpoint wares and an *H* in a diamond with the phrase "Handel Ware" on the Handel products.

A 4- by 6-inch box decorated by Pairpoint should fetch around $750, and a Handel piece of similar size decorated with carnations or some other flower will command about the same price. Carl Helmschmied was yet another maker of white glass dresser boxes and other items, which were often signed "Belle Ware" or "C.V.H.," and the H. M. Rio Company of Philadelphia, Pennsylvania, made Keystone Ware. These items can be just as lovely as Wave Crest et al.—and are perhaps rarer in some cases—but collectors are not currently as interested in these brands, and prices are rather disappointing.

Perhaps the most important clutter on top of the average dressing table is the perfume bottle. In recent years, these have become very collectible, and any perfume container or atomizer with more than a few years on it should be carefully preserved.

Joe remembers going to a dime store when he was a little boy and buying his mother a bottle of Evening in Paris perfume. He wondered why she never wore it, and only years later did he find out that it was because the perfume was more suited for removing the finish from furniture than for wearing as a fragrance (at least in his mother's opinion).

Joe was somewhat surprised when he found out that old Evening in Paris bottles are sought after, and the gift sets with multiple items are particularly desired by collectors. Prices for multi-item gift sets can go over $400, and individual bottles can sell in the $15 to $85 range, depending on size and design.

Although they start much lower (around $500), the high-quality perfume bottles signed "R. Lalique" can bring sums well into the thousands of dollars each, and other pieces signed by Tiffany or Steuben often bring similar amounts. The most expensive "R. Lalique" scent bottles are generally those with color, as opposed to those with clear or frosted glass. A green-tinted Fleurs de Pommier with a tiara stopper is worth in excess of $5,000, while a clear-and-frosted Grecian Maiden is worth about $1,500.

Any product signed "California Perfume" should be saved, and prices here range from $40 into the low hundreds of dollars for the rarer items. Caution should be exercised, however, because these items have been reissued in recent years. California Perfume was the predecessor of Avon, and it saddens us to say so, but the once popular Avon figural bottles seem to have lost much of their appeal at the present moment and are hard to sell. That situation may change in years to come.

Glass perfume bottles made in Czechoslovakia can be very attractive, but they are also plentiful. Prices for these start at $25 and typically go into the low to mid-hundreds. Be warned, however; a great number of new "Art Deco"-style Czechoslovakian perfume bottles are now being imported into this country, and many are being sold as "old" in antiques shops, antiques malls, and on the Internet.

A Parker Lucky Curve fountain pen featuring an entwined snake with "jeweled" eyes.

Fountain Pens

Fountain pens can be found in master bedrooms tucked away among the debris in dresser drawers—because very few people use them anymore. The first time a fountain pen is used, its value diminishes, and the more it is used, the more its value declines. Just the process of filling the ink bladder starts the downward process, which continues with every stroke of the pen against paper.

Name-brand pens are usually the most sought after, and this includes companies such as Parker, Montblanc, Sheaffer, and Waterman. One word of caution, however. Helaine had a client with a small fountain pen collection, and this individual was most proud of an early-twentieth-century Montblanc pen (first made 1910).

The client was convinced that the pen was worth a fortune because new ones are so expensive. It was very difficult to tell her that Montblanc started their business making inexpensive writing implements, and her example was worth only about $35. Quality (and prices) picked up at Montblanc in the 1930s, and it is not unusual to find a pen from this era (1930s, '40s, and '50s) valued in the $200 to $750 range.

Fountain pens are more collectible than the pencils of the same style that often accompanied them. Filigree-decorated pens, pens with jewel-encrusted snakes, and pens made from 14- (and 18-) karat gold often push past the $1,000 mark, and for the rarest, above the $5,000 mark.

Books

The bedroom is also a superb place to look for books—both paperback and hardback. Remember, always save the dust jacket on any hardback book, because destroying it reduces the book's value dramatically. Depending on the writer, first editions of twentieth-century fiction are much desired. Stephen King's first edition of *The Stand,* for example, is worth about $300, and the first edition of *Salem's Lot* brings more than $600 (both prices are for books with their dust jackets).

Anne Rice is another current writer whose first editions are worth keeping, and the boxed, four-volume first edition of her *Vampire Chronicles* is now worth $350. Some first editions by Tom Clancy and John Grisham are also valuable and collected. Keep in mind that first editions of popular or important authors' first books are also very desirable because, as a general rule, fewer of them were printed.

The first edition of Graham Greene's first book, *Babbling April* (1925), is worth in excess of $3,000, while his later efforts seldom rise above $750. The first edition of popular novelist Tony Hillerman's first book, *The Blessing Way,* is worth approximately $1,200 in pristine condition, but the premier printings of his subsequent efforts are valued between $30 and $500.

Little things can also make a big difference. The first edition of Ernest Hemingway's *The Sun Also Rises* had a first printing that has a mistake on page 181 in which the word "stopped" is printed with three p's instead of two. This book is worth $20,000 with its dust jacket and in perfect condition. In the second printing, "stopped" is spelled correctly, but these books are only worth about $1,400 in perfect condition.

Another thing that should be considered is that any book autographed by the author is many times more valuable than an unsigned example. A good example of this is the Hemingway *The Sun Also Rises* mentioned above. As we said, the first edition with the printing error is worth approximately $20,000; with Hemingway's signature, add another $10,000!

Paperback books printed between 1938 and the late 1950s are becoming more sought after and a few prices are hovering around the $100 level. The rule here is that the more lurid and/or sexually suggestive the cover, the more desirable the book.

Bedroom Furniture

The bedroom really is not a great place to scout for "home-run" furniture. Beds are generally fairly inexpensive and have values that start at $100 or a bit less and seldom escalate beyond the $15,000 level—and then only for examples that are very special or large and elaborately decorated.

There is a great deal of interest in some quarters for "tester" beds, which are two- or four-poster beds with canopies of either wood or fabric. The most desired ones seem to be those with wooden canopies that are fabric-covered on the inside. (This fabric-covered area is called the "sky.")

There are "half-tester" beds in which the canopy does not extend the full length of the bed, but stops somewhere near the middle, and "full-tester" beds with tops that are completely enclosed. It is hard to find a massive mid-Victorian full-tester bed for less than $6,000, and fine examples that are attributable to a maker can push past the $10,000 mark. Half-tester beds tend to be a bit less expensive.

Some of the most desired Victorian beds are in the Renaissance Revival substyle. These are usually quite large, and can be so high off the ground that getting into one of them can require the use of a "bed step." Characteristically, Renaissance Revival beds have very high headboards, and they are often decorated with panels of burl walnut, panels medallions, and three-dimensional decorative elements such as the heads of animals and/or people. Prices for these beds start at $3,500 and can rise significantly above the $8,000 level for the best examples.

It is important to understand that Victorian bedroom furniture normally did not come in sets. Bedrooms were usually filled with beds, dressers, chests of drawers, and washstands that harmonized but had not been made as part of a suite or group. Collectors are particularly interested in the Victorian Renaissance Revival dressers that are very tall and have candle shelves, glove boxes attached to the top surface, marble tops or inserts, fancy pulls in the shape of leaves or fruit, mirrored backs, burl inlays, and decorative medallions.

The least of these start at $2,500 and prices escalate from there to around $6,500 for better pieces. Of course, dressers in the Rococo Revival substyle made from rosewood with elaborate pierced carvings, applied rococo embellishments, and full marble tops might bring more than three times that figure if they are attributable to a specific famous maker.

Washstands were and are very popular in American homes, but they have made their way out of the bedroom and are now just as likely to be found in a living room or an entrance hallway. These pieces have survived in great numbers and their value is not as large as many people suppose. It is important that their backsplashes be intact and, if they have marble tops, that the stone be original and intact. Cracked and chipped marble is a big minus on any piece of furniture.

As a general rule, prices for washstands start at $450 for the simplest models made of oak with little more than a drawer, a cabinet, and perhaps a towel bar. Fancier rosewood examples with marble and elaborate decoration can bring sums around $2,000. Exceptional, high-style pieces attributable to a maker should bring more.

We receive a lot of mail about cedar chests from people who report that one has been at the foot of their mother's bed since the beginning of time, and they are wondering how much it might be worth. Many times these chests are quite attractive; at other times they are very plain or even unattractive, but in any case our response to the query is that cedar chests do not command a great deal of money at the present time.

These storage chests were made out of cedar because cedar oil kills moth larvae and is avoided by adult insects. Few cedar chests were made before 1925, and some of the best ones are signed "Lane" for The Lane Company of Altavista, Virginia. Only a small number of cedar chests are worth more than $450, and most do not rise above $150.

Another type of furniture that turns up in the American bedroom is Arts and Crafts, and although it is newer and plainer, it can be much more valuable than its Victorian cousins. A Gustav Stickley two-over-four-drawer chest of drawers with strap hinges and a swing mirror (#906) is worth $10,000, while a Limbert five-drawer chest with C-shaped pulls (#487) commands far less money, at $2,500. Most signed Arts and Crafts chests of drawers seem to run in this range, and even an unsigned specimen is just a bit less if it has good quality and style.

A Gustav Stickley two-drawer dressing table with swing mirror (#914) should be valued at $4,000, but the value for a Stickley Brothers dressing table (#9013) that features two boxes over two drawers, a swing mirror, and a gallery is only about $1,500. Despite its lower price, this piece has a little fancier look to it that may appeal to some of those people who find it hard to warm up to the severity and simplicity of American Arts and Crafts furniture.

Beds in this style are a little hard to find, and a twin bed made and signed by Roycroft is worth $2,400. At this point it might be wise to mention that twin beds are hard to sell in the current marketplace. A double bed branded with Gustav Stickley's mark should be valued at $3,500.

CHAPTER TEN
The Hall Closet

Among the clutter in the average hall closet there are frequently several boxes full of holiday decorations. Christmas is probably the holiday for which people accumulate the most decorations, and it is also the holiday that historically has attracted the most collector following, but Halloween is quickly catching up. Figural light bulbs with Christmas themes originated around 1910, and a bulb in the form of an Indian chief is worth $300. A cat is $100, and a Humpty Dumpty about $50. Joe fondly remembers bubble lights from his childhood, and a set of these sells for about $50.

Starting in about 1870, large numbers of fragile glass ornaments—formed in the shape of everything from angels and Santas to frogs and bulldogs—were imported into the United States from Germany. Today, an airplane is selling for $100, peas in a pod bring $450, turtles fetch $275, and a covered wagon brings about $45. Helaine says she stopped collecting these after she started breaking them faster than she could afford to buy the next one.

Papier-mâché figures of Santa or the anti-Santa known as "Belsnickle," the bringer of switches and ashes, bring considerable money. Later Japanese Belsnickles start at $300, while the earlier German examples can escalate into the thousands. Santa figures tend to bring a bit less because they are more common, but a really detailed piece with a nodding head from the 1930s should command $1,250 or higher.

In recent years, Halloween items have attracted quite a following. Many find the jack-o'-lanterns, witches, and

Late-nineteenth-century Santa Claus candy container.

goblins associated with the holiday to be quite evocative. Jack-o'-lanterns from the early part of the twentieth century (mainly the '20s and '30s) are bringing prices that start at $125 for a small, pressed-cardboard piece, and rise to around $1,200 for a larger, tin one with a paper face. Later plastic jack-o'-lanterns bring much less and range from $5 to $20 depending on their size, condition, and "look."

Masks, costumes, horns and other noisemakers, cardboard cats, trick-or-treat buckets, and all the other items associated with Halloween are desirable. Unfortunately, many of these items were made from paper and cardboard, and have not survived in good condition.

Luggage

Closets are great places to store old luggage, and while most of it is absolutely worthless on the secondary market, some of it is being used by interior designers, who might stack up several pieces, put a piece of glass on top, and call it a table. Of particular interest are old leather bags slathered with colorful and romantic travel stickers, and pieces from the 1920s, '30s, and '40s that have interesting colors and decorations.

Fine luggage made by such names as T. Anthony and Louis Vuitton can bring amazingly high prices. For example, a Vuitton shoe trunk from the first half of the twentieth century with twenty-nine individual shoe boxes tucked away inside sells for about $10,000, and a fitted gentleman's dressing case complete with razor, manicure set, and various bottles and brushes brings about $5,000. Interestingly, a lady's Louis Vuitton dressing case can realize almost twice as much, $9,000.

These prices sound awfully good, but they only apply to items that have not been sideswiped by a bus and have not spent the last forty years rotting in a damp basement. Top-quality luggage must be in top-quality condition or the value has been compromised greatly.

Golfing Equipment

In the back of the closet, behind the boxes of Christmas decorations and the luggage, there might be an old golf bag, and inside that golf bag there may be a real treasure. It is highly unlikely, but there may be something called a "feathery" golf ball, and these have sold for amounts in excess of $40,000.

Why? Well, they are early—at least pre-1860—they are hand-made, and they were so delicate that only a very few survived. The process of making them began when two circular pieces of leather were sewn to a rectangular strip. The resulting sphere was turned inside out so that only smooth seams showed.

Next, the maker took a crutch-like device with a rod on the end and began to stuff the inside with boiled goose or chicken feathers (no, we are *not* putting you on). It was an incredibly hard job, and the problem was that the maker had to get about half a gallon of limp feathers into that small sphere and seal it up to make a ball hard enough to use. It does not take much imagination to understand that after a few whacks with an iron club and a good soaking in a rainstorm, these balls were goners—to say the very least.

That is why they are so valuable. They can be recognized by the H-shaped seam, and by the fact that they are often stamped with their maker's name, such as "T. Morris," or "Allan" for Allan Robertson. One of these in good condition is a real rarity, and the huge price tag is not so hard to understand.

Any pre-1930 gold ball is worth money to a collector, as are books on golf, golf programs, golf prints, golf-themed ceramics, golf playing cards and postcards, and, of course, golf clubs. Pre-1890 clubs with wooden shafts, which are characterized by woods with long "noses" and hand-forged irons, bring prices that easily fly into the low thousands of dollars each. Lesser examples in fair condition start in the low to mid-hundreds.

To be valuable, steel-shafted clubs have to be of high quality from a noted maker, and there is already some indication that, in the future, modern, high-priced graphite-head clubs will be desirable. Unfortunately, many of these are being faked as we compose these lines, and that does not bode well for the future.

Fishing Equipment

Next to the golfing equipment there might be some fishing equipment, and the latter can be almost as valuable as the former. Lures, reels, and fishing rods are all potentially valuable if they have not been abused. In the unlikely event that you discover a 3-inch-long lure shaped and colored like a pickle with a split tail—and if it has black, bulging eyes, and three hooks hanging from its belly (two singles and one triple)—you might have a circa 1890 Heddon hand-carved frog worth about $4,500. The most sought-after fishing plugs seem to be those made between about 1900 and 1940, and most of these sell quickly in the $10 to $150 range. One hint: Unusual items such as frogs, crawfish, bugs, and spearfishing decoys are some of the most desirable—and most expensive—objects.

There are a lot of odd-looking twentieth-century fishing reels out there, but most of them are not worth a significant amount of money. Some modern reels sell in the low hundreds of dollars each, but the devices that are the most desired by collectors are the ones that were made from about 1800 to 1880, and these are rare and costly indeed.

Early fishing rods were long, cumbersome affairs made from wood, and few of these have survived in good condition. In the 1840s, Samuel Phillippe made a rod by gluing together long strips of bamboo, and the descendants of these handmade split-bamboo rods are potentially quite valuable. Look for rods with their own tubes or cases. Rods that have frequent wrappings down their length are early, and German silver fittings are a good sign. Some of these rods command fairly big dollars, but the ones found in typical closets are more likely to run in the $150 to $750 price range.

CHAPTER ELEVEN

The Attic

The attic is the proverbial place to store "old junk" so that it is out of sight and out from underfoot. Unfortunately, the attic is not a good place to store anything that might actually be worth something someday. Dry, roasting heat during the summer, damp cold during the winter, wild fluctuations in temperature from daytime to nighttime, and the distinct possibility of items getting wet if the roof leaks are all potentially detrimental to the well-being of objects stored in such a space.

We do not know how many times we have made the climb into an attic, only to find the contents completely ruined by the climate in which they have been kept. We may call this book *Treasures in Your Attic,* but we know that too many treasures that have been put into attics have turned to trash both because of the harsh environment and because of the outright neglect. If you have treasures or even items that may become treasures in the future, keep in mind that the attic is a less than ideal environment in which to store them.

Trunks and Their Contents

Some of the most commonly found objects in attics are trunks. Many people believe that the trunks themselves are valuable, but for the most part their value is less than $350 unless the example in question is pre-1840 or has some sort of unusual decoration. Both of these circumstances would be very uncommon.

Inside a trunk there may be memorabilia that might range from old photographs and letters to postcards and playbills. We have already discussed photographs at some length, but letters can be surprisingly collectible, and in some instances valuable. Historians are often interested in letters from war zones and letters that discuss important events from a firsthand perspective.

At the moment, most letters that are from after 1870 do not have a great deal of monetary value unless they have very important content or were written by a noteworthy individual. Examples of this might be an account of life among Native Americans, a letter from a survivor of the battleship *Maine,* the *Titanic,* or the Hindenburg, or perhaps letters from Margaret Mitchell that discuss what she was thinking as she wrote *Gone with the Wind.*

A friend of ours had to clear out an attic not long ago, and made a startling discovery. Underneath plastic tubes used to store Styrofoam "peanuts," she uncovered a notebook containing a dozen letters from Margaret Mitchell to a State Department official discussing copyright problems with *Gone with the Wind.* The notebook also contained copies of the official's reply, and the collection proved to be an insightful look into the problems that came with success.

In addition to their great historic and literary significance, these letters were quite valuable. No one knew they were there, and no one had tried to preserve them, but their monetary worth exceeded $50,000!

Many people who find a cache of old letters in the attic think that the stamps are the most valuable part of the letter but in most cases this is incorrect. Canceled stamps have only a small fraction of the value of unused stamps and, for the most part, stamps that are going to have any value at all were issued in the nineteenth century. Of course, there are some notable exceptions to this, but unless it has a printing error, is early airmail (meaning 1918 to the early 1930s), has a high denomination, or is a special usage stamp, the value of most twentieth-century issues is fairly limited.

Postage stamps *per se* were first used in the United States in 1847, during the administration of James K. Polk. Before this time, it was the recipients who paid for mail, and it is said that Polk was besieged with so much unsolicited mail during his presidential campaign that it almost bankrupted him. Once in office, he and his postmaster general adopted the system that had been pioneered by Great Britain in 1840.

Early American stamps have gummed backs but their edges are not perforated. Each stamp had to be cut or torn off the sheet on which it came. These stamps are called "imperforates," and they were made until 1857. If you happen to find an imperforate that has a 10-cent denomination, is black in color, and has the image of George Washington on it, it could be the 1847 first issue, worth approximately $10,000 unused, but only $1,000 used.

The 5-cent version of this stamp is red brown and has the image of Benjamin Franklin. It is worth less than a third of the 10-cent George Washington, and is valued at $3,000 unused and $350 used. But, beware: Both of these stamps were reissued in 1875, and these bring far less money.

Before the United States officially issued postage stamps, postmasters in places such as New York City and Annapolis, Maryland, issued their own stamps, which collectors call "postmaster provisional." Some of these can be extremely valuable, and if you find a stamp that may fall into this category, it should be checked out by a trustworthy professional.

Stampless covers, which are letters written before the advent of postage stamps, and were formed by folding the sheets of the letter in such a way that the back piece of paper became the outside envelope, can have a great deal of monetary worth. Colonial-period letters with unusual place-of-origin stamps or notations can bring prices starting at $1,000. Examples from more common places such as Boston or Philadelphia start at $150.

Stampless covers from territories that later became states are eagerly collected, as are stamped envelopes from such places as Alaska and Arizona mailed during the 1860s or perhaps a bit later. Such letters might command prices above the $5,000 level depending on the stamps used, the condition, and the imprinting on the envelope. Early letters sent during the mid-nineteenth century from Hawaii can also be extremely desirable, and prices generally run in

This letter sent from Honolulu, Hawaii, to San Francisco, California, via the steamship *City of Norfolk* is quite valuable and should sell for $3,500 at auction.

the $1,000 to $10,000 range, depending on how fine and interesting a specimen it happens to be.

Upon encountering a stampless cover or early stamped letter, one of the first things to look for is any notation that states that the piece of mail was transported on a steamship or sailing ship. Imprintings such as "Per: Steamer Isthmus," "China and Japan Steam Service," or just "Steamboat" appear on letters sent using these conveyances. Prices for early mail with these notations start around $350 and can rise into the low thousands.

Letter content can be very important, of course. Examples that contain descriptions of the Revolutionary War, the War of 1812, the various Indian wars, the war with Mexico, and the Civil War are always of interest. Letters about significant people and events are desirable, as are firsthand accounts of slavery. Please remember, however, that ordinary letters sent to ordinary people in ordinary ways from ordinary places have very little value to collectors.

It has been said that more people are collecting picture postcards now than any other single item. The heyday of these colorful cards began in the late 1890s and lasted to the end of World War I, and while more recent postcards have not been as avidly collected, some are now beginning to attract significant collector interest.

Pre-1918 picture postcards were popular because personal photography was expensive and not yet consumer-friendly. This meant that if people wanted souvenir photographs, postcards were the easiest way to supply the need.

Families collected cards as they traveled, and they also collected the cards that friends and relations sent them from faraway places. In many instances, these were kept in an album in the parlor and used as a subject of conversation when company came calling, or for reminiscences on quiet evenings with the family. Radio and television exiled most of these albums to the attic.

Postcards fall into two main categories: "view cards," which show a picture of a location or event; and "topic cards," which deal with specific subjects such as holidays, birthdays, and advertising. "Real" photo views of actual places such as landmarks in small- or medium-sized American towns are becoming very popular with collectors because, as a general rule, fewer of these cards were made. The most interesting of these "real" photo cards are currently experiencing a rapid upward movement in their prices, and they are most valuable in or near the places they depict.

There are rare postcards such as Alphonse Mucha's advertising card for Waverly Cycles (bicycles) that sell above the $5,000 level, but most postcards are much less expensive. The vast number bring less than $5 each, but there are certain types of cards that tend to be more expensive than others.

Mechanicals

These cards have moving parts: a peacock's tail changes colors as a wheel is turned at the side; a boxer's arm swings back and forth. Cards such as these start at $50 and go up to around $150, with a few rare examples bringing more.

Hold-to-light cards

These cards depict a scene that appears one way when it is viewed with light coming from the front, and another way when the piece is "held-to-a-light" and illumination is allowed to come through from the back. With backlighting, elements on the front seem to light up—fireplaces seem to burn, windows glow, the lights on a midway twinkle, and so forth. Prices for these range from $35 to $150, but like the mechanicals, rare examples can bring more.

World's Fair and Exposition cards

The range of these cards is fairly extensive, but the most valuable ones tend to be those from the lesser-known expositions such as the California Midwinter, Cotton States, and Jamestown (Virginia) events. These can bring prices starting at $150 and they can go up to nearly $500. Cards from the big World's Fairs, such as Saint Louis (1904) and the World's Columbian Exposition (1893), generally bring prices of less than $50 each with many commanding $15 or less.

Holiday cards

Collectors are particularly eager to find Christmas cards with images of Santas dressed in clothes in some color other than red, and Halloween cards signed by artists such as Ellen Clappsaddle. Cards by Loundsbury Publishing celebrating Groundhog Day and Labor Day are also desired because they are rare, and Valentine's Day definitely has a following as well. These cards sell in the $10 to $300 range. Cards for Easter, Thanksgiving, New Year's, St. Patrick's Day, and the Fourth of July are seldom valued at more than $5 each and some bring as little as 50 cents.

Advertising cards

These are some of the most sought-after postcards. All types of companies from International Harvester to Coca-Cola used picture postcards for advertising purposes, and some of the most valuable cards fall into this category. Earlier we mentioned that the Alphonse Mucha Waverly Cycle card was outrageously expensive, and some who find a Mucha advertising card for another product or a non-advertising design might feel that it should be just as valuable—but this is not the case. A good example of this is the Mucha advertising card for Warner corsets. This is a really nice card, but its retail value seldom exceeds $500. Coca-Cola advertising cards often bring in excess of $450, but examples from companies such as Cadbury, Chesterfield, Indian Motorcycles, Heinz, and Kellogg usually sell in the $25 to $125 range.

Famous-artist cards

Philip Boileau, Kate Greenaway, Raphael Kirchner, Bessie Pease Guttman, Rose O'Neill, Louis Wain, Eva Daniell, Brunelleschi, Arpad Basch, and of course the aforementioned Alphonse Mucha and Ellen Clapsaddle are just a few of the artists whose names attract collector interest. Usually, however, the cards that bear these names have to have something special about them to raise their value above the $10 level. For example, a Brunelleschi, Arpad Basche, or Eva Daniell card needs to be in the Art Nouveau style, while the Philip Boileau needs to have been published in England by Tuck. The best Louis Wain cards feature paper dolls and not his signature cats, and the best Ellen Clapsaddles are usually Halloween mechanicals. Rose O'Neill cards featuring the "Kewpies" are loved and highly sought after, but her cards featuring women's suffrage themes are as much as five times more valuable. Values for the best of these cards run in the $85 to $600 range.

Transportation-themed cards

Pictures of railroad trains, trolley cars, dirigibles, airplanes, automobiles, ships, and other forms of transportation are very collectible. A period postcard of the *Titanic* is worth around $750, while an image of a Dupont dirigible is valued at $85 to $100. Pictures of identified railroad depots complete with trains are worth $35, and a card featuring a Harley-Davidson motorcycle should fetch $50.

Linen finish

These postcards were popular during the 1940s and are distinguished by a subtle thread-like, or "linen," pattern that can be seen on the surface. These cards are still relatively inexpensive but they seem to have a real future with collectors. Some of the most desired are those that feature early motels, automobiles, tourist attractions, and political campaigns. At present, few rise above the $10 level and most sell in the $1 to $5 range.

Chromes

Popular from the 1950s to the 1970s, these cards feature bright, glossy photographs. Most are still in the 10-cent range, but advertising cards of this vintage are of interest—especially the ones issued by the automobile companies and airlines. Few of these rise above $4 at the current time.

Postcards with small pictures of flowers and portraits of ordinary people are not currently collected. No one is much interested in Uncle Jim or cousin Maude unless he or she is shown engaged in an occupation; holding a toy, doll, or teddy bear; or doing something unusual such as riding in a hot-air balloon. European views, birthday greetings, and other nondescript scenes have very little value on the American market.

For postcards, condition is everything. Tears, writing on the front, bent corners, postmarks that disfigure the picture, stains, and dirt all drastically reduce the value of any postcard.

Joe remembers going through some trunks in an attic in West Virginia. The family, bless their saving hearts, had not thrown anything away since the beginning of the nineteenth century, and they had been lawyers, politicians, and important landowners. Inside one trunk, there were stacks of documents written on vellum (parchment made from the skin of lambs, goats, or calves). They were all neatly folded but were disintegrating from having been in the attic heat for one hundred years or more.

As Joe carefully opened the documents, he found that they were land grants, deeds, and other legal documents signed by presidents Jefferson, Madison, Monroe, and John Quincy Adams, plus other instruments signed by several governors of Virginia, such as Patrick Henry. A few of these turned out to be copies, but most were genuine and the signatures were also genuine, not those of secretaries or assistants.

If they had been in perfect condition, the Jefferson would have been worth $7,000; the Madison, $2,100; the Monroe, $1,500; the John Quincy Adams, $1,250; and the Patrick Henry, $2,700. Unfortunately, the conditions in the attic had degraded the vellum and a few pieces were literally crumbling. This meant that the actual value of the pieces "as found" was 25 to 60 percent of the value quoted.

Now, let's continue digging through the old trunk. Perhaps we might turn up some old sheet music. Most of it will not be very valuable because it will either be in very poor condition or it will not be of a type that interests collectors.

Collectors are interested in sheet music that has interesting and colorful graphics on the cover. Images of modes of transportation (trains, ships, airplanes, and dirigibles), World's Fairs, comic characters, sports themes, military themes, beautiful women, Native Americans, and African Americans all command a premium.

Most of this collectible sheet music is from the late nineteenth and early twentieth centuries. Earlier examples are usually rather monochromatic and bland, and do not attract most collectors unless there is some special aspect to the piece. A good example of this might be "California Gold Digger" from 1849, which highlights the Gold Rush that began the previous year; another good example would be music from about the same time featuring the Christie Minstrels, a group of black musicians, actors, and dancers. Either of these pieces should be valued in the $300 to $350 range.

Most vintage sheet music, however, is somewhat less valuable and sells in the vicinity of $3 to $10. Prices seldom rise above the $50 level unless the item fits into one of the specific categories mentioned above, and then the specimen has to be in pristine condition, have great graphics, and be very rare.

In addition, look for Disney pieces, examples with covers by famous illustrators such as Norman Rockwell, "Ragtime" music (especially by Scott Joplin), and items with pictures of stars such as Ricky Nelson, Elvis Presley, Judy Garland, Al Jolson, Mae West,

This dress is from the 1850 to 1860 period and, in good condition, should be valued approximately $2,000.

and Frank Sinatra. Examples of early blues music are also desired, as are pieces that feature the Glenn Miller Orchestra, and anything with political overtones.

Digging further through the debris in an old trunk, it would not be uncommon to uncover some small white dresses that children wore in the late nineteenth and early twentieth centuries. These were usually made of cotton and were belted, and had at least a small amount of fancywork, such as lace trim or scalloped sleeve edges. If these dresses are not impossibly yellowed or falling to tatters, their value is usually between $150 and $250.

Among these dresses there might be an infant's long, white gown from the mid-nineteenth century. These are often called "christening gowns," and the best of them were very long and very fancy with a great deal of handi-work and lace. These are often treasured heirlooms, and the high-quality examples are valued between $350 and $800. Along with these christening gowns, it is not unusual to find little, white lace caps that sell in the $150 to $350 range.

If, in one of these trunks, you

are lucky enough to pull out a child's fancy outfit, complete with coat and dress, it should start about $750 if it was made before 1895. An adult gown, complete and in excellent condition from the mid-Victorian era, generally brings a price starting at $2,500. Prices for late Victorian outfits (1880s and '90s) start about $1,000.

We have written at great length about the value of designer clothes, and garments from the nineteenth century made by "Worth of Paris" can be exquisitely expensive. Charles Frederick Worth was the leading fashion designer of the day, and gowns by this maker start at $4,000 and escalate to around $12,000 for the best examples. Worth's earlier creations (the firm was founded in 1858 as "Worth and Bobergh") can command more.

These really old fashions can be quite spectacular. An exceptional lace blouse, circa 1900, might be worth $800 to $1,000, while a lesser model might fetch $300 to $500. Short jackets of this period should bring between $250 and $400, and ladies' long coats command prices above $1,000, depending upon their quality and style.

Rolled up in old trunks there are often lengths and pieces of fine lace that were removed from old garments to be reused at a later time on other apparel. These are potentially valuable, and while small or ordinary pieces may bring only a few dollars, larger, finer fragments may bring anywhere from $25 to $300—and a really fine, intricate, handmade specimen of usable size might be worth twice that or even a little more.

Wedding dresses from the first quarter of the twentieth century emerge from trunks with some regularity, and stylish examples that have not been remodeled several times to be worn by a succession of brides bring between $1,500 and $3,000. The higher-priced pieces usually have a great deal of beadwork and lace. The values of vintage wedding dresses from the second quarter of the twentieth century drop somewhat to the $500 to $1,000 range for quality ensembles.

Trunk rummagers are almost always delighted to find fashions from the 1920s, especially the beaded and spangled dresses associated with "flappers." Dresses from this extravagant era that were intended to be worn for dinner and dancing start about $750 and go up to $12,500 if they are by important designers such as Mariano Fortuny. Few, however, sell above $2,500.

Heretofore, we have talked exclusively about women's clothes because they tend to turn up in old trunks and attics. Men's clothes are found far less frequently, but despite this fact they are generally neither as valuable nor as collected as their female counterparts.

If, for example, the clothes worn by a couple while they were having their photograph made in 1900 had been saved, the woman's best, "Sunday-go-to-meeting" dress might be worth as much as $1,000. However, the husband's best "bib and tucker" (say, a three-piece wool suit with shirt and collar) would probably fetch less than $450. Some men's suits of this era do bring as much as $800, but that is rather uncommon. A man's three-piece formal outfit of the time is usually less than $500—minus the top hat.

We could go on discussing vintage and antique fashions, but the point we want to make is that quality old clothes are potentially valuable. Nineteenth- and early-twentieth-century garments in good shape are almost always worth investigating, and items made from luxury fabrics such as silk and lace should be saved if they are in acceptable condition. In short, any garment with style and quality is potentially valuable.

At this time, garments made from polyester are not valuable, and items of low quality and/or ordinary style are of little value as well. Remember, a tattered, moth-eaten rag is still a tattered, moth-eaten rag even if it started out life as an elegant ball gown.

Magazines and Newspapers

There they sit, scattered across the floor of many attics—an abundance of old magazines and newspapers. Despite the fact that once these items have been read, they are a nuisance and a fire hazard, it is surprising how many people have saved them in great heaps and piles. Too many estates that we handle are jammed with old newsprint and magazines going back to the late nineteenth century, and it is amazing how little of it has actual value.

For newspapers, the important thing to remember is that it is the headline and the news that was covered that counts. A two-hundred-year-old newspaper with ho-hum news is worth only $8 to $10, but if it is the *Chicago Tribune* of November 3, 1948, that reads "Dewey Defeats Truman," its value in good condition is $1,000.

We think everyone in the world probably saved the newspaper headline that trumpeted the American landing on the moon in 1969, but despite the fact that it is fairly common, its value is approximately $20. Another newspaper that everyone saved is the one that reported the assassination of President Kennedy on November 22, 1963. The interesting thing here is that the Dallas, Texas, newspapers with this headline are worth about $75, but the newspapers with the same headline from other cities are worth less than $10.

Reprints are a problem, and one of the ones that is most often seen is the *New York Herald* of April 15, 1865, which reports the assassination of Abraham Lincoln. Originals of this edition are worth about $500, but while we have seen plenty of old reprints, we have never seen the real thing.

In a way, magazines are much more fun to collect than newspapers because they have such colorful covers, and because the slick advertising inside is so beguiling. The emphasis here is on personalities, on cover artists, and, to a limited degree, on first issues.

If you saved the March 18, 1950, issue of *TV Guide* with the cover picture of Marilyn Monroe, and it is in good shape, the value would be in excess of $600. But if you happened to have squirreled away the first issue of *Playboy*, which also came out with a likeness of Marilyn Monroe in December 1953, that would be worth close to $3,000 on the current market.

A lot of people have stacks of old *Life* magazines piled up in their attics and basements, and some of these can have a small value. How much depends on who appears on the cover. Liz Taylor and Dick Burton from 1962 brings about $125, while Ted Williams from 1941 sells for about $50, Hopalong Cassidy from 1950 about $40, and Lucy and Desi from 1953 about $30.

Editions of *The Saturday Evening Post* with covers illustrated by Norman Rockwell can also have value—but not as much as many people suppose. His first cover, which appeared on the May 20, 1916, issue, is worth only about $50, and subsequent numbers with his covers sell in the $20 to $40 range.

The National Geographic Magazine, which first appeared in 1888, is another one of the magazines that many people save. If you have the initial issue, it is worth in excess of $3,000, and the next three editions are worth more than $1,000 each. But prices after that fall off dramatically. Magazines from the ten years between 1890 and 1900 are worth between $100 and $400, with the higher prices generally going to the older magazines.

Finding a pre-1950 *National Geographic* around an average home is a rare occurrence indeed, but post-1950 examples abound. Unfortunately, these are worth on average around $2 each or less, and selling them for even $1 each can be a daunting task.

In our continuing effort to point out that some very new things are very collectible and, in some cases, very expensive, we need to mention a fashion magazine that originated in the 1990s. Called *Visionaire,* only 6,000 copies were printed of each of its quarterly issues, and these have a $150 retail price.

Yes, that is very expensive for a magazine, and not many are going to be sold in the supermarket checkout line. To keep things in perspective, however, its issue #18 came in a Louis Vuitton case, and it is said that it now brings considerably more than $5,000! To demonstrate that this is not a fluke, the #20 issue sells on the secondary market for around $3,000.

Old Television Sets

Not long ago, Helaine was dragged up the stairs to an attic to see an old television set from the 1950s. It did not work, it was unexceptional in almost every way, and it was practically worthless. This information surprised the owner, who imagined that a forty-five-year-old television set must be quite rare and valuable despite the fact that it did not work.

It amazes many people to learn that television is pre–World War II technology, and that the first TV transmission took place in England in 1925. The technology was prominently displayed at the New York World's Fair in 1939, but sets did not start to become fixtures in American homes until after the war.

Pre-1943 televisions can be worth as much as $6,000, although there are models that sell for as little as $750. Early televisions can be distinguished by the fact that they were designed to receive only between one and five channels. Television sets made from the late 1930s to the early 1940s with small screens are the focus of many collectors' interests, but sets with cabinets made from other materials (metal and plastic) and with large screens are not yet in vogue.

Circa 1928 Western Television #V-00151. A scanning-disk television worth $3,000—note the tiny screen.

Color televisions from the 1950s are getting to be moderately collectible, but the ones that are most desired are the ones with screens smaller than 16 inches. Most sets from the mid-1940s through the 1950s sell for less than $250 each, with only a few approaching the $500 mark.

Collectors have more than a passing interest in a group of more modern televisions sets made by Philco between 1958 and 1960. Called the "Predicta" line, these sets are very distinctive, with picture tubes that swivel or are mounted as separate units on a cabinet. The H4730 Danish Modern set is now valued at $850 in good working order, and the H4744 Townhouse is valued at almost $1,200. Values for other Predictas start at about $300.

It is not known what will happen to the collectible television set market once the new digital standard is fully operational and old, non-digital sets will no longer receive a picture. Right now, collectors are insistent that sets be functional, but in the very near future, when there are no longer signals for these devices to pick up, the criteria may change, and age, style, and the presence of all the original components may become more important than whether or not the set is in actual working order.

Radios

Earlier we said that the first television transmission was in 1925. It may surprise you to know that radio technology was not developed that much earlier. Morse code had been used to transmit "wireless" messages through the air for some time, but transmitting actual voices into homes had to wait until the 1920s.

The first voice transmission in this country was from Brant Rock, Massachusetts, in 1906, and serious experimentation began in 1916 in a garage in Pittsburgh, Pennsylvania. When radio finally arrived in American homes in the early '20s, it was an instant success even though radio receivers ran on batteries, often required headphones, and were hard to tune.

Current collectors are most interested in "breadboard radios," early units that did not have cabinets, just exposed works; Cathedral models, which were originally called "Gothics," and had cabinets that were shaped like pointed or rounded arches; and colorful plastic or mirrored varieties. Large, floor-model consoles in unexceptional cabinets are still fairly inexpensive because they are too bulky to be collected and displayed in large number, but some table models are commanding nice sums of money.

Atwater Kent made a number of different breadboard units, some of which are very valuable today. Atwater Kent was originally in the automobile parts business, but began making radio components, and then entire sets. The company's breadboard model #5 was made in 1921, and its current value is over $2,500. Most of Atwater Kent's other breadboard models sell in the $750 to $1,500 range.

Cathedral radios, as they are now called, were made between 1930 and 1934, and their pointed or rounded arch profile says "1930s" to many people. A number of companies made these sets; an Atwater Kent model 84D from 1931 should retail for around $600, while a Majestic model 20 fetches $250.

Some of the most valuable vintage radios are the table models with bright, two-toned Catalin or urea plastic cases. Addison, DeWald, and Emerson made some of the most valuable examples, and the Addison model 5F (circa 1940) with a butterscotch and burgundy Catalin case, has a value in excess of $1,800. In yellow Catalin, the value of the 5F drops to $1,000, and in green and caramel, to around $1,200. Plain, single-color plastic radios are generally very inexpensive.

A Sparton #506 Bluebird mirrored radio. Watch out for reproductions.

A very special grouping of radios are the mirror-fronted ones made by Sparton. Their circa 1935 #506 Bluebird with round, blue mirror and chrome accents is now worth in excess of $3,500, and their #558 with a peach-colored mirror is worth more than $5,000. Exact prices for these and some of the rare Catalin models are a little difficult to specify because they sell so rarely. Therefore, please consider the foregoing values to be "ballpark" prices—or values that are in the right neighborhood but are by no means exact.

Also, keep in mind that the cathedral and mirrored radios are being reproduced.

Fans

While grubbing around the attic, it would not be unusual to trip over an old fan that had been banished to this no-man's land when central air-conditioning was installed. The first electric fans were made by Westinghouse Electric using a motor powered by alternating induction current (based on the work of Nikola Tesla).

A circa 1905 Westinghouse pancake fan. The name derives from the flat motor on the back.

Early models of this fan, which generally had a distinctive ribbed circular base and four 12-inch blades, are now worth $7,500 in like-new condition. Another valuable Westinghouse fan is the circa 1905 "pancake" fan, which has a motor that is relatively flat and round, thus the name. This fan also has four 12-inch blades, but they are shaped like the blades found on windmills. Valued at $6,000 in great condition, a pancake fan in very poor condition is worth less than $300.

Some of the best electric fans made in America were manufactured by the Emerson Electric and Manufacturing Company of St. Louis, Missouri, starting in 1891. Their first fan was based on a patent obtained by the Meston brothers for an alternating-current motor. Emerson's Meston fan had wing-shaped 12-inch blades, a fancy tripod base decorated with hand-painted flowers, and fancy bronze plates on the front and back. At retail, one in perfect condition with its original blade guard is worth $7,000. The same fan in poor condition is worth $1,000, and one missing major parts brings about $250.

Other nineteenth-century Emerson fans sell in the $3,000 to $4,500 range in pristine condition, except for the model PI 241, which is worth a little less than $1,000. Pre–World War I models #1020, 1120, and 5610 sell in the $150 to $1,800 range.

General Electric made its first electric fan in 1894. The first models had six 12-inch blades, but by 1899 they only had four. General Electric fans were very successful and few now command prices above the $1,000 mark. The exception to this is their early oscillating fans, which were introduced in 1909. The very large "sidewinder" fan with 16-inch blades (model 427220) is valued at $4,000 in pristine condition, while the smaller model 394950 sidewinder oscillator with 12-inch blades is worth a bit less at $2,500. In very rough condition, prices for both these fans drop below $200.

Most fans from the 1930s, '40s, and '50s found in an attic are priced at less than $100. A few approach the $500 level, but most sell in the $35 to $75 range in mint condition.

Almost anything might turn up in an attic. Over the years, we have found crates of sterling silver, Tiffany lamps, carousel horses, jars of money . . . and more pure trash than it is possible to describe. One place you should always explore is the rafters, because this is a favorite hiding place for valuables.

Seeking to thwart burglars, one of our clients hid the family silver in the attic and there it stayed for years. When it came time to move, he went looking for it and could not find it. Chances are that it is still there waiting for a subsequent owner to make a real find.

CHAPTER TWELVE

The Garage

The garage is a great place for storage. Out there, you might find an old bicycle, a few winter sleds, perhaps an old pedal car, or some Coca-Cola bottles from long ago. During estate sales, men in particular love rooting around in the garage. The things that they find are generally not too expensive, but the act of finding them is definitely the point—and the fun!

Tools

Tools are the main attraction, and among these implements there is always a following for examples made by Stanley. Imagine the internal excitement when an eager explorer finds a #212 single-handled scraper plane, which is valued at $600, or a complete set of No. 6 trammel points, which are worth $200. As a general rule, planes and levels are some of the most expensive tools found in a garage, but there is a market for everything from augers to miter boxes.

Much of the fun of looking through old tools is trying to decide the purpose and use of what you find. Manufactured tools with makers' names on them provide little challenge, but blacksmith-made tools can be tricky. Collectors love to find these hand-forged tools, as well as the unique tools that craftsmen, carpenters, and farmers created to perform specific jobs. Many times, these tools are worth more in speculation and conversation than in dollars and cents, because few of them are valued at more than $100, and most can be bought for less than $50.

Bicycles

The vintage bicycles that turn up in garages are not likely to be in good condition, and we have rarely seen one that did not look like it was being used commercially to grow rust. Bicycles that are falling apart and are in need of repainting are worth very little in their dilapidated condition, and a derelict example might bring less than $100 even if the same bike in mint condition is valued at several thousand dollars.

A sleek boy's bike from the 1950s might be worth $300 to $500 if it is in decent shape, and some high-styled bicycles from the 1920s, '30s, and '40s have been known to bring between $2,000 and $8,000 in mint condition. It was the lucky child who, in the 1950s, had a shiny red Bowden futuristic bicycle with chrome trim and white-wall tires. Its sleek lines were like nothing else on the street, and in like-new condition its value today is $4,000.

A boy's Schwinn Black Phantom with saddlebags and other accessories brings a little more than $1,500 in pristine condition, and a circa 1949 girl's Donald Duck model by Shelby can bring about the same price if it is in great shape. The Donald Duck model can be identified easily enough when you spot the head of that irascible cartoon waterfowl between the handlebars and the front wheel.

Pedal Cars

Pedal cars have a large following, and a rare one in like-new condition might bring as much as $10,000. Top pedal-car items include the *Spirit of America* "airplane," the 1935 American National Fire Truck, and the 1927 American National Buick Roadster. Lesser models from the 1960s start at $300, but for desirable models from the 1930s, '40s, and '50s, price tags in the $1,000 to $2,500 range are not uncommon.

These include items such as the Murray Station Wagon and the Garton Ford. Some restoration on these pedal cars is acceptable, but there is a great deal of debate as to how extensive that restoration may be. Many collectors want these to be as original as possible, while others advocate completely new paint jobs to make the cars look fresh.

Joe is fond of the 1955 model of the Bel Air Chevrolet. It is 38 inches long and as cool as its big brother. In restored condition, this beauty is worth $2,500. While Helaine likes this one, too, she is a little more partial to the 1941 Steelcraft fire engine, complete with wooden ladders. In restored condition this also should be valued at $2,500.

Oil Cans

It is amazing what valuable things can be picked up in a garage! Even some of the old motor oil cans may be worth money. Unlike the modern ones with boring graphics, the pre-1950 ones had wonderful pictorial images on them. One of the most interesting of these is a Marathon Oil can shaped and decorated like an oil derrick. In good condition, this circa 1927 item should be worth about $400.

Other vintage oil cans start at $10 and commonly go up to around $300. Gallon- and half-gallon-size cans are usually the most decorative and the most desirable. Along this same line, save anything related to gas, oil, gas stations, aviation, or motorcycles. Harley-Davidson items are particularly good.

Coca-Cola Bottles

We think that most people know that Coca-Cola-related objects are collectible, but how many of you know that some Coke bottles are worth $2,000? Right at the turn of the century, about a dozen Coca-Cola bottling plants used a straight-sided bottle with the Coca-Cola brand name embossed on the side plus the location of the bottling plant.

These are known as "Hutchinson" bottles, and one from Jasper, Alabama, brings $2,000, while a similar one from Chattanooga, Tennessee, sells for about half that amount. One Hutchinson variety has "Property of Coca-Cola Bottling Company" on it, and does not give the place of origin; it is worth about $1,500. Other pre-1916 Coca-Cola bottles sell in the $40 to $250 range, and after that date the prices fall off sharply unless you happen to have a large display bottle.

The 36-inch-tall, leaded glass Coke display bottle from the 1920s brings in excess of $10,000, and the various bottle-shaped lamps from the same era bring $5,000 to $7,000 depending on the model. All genuine, company-produced Coca-Cola memorabilia is collectible, but beware of fakes and reproductions.

Actually, items of all sorts relating to other soft-drink products should be preserved. Pepsi, Dr Pepper, Moxie, and other soft drinks have a following, and in fact if something in your garage carries an advertisement for a cola product, and it is more than a few years old, save it. It has a good chance of being worth money.

Flowerpots and Planters

Garages are great places to store old pots that once contained plants that have since become deceased or are on the brink of going to glory. We are always finding these pots half-filled with dirt—sometimes with the corpse of some poor flower lying in state—sitting on shelves and looking forlorn and valueless.

Many of these pots are Japanese from the 1950s and later, and if they are in the shape of some object—an animal, a vehicle, a building—they are now being collected. To be sure, they are not yet bringing a great deal of money (usually in the $10 to $45 range), but there is a growing interest in these because they are so cute.

Unsigned planters, jardinières, and vases could have been made by any one of a number of manufacturers, and it should be kept in mind that major makers such as Weller and Roseville often did not sign their products—especially those made before the middle 1930s.

Two commonly
seen marks of the
Nelson McCoy
Pottery.

This means that if you find a piece of pottery out in the garage that is completely unmarked, do not assume it is junk. It may be a treasure that just needs to be identified—or it could be commercial florist ware worth only a dollar or two.

The flowerpots or planters that are seen in garages often bear the mark "McCoy," for the Nelson McCoy Pottery Company of Roseville, Ohio. The history of the various McCoy potteries is more than a little convoluted, but suffice it to say that there was also a J. W. McCoy Pottery, which later became Brush-McCoy. This other company did not sign its products "McCoy."

We have seen few houses that did not have at least a piece or two of McCoy (that is, Nelson McCoy) pottery. Most of these pieces are not very valuable—no one is going to retire or send their child to college by selling one of these—but values in the neighborhood of $25 to $150 are standard.

A McCoy planter shaped like a goose pulling a cart is valued at $45, while a planter shaped like a fish (pink with green fins) has reportedly sold for as much as $500. There is a much-desired McCoy pair of bookends/planters in the shape of a bird dog with a bird in its mouth, which should retail around $200.

Currently somewhat more valuable than the McCoy pieces are the pottery pieces made by the A. E. Hull Pottery Company of Crooksville, Ohio. They were in business between 1905 and 1986, and they are famous for their commercial art wares made with a matte glaze. This was the preferred glaze at Hull until 1950, when a flood caused the kilns to explode, which resulted in a fire that completely destroyed the factory. When they rebuilt with modern equipment, they found that their matte glaze could not be duplicated and they switched to a glossy glaze.

One of the casualities of this disaster was a line inaugurated in 1949 called "Bow Knot." It is a very feminine line with puffy bows and pastel flowers. Should you run across the 12-inch basket out in the garage (marked "Hull" and "B-29-12"), value it at $2,500. The

12½-inch-tall vase (B-14-12½) is worth $1,800, but a more common piece such as a flower-pot with attached saucer (B-6-6½) is worth $300, and a jardinière (B-19-9⅜) $1,400.

The value of other pieces of Hull pottery have to be evaluated piece by piece and pattern by pattern. In general, however, examples with the glossy glaze are less desired than the ones with the non-shiny, or matte, glaze. Glossy, glazed items from the 1950s are beginning to attract more positive collector attention, and a shell-shaped planter basket in the glossy Ebb Tide pattern is $350 because of its large size (16½ inches long) and its attractive design.

A Hull basket in the Bow Knot pattern.

Some of the sought-after Hull patterns include Orchid, Magnolia Matte, and Woodland Matte. The price range for Hull pottery can be enormous, because a few of the newer pieces are still available for less than $20, while some of the more uncommon items can command prices into the low thousands. The most desired shapes are baskets, large vases, jardinières, wall plaques, and wall pockets.

Haeger is another pottery whose wares can be found languishing in garages. This company was founded in Dundee, Illinois, as a maker of bricks and tiles and began producing commercial art wares in 1914. The company continues in business today. Early wares are marked "Haeger," which is written on the crossbar of a large *H,* but, beginning in 1938, pieces started being marked "Royal Haeger" in conjunction with premium wares designed by Royal Hickman. Some pieces were marked with only a paper label, which often came off over time.

We mention Haeger here because they have made a lot of pottery over the years, but until quite recently collectors were rather cool. Now that is rapidly changing, and Haeger pottery has all the earmarks of being a future hot item! Prices are still fairly inexpensive (for the most part), but that should change as people start to collect Haeger more avidly.

Items to look for include pieces that have silver overlays, sculptural and figural objects, the Rudolph the Red-Nosed Reindeer planter, clocks, lavaboes (two-piece, wall-mounted washbasins with a water container above and a bowl below), World's Fair items, and pieces that contain music boxes.

Remember, when you start poking around in the garage, just because the flowerpots, tools, and oil cans have dirt on them does not mean that they are not valuable. In some cases, their value may be considerable.

CHAPTER THIRTEEN

The Garden

On several occasions, we have worked our way through the inside of a house without finding anything that piqued our interest—but the outside was a different story. The gardens of old homes are often strewn with urns, benches, birdbaths, and statues made from a variety of materials such as cast iron, bronze, marble, and concrete. Some of these are snapped up avidly by collectors.

An old sundial, for example, can be quite a find, since an eighteenth-century piece signed by an important maker and sitting on its original stone column can be worth as much as $10,000! Of course, unsigned late-nineteenth- and early-twentieth-century models bring much less, but good specimens from later periods might be valued in the vicinity of $1,000 to $2,500.

Most of the objects found in modern gardens and backyards are made from concrete, and they tend to be more cute than hugely valuable. The charming gnomes, geese, saints, pagodas, and other objects that pepper the landscape have only modest value—and that value is often more in the world of gardeners and landscapers than in that of collectors. In other words, individuals who are looking to buy these items are interested in using them, not in forming a collection per se.

People who are interested in these ornaments are looking for pieces with character, for pieces that are covered in moss and look like they have been around for a long time. There is a tendency to search for these items in the late winter and early spring, when thoughts and plans are turning toward the outdoors and the coming growing season.

It is rather amusing to watch people who are attending February or March estate sales running around in cold, desolate gardens or backyards, diving into bushes looking for lawn decorations. Oftentimes, their manic efforts are rewarded with the discovery of some piece that has fallen over and been unseen for years. Normally, this "find" is covered with a green patina (actually, "green slime" might be a better description), and if it is undamaged, it is laboriously hauled up and taken to a new home. Damage is deadly on these pieces, and any object with a crack or broken-off piece is almost unsalable.

In addition to coveting the charming figural ornaments, collectors are interested in modern concrete urns, benches, and birdbaths, but while these sell very readily, they do not bring a great deal of money. Most of the figures bring less than $200, and other items such as tables and benches fetch less than $750 for a set. However, some earlier sets and better pieces can go into the thousands of dollars.

Urns

A few years ago, Joe and a collector-acquaintance were walking down the main thoroughfare in a small town in Virginia. As they passed an old hotel building, they noticed a pair of elaborate cast iron urns on pedestals in front of the building. The urns were from the third quarter of the nineteenth century and, against Joe's strenuous objections, the acquaintance trotted up to the hotel with acquisition fever burning in his eyes. He offered the lady $2,000 for the pair but she turned him down flat.

This was a good decision on the proprietor's part because almost any pair of 34-inch-tall urns with fancy handles and a plain base is worth at least $3,000 if they are signed by the maker. These particular urns, however, were much larger (taller, broader, and more massive), had decorated bases and extravagant handles, and were signed by a Virginia maker that had made artillery pieces for the Confederacy. At the time, the pair was worth between $10,000 and $15,000!

Footed cast iron urns that do not sit on separate bases or pedestals can be of considerable interest, too. To be prime examples, they need to be large (at least 16 to 18 inches tall), be signed by the maker, and have decorations on them such as leaves and flowers. Such urns can bring from $5,000 to as much as $15,000!

When it comes to cast iron urns, collectors insist that they be in pairs, and prefer that they be signed by the maker. Unsigned examples usually bring one-third to one-half the value of similar signed pieces. Collectors also prefer pieces that are Neoclassical in inspiration or are decorated with elaborate Rococo designs, and are fairly rust-free. Specimens that have developed significant holes due to years of standing water are passed over.

Elegant garden urns made from other materials can also ignite a collector's interest. Pairs of white marble urns in the 30- to 45-inch-tall range start at $3,000 for nicely carved models and go up to over $10,000 for special pieces with elaborate decoration. Occasionally, similar urns made from terra-cotta turn up. A 40-inch-tall example composed of a neoclassically shaped urn with leaf and flower decoration around the rim and a pedestal decorated with a raised garland of flowers is worth between $800 and $1,000.

Garden Benches

What garden is complete unless there is a place to sit and contemplate the posies and peacefulness? Stone and marble benches from the nineteenth century with some carving or figural supports in the shape of lions or sphinxes bring prices in the $1,500 to $4,000 level. More intricate, stylish, and special pieces can bring sums over $20,000, but these are most likely to be found in public or institutional gardens or in outdoor spaces belonging to the very wealthy.

It is far more common to find a wrought iron seat in the garden than a marble one, and some of these from the nineteenth century can bring big bucks. Helaine is taken with the European-made examples that are composed of flat straps of metal arranged either

Mid-nineteenth-century metal benches such as this one are usually English or Continental European and are very elegant in their simplicity.

in straight lines or in arches and ovals, or a combination of straight and curved lines.

A mid-nineteenth-century long bench (125 inches) with a slatted seat, a back made from five lengths of metal with X-shaped supports, and curlicue arms is worth as much as $3,000. A somewhat smaller example (70 inches) with a back composed of pointed ellipses and graceful arches should bring $4,000 because the design is more graceful and pleasing to the eye. A pair of armchairs to match these pieces is worth somewhere in the $1,500 to $2,000 range.

All these pieces are deceptively simple and are the sort of things that homeowners overlook when they are trying to decide what has value. Although Joe recognizes how elegant these pieces can be in a restrained sort of way, he is a little more taken with the elaborate cast iron seats that feature dense, three-dimensional designs of such things as ferns, flowers, tree branches, and Gothic quatrefoils.

Those with interlacing tree branches and leaves start at $2,000 if they are in what might be called a "loveseat" size. Prices for the more common patterns start a little lower, around $1,500 for a 60-

inch piece with fern motifs, and up to $15,000 for an example extravagantly festooned with a Nasturtium pattern and signed "C B Dale" (for the English Coalbrookdale Company).

On average, prices for most examples of nineteenth-century wrought iron settees run in the $2,000 to $5,000 range. Be very careful when buying this type of outdoor furniture, because reproductions abound. Most imitations, however, are made from cast aluminum and should be easy to spot.

Statuary

From time to time, Helaine has been to homes with marble and bronze statuary scattered around on the lawn, and some of these statues have ultimately been valued at hundreds of thousands of dollars each. As might be expected, such pieces are not found around most American homes.

Lesser stone and marble carvings from the nineteenth and early twentieth centuries do turn up, and a large (5-foot-long), nicely executed recumbent stone lion should be valued approximately $25,000. One that is half that size and slightly less well-carved might bring only about $4,000, and still smaller stone lions made from composition stone are worth even less, at $1,000 to $2,000.

An important point to make here is that prices for these objects can be all over the board, and each piece has to be evaluated and valued on its own merits. Some of these items are considered to be art and they can command large sums of money, but other items are just decorative and are less valuable. Usually, an art object is signed by the maker, its design is aesthetically pleasing, and the workmanship is superb. Size is important as well. Generally, bigger means better.

Other forms of statuary that might turn up (and are less difficult to evaluate) include such things as lead figures of children or cupids. If a piece is from the mid-nineteenth century and about 45 inches tall, its value might be in the neighborhood of $2,000. Cast iron figures of animals are occasionally found, and a nice pair of nineteenth-century, 2-foot-tall reclining bird dogs should be valued around $12,000, while a 6-foot-tall pair of lead stags on stone bases should bring just a bit less.

Fountains

Some of the more valuable objects found in gardens are fountains. A well-carved marble example from the mid-nineteenth century with a *putto* (or cupid) sitting on a dolphin might sell for somewhere in the $7,000 to $10,000 range, but a 5-foot-tall cast iron fountain featuring a standing woman is potentially worth about half of the larger amount. Simpler nineteenth-century cast iron fountains seldom rise above the $3,000 level. Condition, again, is very important.

Other objects to look for in the garden include iron gates and fencing, stone or terra-cotta baskets of fruit and flowers, marble or carved-stone wellheads, columns and capitals, lampposts, lanterns, decorative cisterns, weathervanes, and cast iron or wooden shutters.

Part Three: Professional Advice

CHAPTER FOURTEEN

Buying and Selling

We have spent a great deal of time discussing objects found in and around American homes that are potentially valuable. We have been from the top to the bottom of a typical American home—not to mention outside it—and have called attention to many of the objects of value that can be found there. We hope that those of you who have come this far with us will think twice before you throw anything away, and that before you actually consider selling an object, you will have a professional appraiser evaluate its value.

Perils of Self-Appraisal

No matter how much you have learned from these pages, opting to perform a self-appraisal is not a good idea because there are just too many ways in which a nonprofessional can make a costly mistake. We have tried to impart a body of knowledge that has taken us at least twenty-five years each to amass, but there are numerous nuances that require years of hands-on experience to be understood fully.

Appraising a given item can require intensive research, and this can be much harder than it sounds. Joe tells the story of a gentleman who was sure he had a very valuable piece of glass. Since a relative had bought the piece from an antiques shop in the 1970s, he reasoned that the piece must be "old." He had done research on the Internet and had found out that Burmese glass (see chapter 2) shades from pink to yellow, and the vase he had did indeed shade from pink to yellow.

Unfortunately, he had never seen a genuine piece of old Burmese in person and did not know that the colors are very soft, that there is no demarcation between the two colors—one just fades into the other—and that real pieces should have a polished and unfrosted pontil. When Joe saw the piece, he immediately saw that the "bubblegum pink" was not authentic and that the pontil was frosted, so it was clear that it was an Italian reproduction from the late 1960s or early 1970s with very little value.

To the trained professional this was a quick evaluation, based on the experience of having seen countless real pieces and a boatload of spurious pieces as well. The owner, however, had labored mightily and come up with the wrong assessment because the pictures in the books and the images on the Internet were not good enough to tell him what the real thing actually looked like when compared to a very similarly colored reproduction.

This is a serious problem for the private individual who wants to learn about the objects in his or her possession. No amount of reading or Internet research can substitute for seeing an actual example in person. Reading and research are essential first steps, but they need to be coupled with the experience of seeing real items in museums and at antiques shows. But be careful—spurious merchandise does turn up at even top-quality shows, and knowingly or unknowingly, some dealers do have fakes and reproductions.

It is amazing how holding a genuine Tiffany vase in your hands, studying the signature, and noting the color and texture of the glass can bring all the reading and research into instant focus. Pulling out a drawer on a genuine eighteenth-century desk can make all the diagrams and descriptions you have encountered suddenly seem clear, and can make all the pieces of information you have read fall into place. In other words, you can read and read and read, but the light bulb may not go on until you are in the presence of the actual object and can examine it in detail.

Too many people base their valuation of an object on family history, and Helaine can attest that an unsubstantiated family history can lead a homeowner astray. Not long ago, when she was doing an appraisal clinic, a lady brought in a chair, sat it down, and announced that it had come over on the *Mayflower*. When asked how she knew that, she said that her family had arrived on the particular vessel and that the chair had come with them—it was cherished family history.

On its face, the notion that the chair had come over on the tiny and crowded *Mayflower* was unlikely, and on examining the chair it took Helaine just a second or two to spot that the piece was a late-nineteenth-century reproduction of a Jacobean chair. Helaine had to talk for quite a while about construction, design details, and signs of wear before the woman would even consider the idea that the chair might not be what it was supposed to be. This information was a little difficult for the owner to accept because the chair she had supposed to be worth tens of thousand of dollars was only worth a few hundred. That realization was quite a blow.

There are any number of reasons why family histories wind up being inaccurate, but it is not uncommon for homeowners who are self-appraising to give too much weight to these stories when they are arriving at their valuation. Professional appraisers do not make this mistake. They are there to provide an unbiased opinion based on data drawn from the marketplace, not from family pride or wishful thinking.

Lastly, homeowners often try to value their possessions by taking them to antiques dealers. In most cases, this information is free—and worth every cent paid for it. Recently we received a letter from a woman who had taken an item to an antiques dealer some eighteen years before. She was carrying her newborn daughter, and the dealer told her that although the item was not valuable at the moment, when her baby was ready to go to college, she would be able to sell it to pay for her child's education.

The woman went home and carefully put the object away until eighteen years later, when she wrote to us asking how much her treasure was worth and how she could sell it to pay for her daughter's tuition. Frankly, we were flummoxed because the piece was worth only about $300 at retail, and we had to tell this woman that the plans she had been making for her daughter's future had hit a substantial bump in the road.

As outrageous as this sounds, it is not all that surprising. We get letters and telephone calls every day from people who preface their remarks by saying, "I have taken this piece to every antiques dealer in town." The statement then ends with either "I have been to ten shops and gotten ten different answers" or "No one seems to know what I have."

This is not surprising, since most antiques dealers are not appraisers. Antiques dealers are in the business of buying and selling, and most of them function within a very narrow range. They buy items they know about and everything else is more or less an unknown quantity. An appraiser, on the other hand, is often a generalist and research specialist who knows and understands a very broad spectrum of items. He or she also knows how to find reliable answers about market trends and pricing.

Finding an Appraiser

Many of you who have gone with us on the room-by-room exploration of an American home probably recognize that you may have many valuable things in your homes. Some of you will want to insure these objects and protect them, while others will want to sell. To insure, the services of an appraiser are necessary; to sell, as we have just discussed, it is advisable to secure professional appraisal services as well.

How do you find a reliable professional appraiser? We wish the answer to that question was simple, but it is not. There are some parts of the country in which a first-class appraiser is simply not available. This is a fact of life. If you happen to be in one of those areas, you might find someone through one of the larger of the appraiser organizations: the Appraisers Association of America, the American Society of Appraisers, or the International Society of Appraisers.

The associations may be able to point you in the direction of an appraiser close enough for you to visit, or one who will come to you, or one who would be able to do at least some of the work from photographs. Now, there are some things that just cannot be appraised using photographs alone, and this includes fine art and jewelry, but as we can tell you from the thousands of photographs we receive each year for our newspaper and magazine work, appraising from good-quality photographs may not be ideal, but it can be done.

Locating one of these appraisers' associations is as easy as looking up a telephone number and address in a New York City telephone book, which is available in most public libraries across the nation, but there are other approaches to locating a reliable appraiser. The first thing to do is ask your lawyer, banker, and/or insurance agent for a recommendation. These individuals often need appraisers in their professional capacities and may be able to make a suggestion.

Also, call the local art or university museums. These institutions do not do appraisals themselves, but they are asked on a daily basis to provide this kind of service. In self-defense, most museums have a list of appraisers with good reputations that they can supply to those making inquiries. Few want to recommend someone who is not up to par.

It might also be advisable to inquire among friends to find out if anyone has used an appraiser who they felt did a good job. This kind of personal endorsement from a trusted friend is always worth investigating.

Once you have determined who is doing antiques appraisals in your area, an interview is appropriate. Ask to see references, and if there is an item in your home that you feel you understand, ask the appraiser to tell you about its history. If he or she can speak confidently on the subject and demonstrate why what is being said is valid, this is a positive sign. Do not, however, expect the appraiser to price the piece on the spot because pricing requires research, and answers off the top of someone's head may be irresponsible.

As we said in an earlier chapter, if at any time the appraiser gives any indication that he or she wants to buy your piece, or suggests that part of the fee might be discharged if you gave him or her some of your personal property, discontinue the interview and ask the person to leave your home immediately. It is unethical for an appraiser to buy from a client, and an attempt to exchange goods for services indicates that the appraiser is more interested in working for him- or herself than for you.

During the selection process, explain to the appraiser what you want. Specify either that you are interested in an insurance appraisal or that you are considering selling. Make sure the appraiser knows that these are two different types of appraisals (see chapter 1), and two different kinds of value structures.

How much will all this cost? It depends on where you are located, and whom you choose to do the appraising. In some areas, appraisers can be hired for as little as $50 an hour, but in most parts of the country the rate runs between $75 and $100 per hour. In large urban areas such as New York City, the fees generally are much higher and customarily start at about $150 to $200 per hour.

That is a lot of money, so you will surely wonder how long it will take to do the job. That is a good question to ask the appraiser before he or she starts working. The procedure usually involves coming to the home, examining the items to be appraised, and making notes. Sometimes photographs are taken. Then the appraiser does the necessary research, prepares a document with descriptions and prices, and returns it to the client.

If the initial visit to the home takes two hours, the final bill will probably be in the four- to six-hour range, unless an unusual amount of research is required. Should the appraiser see that the job will take more time than normal, this situation should be discussed with the client as soon as this circumstance becomes apparent to the appraiser.

Selling

Too many times, people decide to forgo the careful approach that requires pricing their goods before selling them, and they just haul them down to the local antiques shop or mall to sell. This sounds terribly foolish—and it is—but it happens countless times every day.

Most antiques dealers are not crooks, but they are human and they do want to buy the goods they will be selling as cheaply as possible. When unprepared individuals come into their places of business, the normal question that the dealer asks the seller (if indeed the dealer is interested in the item at all) is "How much do you want for it?"

If the seller answers that question with a sum of money and the dealer says, "Okay," and pays the sum that was requested, the goods now belong to the dealer, and even if $20 was paid for a $20,000 item, the seller probably has no legal recourse should he or she find out later that a "mistake" was made. *But,* if the dealer says, "I will give you twenty dollars" for that item, and the seller accepts, the seller may be able to recover his goods at a later date if he can prove the price paid was too low. The idea is that the dealer is an "expert" who took advantage of the seller.

At this point there is one thing that needs to be made painfully clear. If you have found out that the "retail" value of what you want to sell is $500, DO NOT—we repeat, DO NOT—expect to get that sum when you go to sell an item yourself. Realistically, you may expect to receive between 40 and 60 percent of that amount, which for a $500 item is between $200 and $300. There are circumstances in which you might receive more, but that would be a fluke or a lucky occurrence and you cannot count on that.

Estate Sales

Many times people find themselves in the possession of an estate that belonged to a deceased relative or friend. When this happens, the desire to sell can be overwhelming, and all too often the person in this position just calls in someone to buy the entire contents. This can be a terrible mistake.

Those who buy estates like this usually pay very little, and hope that they will uncover buried treasure that will bring them a real windfall profit. Estates should be treated like any other asset: They should be examined and quantified before they are sold.

If it is determined that there is very little of value in the estate, it should probably be sold as a whole to whomever will take it. On other occasions it may be determined that an estate sale is the appropriate means of disposal and many times the owners or custodians of the estate are amazed at how much money was actually generated from what they considered to be "junk."

An estate sale can be a wonderful solution for heirs who have no idea how to proceed with clearing out Grandma's belongings. The estate sale professional identifies, prices, cleans, arranges, advertises, provides help and security, disposes of unsalable items, and, in the end, turns over the proceeds of the sale minus the previously agreed-upon commission. People who have this done for them are often surprised at how much money the flotsam and jetsam bring, and how a dollar here and a quarter there can mount up to significant dollars.

The other option for people who need to dispose of an estate is to send every last item to auction. Here, we are not referring to the large international houses that employ professional staffs and print impressive, glossy catalogs. No, most of the time when estates go to auction, they go to small establishments often called "country auctions."

Estate Auctions

The "up side" to an auction held by one of these smaller auction companies is that the competitive nature of the process means that some things will bring more than they would in almost any other setting. It also means that because large numbers of items are being sold in a short period of time, some objects will be unappreciated and will bring less money than they should.

The "down side" to selling an estate at auction is that auction-eers prefer to concentrate their energy on selling expensive items and do not want to sell cheaper things individually. The items that the auctioneer perceives to be valuable will be sold separately, but the pieces with values of less than, say, $25 will be grouped together and sold as multiples or "lots."

This really is a necessity because time is always a factor at an auction. For example, if an auctioneer has eight hours to sell an estate, he knows that during that period he can sell 60 to 100 lots per hour, so for the entire day he can move only between 480 and 800 objects or groups of objects.

If an estate has two thousand items in it, that means that more than two-thirds of them will have to be grouped together and sold as one unit. Therefore, "big-ticket" items are going to be sold indi-vidually, while small, less valuable items are going to be sold as groups, and damaged items or pieces that are perceived to be insignificant are going to be placed into a conglomeration called a "box lot."

The problem here is that these box lots sometimes end up con-taining some of the most valuable items in the sale. Joe remembers perusing the box lots in one of these country auctions and finding six art glass plates. The auctioneer had presumed that they were recent reproductions because they were not signed. What the auc-tioneer did not know was that Tiffany did not sign their plates in or around the pontil but on the rim, and very discreetly, on the edge of each of these plates, there was a genuine Tiffany signature. The entire box sold for $85, and the plates alone were worth thirty times that figure.

These kinds of mistakes happen because, with a few notable exceptions, most of the proprietors of these smaller auction compa-nies do not know or understand antiques. They may know the basics of the antiques world, but their job is to sell, sell, sell. Mis-takes, however, can be made by even the larger auction companies.

Helaine was attending an estate auction held by a highly regarded company. As she walked through the house looking at the catalog and comparing it to the merchandise, she noticed a very nice silver pitcher that was listed as a "nineteenth-century silver-plated pitcher." It had an auction estimate of just $80 to $100. A quick examination told her that the pitcher was not silverplated, but American coin silver from the early nineteenth century and worth between $2,500 and $3,000.

After noting the piece's catalog number, she walked away thinking that she might be able to get a real bargain. When the pitcher crossed the block, the auctioneer tried to start the bidding at a mere $50, but hands flew up so frenetically that the bidding flew past $1,200 in a matter of seconds. At this point, the auctioneer looked up at the audience and said, "Well, I guess you know something we don't."

With this damning statement of ineptitude, the bidding progressed to the $1,500 level and Helaine got neither a bargain nor a coin silver pitcher. Luckily, this mistake did not cost the estate any money, but sometimes other commonly made errors do.

When choosing an auction company, find out how they treat their consignments. Sometimes these companies sell items that belong (at least in part) to themselves, and they will work and work and work to get good prices for these things, but will sell the items owned by other people at bargain prices.

Joe is familiar with one auction company that will take consignments and small estates, and on sale day sell everything belonging to the auction house first and then sell the consignments at the very last. By this time the bidders have spent most of their money, and the property belonging to other people brings far less than it should.

Prior to choosing an auctioneer, visit an actual sale and see how business is conducted. Speak to the auctioneer and find out how he or she intends to sell your goods; if he indicates that your items will be sold first or last, this is reason to be concerned. During the conversation with the auctioneer, make sure he or she understands your property and can present it to the audience in a positive way. Sometimes an auctioneer needs information that you have, and supplying it can help him or her prepare a way to present your merchandise to bidders in the best possible light.

We remember representing the interests of family members who were selling a very large and very fine estate. There was a chest in the living room that had belonged to the original owner of the house and had come into the home at the time of his wedding. The chest was Chippendale style but it was circa 1830, not circa 1770. The auctioneer took this fact and began to proclaim grandly to all who would listen that this was the "Samantha Jones Chippendale Chest," and told the story of how the bride, Samantha Jones, had brought this particular piece into the family at the time of her marriage and that it had been cherished through the generations. It was all absolutely true, but it left out the fact that this piece was made a little late to be called a period Chippendale chest.

On the day of the auction, the chest was hauled out onto the front porch with great style and the story was retold in a grand manner. When the bidding started, it began with a fury, and when it ended, the price was set at just a little less than $20,000—which was great for a piece that was worth no more than $4,500 at retail!

The point of all this is that before you send your possessions to auction, make sure that the auctioneer is working for *you*. Make sure he or she is competent, and has some basic knowledge of the objects that are to be sold. And make sure he or she has all the information you have and is willing to use it in a positive manner.

Internet Sales

Whenever we teach a class, there is always someone squirming in his or her seat, desperate to ask us how we feel about buying and selling on the Internet. In a nutshell, Helaine is not comfortable with the Internet, but Joe is all for it.

Helaine feels that the buying and selling of antiques and collectibles is a very personal activity. You see an item, you fall in love—and somewhere in that process, a lot of touching and examining takes place (expressed like this, it sounds like the story line of a particularly cheesy soap opera). To Helaine's mind, going to antiques shows and traveling around to out-of-the-way antiques shops may be the old way to buy, but it is still the best way, and selling should be handled in the same "person-to-person" manner.

Joe feels quite differently about the Internet, and thinks that it is just a logical extension of the mail-order business in which antiques dealers have engaged for decades. As he travels around the country, he has noticed that some antiques malls are beginning to sell their better small items on the Internet. In fact, some larger malls have opened up Internet departments. They photograph items, list them on their website, and then ship the pieces out after they have sold if they indeed do sell.

This can be a great boost to the malls because it makes it possible to "move" an item in a matter of days rather than having that item sit on a shelf or be locked in a case for months or even years. Having a website is like having several million customers walking through your place of business at all hours of the day and night and seriously shopping for merchandise without subjecting the premises to all the security problems and wear and tear on the linoleum.

Joe thinks—and Helaine reluctantly recognizes—that the Internet will change forever how antiques and collectibles are sold around the world. Antiques shops and malls that use the Internet wisely will be stronger and more profitable, but it will put other, more conventional antiques shops and malls out of business, because it will make it difficult for them to get good merchandise. After all, who would want to put his or her wares into a shop or mall that might take six months to sell them, when the same items can be sold in ten days on the Internet?

Many sales on the Internet are made through the auction process, but there are sites that allow items to be posted for sale with a set price. Usually, these sites belong to antiques dealers who are selling their own goods exclusively.

For the most part, the Internet auction format seems to appeal to individuals who want to sell their own art, antiques, and collectibles. Such sites as eBay, Yahoo Auctions, Amazon, eHammer, and Ubid are all out there taking bids on items—both new and old—that are owned by private individuals as well as professionals.

To get started selling on the Internet, the homeowner needs some equipment and determination. It goes without saying that the first thing required is a computer, the ability to use it, and access to the Internet. Once this is accomplished, the would-be Internet seller needs a scanner and a digital camera.

We are not going to go into all the ins and outs of setting up a scanner, using a digital camera, and uploading pictures, because the processes are different for every device, operating system, and Internet service provider (ISP). All we are going to say is that if you are going to sell on the Internet, you must be able to produce and upload a clear picture of the object being sold. This includes photographs and/or scans of the piece itself, of all its markings (if any), and close-up shots of defects (again, if any). This is critical. Buyers like to see what they are bidding on, and no photograph often means no sale.

The scanner is really helpful because it is a good device for capturing the image of basically flat items such as jewelry, flat silver, plates, postcards, books, and the like. When scanning a flat piece, try putting a square of colorful cloth under the item before starting the scan. The finished image will have an attractive backdrop that will make the picture look like it was taken by a professional and the object look like it came from an upscale store.

When all the equipment is hooked up and you understand how to use it, choose a site for merchandising your items and become a registered seller. Although the procedures and rules differ from site to site, this is usually an easy process. Generally, however, it does require a credit card so that the charges and commissions associated with the site can be charged to you automatically. Often, these charges consist of a listing fee and a percentage of the amount for which the object eventually sells. Listing fees are generally modest and the percentages reasonable, and selling on the Internet is amazingly cost-effective. Of course, if the item does not sell there is no percentage charged, but you do pay the listing fee no matter what.

Next, decide what you want to sell. The best items are usually those with name recognition, such as the products of Roseville, Tiffany, Harmony Kingdom, Wedgwood, and Heisey. It is always best to choose pieces that fall into categories that have a strong collector following. Esoteric objects often do not do well, but sometimes that unappreciated "mystery" piece can take off and bring a really high price.

Try to choose objects that do not have a tremendous value. Most sales on the Internet are under $100, and it can be difficult to break the $2,000 barrier. Stories of items selling for tens of thousands of dollars are told and retold, but, realistically, sales of this magnitude are uncommon and the odds are against you. Although some professional dealers and upscale galleries do sell expensive items all the time, at the current moment the Internet seems to work best for low- to medium-priced goods. In many cases, upper-echelon items need to be sold in other venues where the items can be carefully examined.

It is also a good idea to choose objects that are not too large. Furniture can be a real problem, but they are not the only bulky objects that can present a challenge when they need to be shipped. The largest Internet site, eBay, now allows for regional listings, which means that items are offered only in a limited geographic area so that pickup or delivery is a feasible option. Keep in mind that many conventional shippers have size limitations and you need to know what they are before you begin selling.

Internet buyers are very sensitive to damage, and if you decide to offer a less-than-perfect piece for sale, be sure to note the damage in your description with great care. If the decoration is rubbed, say so. If there is a teeny chip on the base or inside a lip that cannot be seen, say so. If there are scratches, say so. If possible, show the problem in a photograph or scan. If you do not do this scrupulously, the merchandise probably will be refused by the buyer and returned to you.

After you have chosen the objects you want to put on the Internet, descriptions have to be written and sales strategies need to be decided upon. Before you begin this process, please be careful to have your facts right. A large percentage of the items on the Internet are described incorrectly, sometimes so incorrectly that they prevent a sale from being made.

The description of the item needs to be informative, not fulsome. Control the urge to gush and to pile words like "unique," "fabulous," "glorious," and "incredible" together into a conglomeration that can only be read as a self-serving overstatement. These words are overused and are more likely to generate a derisive response from buyers than a positive one.

Yes, of course you should describe your piece very positively, but do not go so far as to make people giggle when they match the description to the article being sold. Tell the story correctly and let the object being sold speak for itself. Be sure to include the material the item is made from (glass, pottery, porcelain, wood, silver, cream cheese, whatever), its size, any marks it might have, its condition (and this includes repairs), its provenance (previous ownership history), age, and any references found in collecting literature.

At this point, the piece needs either a title or a concise description that will appear on the website's directory and will serve as a means for customers to find your listing. This phrase can only be about 45 characters long at most, and it needs to impart the most significant and compelling facts. Something like "Tiffany, gold Favrile vase, signed" or "Rookwood pitcher, artist-signed, dated 1908" should do the trick. The big selling words, "Tiffany" and "Rookwood," are up front, and the rest of the information tells the shopper what to expect. Again, superfluous words like "fabulous" are left out of this brief entry.

From there you need to decide whether or not to put a reserve on the piece to be sold. A reserve is the amount of money the bidding must reach before an item will actually sell. This is really the figure that the seller is willing to take for his or her property, and setting a reserve prevents a $1,000 item from selling for $5.

When setting a reserve, be realistic. Despite the widely held view that everything sells for a lot of money on the Internet, the truth is that this is primarily a wholesale venue. Items usually sell around their "fair market value" (see chapter 1), normally 40 to 60 percent of the retail value. This means that an object that is "worth" $1,000 will most likely sell in the $400 to $600 range, and if the seller is serious about selling the merchandise, $400 is a reasonable reserve.

The amount of the reserve is generally not divulged to the bidders, but some sellers reveal it in their descriptions and others will supply the information to potential buyers who ask via e-mail. Joe likes the e-mail approach, but he knows that some sellers protect the amount of their reserve as if it were a state secret and will snap the head off anyone who asks. Buyers like to know what the reserve is because if it is too high there is no point in bidding.

Some sellers decide not to reserve their items, especially if they feel they may only have a modest value. They protect themselves by setting an opening bid that covers their expectation. Opening bid requirements of $5 to $100 with no reserve tell the buyer exactly what is required to buy the item.

Buyers are often annoyed if the bidding on items with high reserves start at $1. Sellers sometimes designate low opening bids because sites often base their listing fee on this amount—the lower the opening bid, the lower the fee. This is a false economy because it saves only 25¢ to $2 at most and is viewed very negatively by buyers.

The last things that need to be decided upon when you embark upon an Internet sale are the business details that need to be part of your listing: the way you want to be paid, the fact that the cost of shipping and insurance are extra (that is, the responsibility of the buyer), and the time frame in which you expect payment. Method of payment is generally personal check or money order, but there is a movement by some sellers toward using services such as "BidPay," "Billpoint," or "PayPal," which allow buyers to use their credit cards.

The buyer pays the service for the item and any charge the service might have, and the service pays the seller the full amount immediately—but sellers must subscribe to one of these before they can avail themselves of this convenience. Some sellers accept credit cards on their own, but it is hard for private individuals to make the necessary arrangements with a financial institution to take plastic money.

You should state in your listing that you will hold an item sold by personal check for ten days or until the check clears the bank, but money order payment will get immediate shipment. On occasion, someone overseas may want to buy an item you have for sale. Payment in this instance is done either by one of the services listed above (BidPay, etc.) or by international money order, which is available in this country at the main branch of your post office—but the foreign buyer will know how this is done in his or her country.

Funds should always be tendered as U.S. dollars. Also, for overseas sales, it will be necessary to go to the post office to find out precisely what the shipping costs will be. Joe remembers selling a $5 item to a gentleman in Japan. The shipping amounted to $27!

One last word on shipping: We think it is best to list the shipping costs with the description of the item. This is because some buyers suspect that some sellers charge huge shipping costs if the item being sold does not bring as much as the seller hoped. We have heard of several instances in which this did seem to be the case, and in order to allay buyers' fears, it is a good idea to be upfront with these add-on costs. Remember, the buyer should pay for the shipping insurance, too.

The last thing to do before the sale begins is to choose how long you want it to run. One theory is that the longer the run, the more people will see your listing. This may be true, but long runs of around thirty days tend to bore buyers, who can lose interest or just forget when the sale closes. Five to ten days is a better length. It is always a good idea to have sales end on a weekend at a time of day or evening when West Coast buyers can be at their computers. This can be critical.

Once an item sells, it is the responsibility of the seller to e-mail the buyer immediately. Send congratulations on being the winning bidder, and give the address where the funds are to be sent. One good trick is to ask the winning bidder to acknowledge your e-mail so that you will know that you are communicating. Sometimes the winning bidder just mails the check or money order and the seller has no idea if the transaction is complete until the funds arrive. Asking for an acknowledgment cuts down on anxiety, and provides you with further assurance that you have reached the buyer and all is well.

Shipping the antique to the buyer is not like sending a fruitcake to Aunt Maude in Albuquerque. First, wrap the item in some soft, non-abrasive tissue, then wrap it in a layer of bubble wrap and tape it so that this cushioning does not shift. Next, put it in a box with Styrofoam peanuts and tape the box shut. Finally, put this box into a larger box with more Styrofoam peanuts and seal that. Use U.S. Postal Service–approved tape and boxes whenever possible. The U.S. Postal Service may supply the boxes and tape for free if you send the package via Priority Mail.

When choosing a carrier to deliver your package, remember that some companies (such as UPS) do not accept antiques or one-of-a-kind items. Do not ship with a company that has these restrictions, because if a one-of-a-kind or antique item gets damaged, the company has every right not to honor your claim.

When the buyer receives the package from you, he or she has the right to refuse it and return it to you if it is not as advertised or has flaws that were not disclosed. We feel that a buyer should be able to return any item for any reason within a three-day period with no questions asked. There are those who disagree, but if online selling is going to prosper, this policy will have to be adopted for buyers to feel comfortable about buying. The accepted procedure is that the buyer returns the merchandise, then you return the funds.

If an item does not sell, do a little re-evaluation. Make sure your description is right and your reserve is not too high. Then give it another try. There are literally millions of items on the Web and it is easy for one not to be noticed. We are surprised at how often an item that did not sell the first time around will find a buyer right away the second time around.

Buying

The emphasis of *Treasures in Your Attic* has been on objects that people already own, but individuals who own antiques and collectibles often want to buy more items. Those of us who are interested in this sort of thing tend to be eternal—some say compulsive—shoppers.

Shopping for antiques, however, can require some skill, and it is nice to know the rules of the game. We have some friends—a married couple—who love to shop for antiques. They also love to play a game while they are doing it that they call "good cop, bad cop."

When they go into a shop and see something they like, the wife becomes the "good cop" and the husband becomes the "bad cop." She admires the piece while he complains that it is "too big," "more money than we can afford," "not the right size to fit in the living room," or whatever.

While the husband is carping and trying to drag his long-suffering spouse to the car, the wife is smiling sweetly at the owner and praising the item with which she has "fallen in love." She says, "Maybe if you will take a bit less, I can convince him to buy it for me." Sometimes the feuding couple goes outside and talks by the car, and then the "good cop" returns for one last look. Many times, the dealer offers a really good price to the abused and put-upon wife, and the husband "reluctantly" shells out the money. Then they load the item into the car while trying not to giggle until they are safely out of sight.

We do not recommend this particular psychodrama, but shoppers try similar tactics every day. One approach that is often attempted is one that should never be used. A customer goes into a shop, finds an item that he or she is interested in, and begins to belittle it: "It's the wrong color," "It's ugly," "Too bad it isn't just a tad smaller," and so on.

The purpose may be to get a better price, but antiques dealers are not stupid and they know that a customer who really found an item to be unsightly or unsuitable would not want to buy it a few moments later even at a reduced price. This tactic makes antiques dealers angry. Most of them really like their merchandise, and to have it besmirched in an effort to get a better price is like waving a red flag at a bad-tempered bull.

Joe has a good friend who is an antiques-show dealer, and Joe remembers hearing him talk about sitting in his booth at an antiques show and watching as a lady and her friend approached. As the woman walked down the aisle, she would turn to her friend, point at an object, and say, "I gave that to my maid," or, "I wouldn't have that tacky thing in my house." When she came to the booth with Joe's friend in it, she stopped and looked at a very nice piece of American porcelain. She looked at the $500 price tag, turned to her friend, and said, "I threw that away!" Joe's friend casually looked up and said, "Well, *now* you know how stupid you were!" The lady left in a huff, but the point is that customers should not denigrate merchandise to antiques dealers—they do not react well at all to such treatment.

When shopping in an antiques store, it is always a good idea to get to know the owner. Ask him or her to tell you about the merchandise, because this is a great way to learn about antiques and it is also a great way to form a relationship that may lead to your getting first choice of items and a better price, too, as new items come into the shop.

In an antiques shop, antiques mall, or at an antiques show, it is wise to remember that dickering is a gentle art form, not a type of demolition derby. Making an offer at a shop or show is a fairly common way of doing business, but if the piece you are interested in is marked $1,000, do not start the process by offering the dealer $100. This is an insult, and a tactic not destined to produce a good result.

Start with a reasonable sum. On a $1,000 item, $700 might be a good start, and you could reasonably hope to agree somewhere in the $800 to $850 range. One important point: Do not dicker with a dealer unless you intend to buy once a price is agreed upon. Nothing irritates a dealer more than to go through the process of arriving at a price, only to have the customer walk off with an airy wave of the hand and an "I'll think about it." If you do this, do not expect the dealer to honor the price he or she originally gave you, and do not expect the dealer to negotiate prices with you again.

At an antiques mall, you can usually get a 10 percent discount unless there is an extenuating circumstance, such as discounts given only for items priced over $50, or discounts not given on purchases by credit card. If you want a bigger discount—and 20 percent is about the best you can expect—ask the mall to try and call the dealer who owns the merchandise you are contemplating and make an offer directly to the dealer. This sometimes works very nicely.

At an antiques show, ask politely, "Is that your best price?" Usually that query will get a discount of up to 20 percent, but on occasion the dealer will say that the price is firm. At an antiques show it is a good idea to admire the piece you are interested in and talk to the dealer. Make it clear that you like what you are seeing, and many times the dealer will give you a better price because there is a sense that the item is going someplace where it will be appreciated.

There are usually two great times to buy at an antiques show: before it opens, and just before it closes. Before a show opens, the dealers are a little apprehensive, and many of them want to make a sale as a kind of good luck omen. They want to start their show off right, and they are ready to sell.

This is the also the moment when all the bargains are still available, and there is a real possibility of finding an unrecognized treasure. There are many people who believe that there are no bargains at antiques shows, but nothing could be further from the truth. Even at the best shows bargains turn up, and the best time to find them is when the dealers are setting up their booths.

Many shows do not allow early buying, but those that do can be a buyer's paradise. The Scott show in Atlanta, Georgia (and Columbus, Ohio), is a great example. Early in the morning when the trucks begin to roll onto the floor, there is always a dedicated crowd of collectors and dealers who congregate around the tailgates as the merchandise comes down onto the floor. The selling is always brisk, and the bargains can be incredible.

If there is a show in your area, check to see if it allows early buying or if there is a preview party. It may cost more to get in before the general public, but this is prime buying time and well worth the extra cost if you are a serious collector.

There is a legend that says that prices get better when an antiques show is about to close. There is some truth to this, but it can be very hit-or-miss. Dealers who are desperate for cash because they have had a bad show (or a series of bad shows) might sell at bargain-basement prices, but this will be true of only a small percentage of the exhibitors. Some dealers will sell things cheaply at the end of a show because they do not want to pack them up and take them home. Usually these items are too fragile, too bulky, or too different from the rest of the dealer's stock, and the dealer just wants to make them go away.

Earlier, we discussed selling at auction, but buying at auction can be even more of a challenge. Auctions can be very exciting places, with all the exotic merchandise, the milling crowds, and the palpable hope that goodies will be found and bargains will be had by all. This festive atmosphere can mask the reality that serious business is being conducted. Many auction-goers do not understand that when the auctioneer stands up before the crowd and states that, "Everything is sold as is, where is, with no warranties," he or she is establishing a legal contract between the seller and the audience as buyer.

This means that if a damaged piece is sold, it is the responsibility of the buyer to know that the piece is damaged. This also means that no guarantee is provided that any piece of merchandise is authentic (unless specifically guaranteed from the podium or in a catalog), and it means that the buyer must remove his or her purchases immediately after the end of the sale. At an auction the buyer is on his or her own, and the auction house's obligation is to sell to the highest bidder and not to misrepresent anything knowingly.

The most important thing to do at an auction is to inspect everything carefully before you bid on it. Before the sale there is always a preview, and buyers need to go and diligently examine every item that they may want to bid on and make notes as to condition and how much they are willing to pay for the item. The first rule of auction-going is *never* to bid on anything you have not inspected.

Joe recalls with some chagrin going to an auction and seeing a nice-looking armchair go up for sale. He had not noticed it before the auction, but it looked very attractive from where he was standing and the bidding was very low. He bought the piece, and subsequently went to look it over. What he found on close inspection was a poor, bedraggled thing with one arm completely broken off and a leg hanging on by a splinter. It was his fault and his loss.

Once you have made up your list of what you want to buy, it is vital that you pay attention to it during the heat of bidding. Bid only on items that are on the list, and bid only the amounts that you decided on beforehand. Some items may be "must-haves," and on these it is permissible to go above the noted price, but by no more than 20 percent. If the bidding goes that much above what you initially wanted to pay, you may have underestimated the value of the piece, but it is still time to stop bidding. Getting carried away is not in your best interest.

There are certain bidding techniques that may help you to be successful at an auction. The auctioneer will usually start the process by asking for a high sum, usually the amount that he or she thinks the item is worth. He or she expects the bidding actually to start at a mere fraction of this amount, but occasionally the auctioneer will make a mistake in assessing the value of the piece. If the item happens to be something you want, and if the initial price asked by the auctioneer is within your range, bid it. This is called a "preemptive bid," and it may so shock the audience and the auctioneer that it will be the one and only bid.

This works best on expensive items that may have attracted a lot of pre-sale interest. If it works (and it is risky), this tactic may be the only way to get the piece for a reasonable price. If it does not work, the audience will jump on this bid and the price will soar to the moon and beyond.

Another tactic that sometimes works is called "jump bidding." Auction prices tend to escalate at set dollar intervals. Each successive bid must be $5, $10, $25, $100, or $1,000 greater than the last one. If there is an item you want and the bidding has started low and is going up rapidly in $5 (or so) increments, give the auctioneer a $25 or $50 jump bid. If someone comes back with another $5 bid, jump it again. Do this firmly and with a determined look. This usually slows the bidding and may end it quickly in your favor. Of course, this only works within the price perimeter you set for yourself before the bidding started.

Bidding can sometimes seem to take a very long time, and as it progresses to higher levels, it can slow down. Couples begin to confer, asking, "Do you really want to spend that much on that?" If you are committed to the piece on the block, every time the conferring couple makes a bid, do not give them even a second to catch their breaths. Fire a bid right back and make them confer again. The conferring couple will usually surrender fairly quickly.

One last thing you might try is *not* bidding on an item until the very last second. When the action starts to flag, jump in. This serves two purposes: Your bids do not contribute to the escalation of the price, and the new bid discourages the person who thought he or she just about had the item bought.

If buying at a live auction is a challenge, buying at an Internet auction can be even more daunting. The very first thing you have to keep in mind is that much of the information in the listings is either incorrect or overblown. As we scroll through the merchandise offered on an Internet auction, we are amazed at the amount of misinformation that is there, and it is obvious that in many cases, the seller has no idea of what he or she is selling.

The Internet really is not an ideal place for novices to buy because purchasing objects from a photograph and description can be very tricky even for a seasoned veteran. There is too much margin for error, and the only people who should be buying on the

Web are those who know what they are looking for and what it actually looks like when they find it. If you do not have a very firm grasp of what the fakes and reproductions within a category look like, this is just a bad place to shop. Novices who do shop on the Web should start small and work their way up to bigger purchases as their experience and knowledge grows.

Before buying an expensive item on the Internet, you might want to ask the seller if he or she will approve the use of an escrow service. How this works is that the buyer pays the escrow company for the purchase, and then the seller ships the merchandise. When the buyer receives the merchandise and finds it to be satisfactory, the escrow service pays the seller in full. The buyer is usually responsible for the escrow company's fees, but it can be worth the money.

These arrangements should be made well before the close of the sale, and if the seller refuses the escrow service, the buyer has every reason to reconsider making the purchase. Escrow services can be located either through the auction site or by using a search engine.

Bidding online can present something of a challenge, and we feel that there are many times when you should not even think about placing a bid until a sale is about to close. It is like the last two minutes of a basketball game—that is the time when all the important action happens, and what has gone on before can be fairly meaningless.

In any auction—on site or on the Internet—it is a good idea to decide how much you are willing to spend before you start bidding. If there is a reserve and the reserve has not been met (remember, in an auction, a reserve is the price that must be reached before an item will sell), it is a good idea to start bidding to see if it is possible to arrive at a sale figure before the price goes over your spending limit.

If you come to your spending limit and the reserve has not been met, it is time to move on and let the item go to someone who is willing to pay more. If, however, the reserve is met, or there is no reserve, you might want to wait until the auction has just a few minutes to go before placing your final bid.

As the clock ticks down to the final seconds, enter a bid of a significant amount above the current high bid. With any luck, yours will be the high bid and no one will be able to counter your offer because of the time limit. This is called "sniping," and it tends to anger the bidder who was winning until the last few seconds.

CHAPTER FIFTEEN

A Few Last Words

In the course of writing this book, every now and then one of us would jump up and exclaim that we should have included this thing or that thing. Pez dispensers, figural lawn sprinklers, Warner Brothers collectibles, Goofus glass, and fireplace equipment . . . the list of items to write about is practically endless.

We know we have said it before, but it still worries us that people reading this book will get the impression that everything in their house is valuable. Sadly, this is simply not the case. Many times we go into houses that have absolutely nothing of any significant value in them. This is a grave disappointment to both the owners and to us.

At best, the homes of noncollectors and the people who did not inherit the family's treasures have only a few things of present value, and a few more items that are going to be valuable someday. We have tried to show the possible value of what may be in your home, and to encourage everyone who reads this book not to throw things away without giving the objects some thought and evaluation before they are tossed out.

We hope our road map has helped you to navigate through your home and find the unrecognized treasures it contains. Our goal has been to supply some answers, and open your eyes to the potential value of some of the "stuff" that might otherwise look like junk.

Every week we get phone calls from people who have just inherited large quantities of items, and they have no idea what to make of their windfall. They want us to tell them over the phone that such and such is worth X amount of dollars, and that it can be sold to Mr. Y or Mrs. Z.

We, of course, cannot do that, because we cannot identify or quantify any item without actually seeing it—at least we will not be able to do so until we get our crystal ball tuned up and pass our mind-reading course. We hope we have answered some of your questions about antiques and collectibles in your possession, but for a proper evaluation you need an in-house visit by a professional appraiser who can evaluate exactly what you have and advise you about your insurance needs, what can be readily sold, and how to preserve your treasures for posterity.

Decisions of this kind can have a significant financial consequence, and they need to be made very carefully. After reading this book, you should be able to make some of these important judgments with more confidence. And, remember, there may be TREASURES IN YOUR ATTIC!

INDEX